Joomla! VirtueMart 1.1 Theme and Template Design

Give a unique look and feel to your VirtueMart
e-commerce store

Joseph Kwan

BIRMINGHAM - MUMBAI

Joomla! VirtueMart 1.1 Theme and Template Design

First published: May 2011

Production Reference: 1190511

Published by Packt Publishing Ltd.
32 Lincoln Road
Olton
Birmingham, B27 6PA, UK.

ISBN 978-1-849514-54-5

www.packtpub.com

Cover Image by Charwak A (charwak86@gmail.com)

Credits

Author
Joseph Kwan

Reviewer
Nicholas Rhodes

Acquisition Editor
Usha Iyer

Development Editor
Meeta Rajani

Technical Editor
Manasi Poonthottam

Copy Editor
Leonard D'Silva

Project Coordinator
Srimoyee Ghoshal

Proofreader
Kelly Hutchinson

Indexer
Tejal Daruwale

Production Coordinator
Adline Swetha Jesuthas

Cover Work
Adline Swetha Jesuthas

About the Author

Joseph Kwan has been a professional programmer for 12 years. He has thorough understanding of all major web technologies including HTML, XML, CSS, XSL, PHP, ASP, .NET, JS, Ajax, Apache, MySQL, MSSQL, and so on, on both Linux and Windows systems.

In the past five years or so, he has specialized himself in Joomla!/VirtueMart. Besides customizing/building many Joomla! components and modules, Joseph is also considered as one of the few VirtueMart experts who know the system from front to back. He is highly regarded in the VirtueMart community and is renowned for building robust and quality extensions to Joomla!/VirtueMart. Joseph is also very active in the forum. He works in Burnaby, BC Canada.

I would like to thank all the people at Packt Publishing who made this book possible, especially thankful for the advice of Usha Iyer and Meeta Rajani.

I am also greatly indebted to my wife Susan, and also the whole family, for allowing me to write this book on my already hectic life.

About the Reviewer

Nicholas Rhodes owns and operates Asgard Development. His company provides a wide range of web development services including content management systems and custom-designed solutions. He has been a web developer for six years and has been running his own business for two years. He graduated from Thiel College with a Bachelor's Degree in Computer Science. His content management skillset includes Joomla!, Drupal, and WordPress. He works primarily with PHP, MySql, HTML, CSS, and JavaScript and has worked with Visual Basic, C++, ColdFusion, and other languages in the past.

Nicholas is a co-founder of the NEO Technical Co-op based in northeastern Ohio and northwestern Pennsylvania, USA. He enjoys working with non-profit and education based organizations. In his free time, he has donated several websites to libraries and other non-profit organizations. When not sitting at his computer, he enjoys hiking, biking, kayaking, and traveling.

www.PacktPub.com

Support files, eBooks, discount offers and more

You might want to visit www.PacktPub.com for support files and downloads related to your book.

Did you know that Packt offers eBook versions of every book published, with PDF and ePub files available? You can upgrade to the eBook version at www.PacktPub.com and as a print book customer, you are entitled to a discount on the eBook copy. Get in touch with us at service@packtpub.com for more details.

At www.PacktPub.com, you can also read a collection of free technical articles, sign up for a range of free newsletters and receive exclusive discounts and offers on Packt books and eBooks.

http://PacktLib.PacktPub.com

Do you need instant solutions to your IT questions? PacktLib is Packt's online digital book library. Here, you can access, read and search across Packt's entire library of books.

Why Subscribe?

- Fully searchable across every book published by Packt
- Copy and paste, print and bookmark content
- On demand and accessible via web browser

Free Access for Packt account holders

If you have an account with Packt at www.PacktPub.com, you can use this to access PacktLib today and view nine entirely free books. Simply use your login credentials for immediate access.

Table of Contents

Appendix

This appendix is not present in the book but is available as a free download from `http://www.packtpub.com/sites/default/files/downloads/Appendix.pdf`.

Preface

Since you picked this book, the odds will be that you are already familiar with Joomla! VirtueMart. You will agree that this open source e-commerce solution is definitely amazing and feature-rich. That's why you want to stick with it. However, you still find there are some things here and there that don't quite fit your requirements. So you want to hack into the files to customize them to make them work for you. The main purpose of writing this book is to help you do things like that!

VirtueMart is a feature-rich e-commerce component that extends Joomla!. There are many complexities inside the package and also lots of customization possibilities. And because the complexities and documentation are not that easy to understand, hacking into VirtueMart can be a steep learning curve. Simply customizing the templates, which are meant for modifications, may not be easy for some readers. Working on any sizeable project can quickly turn into a nightmare. The purpose of this little book is to unravel the secrets of themes and templates in order to get you started with your customization project.

Before you roll up your sleeves and start plunging into the real stuff, there are a few important things that we should discuss. This is what the introduction is for.

What this book covers

We will explain the basic structure of the VirtueMart themes and templates and go into the detail of all important templates. We will also show you how to customize the templates and add new features to your theme with lots of real-world exercises. The customization is not just on HTML elements and CSS styles. Many of them involve changing the PHP and JavaScript code, adding new features and behaviors. We even included exercises that demonstrate how to integrate Joomla! plugins, JavaScript frameworks, existing JavaScript code, and Joomla! components into VirtueMart themes and templates.

We understand your customization projects will have many diverse varieties. So we've tried to include examples of different types, templates, and module pages as much as possible within the limitation of the text. Yet there may be areas we cannot touch on in the exercises or areas we didn't go into as much details as you would have liked. In that case, you can refer to the comprehensive template reference in *Appendix, VirtueMart Template Reference*, where we have covered all 86 templates in seven different template groups (up to version 1.1.5).

VirtueMart is one of the most complex components in Joomla!. It is impossible to cover every area of VirtueMart in a little book like this. The main subject of this book is VirtueMart themes and templates. Themes and templates are those parts of VirtueMart responsible for the final presentation of data to the browser. In particular, most of the templates, if not all, only deal with the frontend. While we will explain the VirtueMart engine in some detail and touch on other areas, our focus will remain on themes and templates. That means we will not touch on the many details of classes and module pages, except when they are related directly to the themes and templates. That also means we will not discuss customization of the backend VirtueMart modules. Creation or customization of payment modules and shipping modules are not part of the presentation engine and so they will not be discussed in this book. Also, we will not talk about the VirtueMart database structure.

If you are seeking help solely for a VirtueMart backend project or for payment and shipping module, this book is not for you. You can treat this book as a first step in knowing how VirtueMart works, though. After you thoroughly grasped the idea presented here, you will definitely have a solid foundation in researching ways to hack into the backend.

To be successful in your customization project, you will probably need to tweak some PHP code or include some JavaScript handlers. However, this book is not a textbook on programming and so will not tell you all the bells and whistles of writing PHP or JavaScript programs. We will give you a basic idea of how to tweak code but do not expect that you will become a seasoned programmer after reading this book.

While we will touch on simple techniques on tweaking Joomla! to work in our way, this book will not tell you the detailed structure of Joomla!. In some exercises, we may step into Joomla! technicalities such as customizing a Joomla! module. However, Joomla! is not the focus of this book and so you may need to refer to other textbooks on Joomla! if you want to work further on the modules.

Chapter 1, *The Virtuemart Engine*, will briefly review the Joomla!/VirtueMart file structure. We will then continue to explain the presentation framework of Joomla! and VirtueMart. A high-level view of the VirtueMart engine will be presented and we will see how the VirtueMart theme and template fits in the whole system. After that, we will be able to understand the various ways to customize the VirtueMart shop and provide a list of items we need to consider before heading on a customization project.

Chapter 2, *The VirtueMart Default Theme*, will focus on the default theme and its accompanied template structure. We will start with the shopping life cycle in VirtueMart, the backbone of the theme and template system. We will then give a general description of the VirtueMart configuration settings with a closer look at the Site configurations that relate closely to the frontend presentation. After that, we will concentrate on exploring the `default` theme. We will see the options that are available in the `default` theme configuration. Finally, we will give a brief introduction to the seven template groups under the `default` theme and understand their basic usage.

Chapter 3, *Product List Templates*, is the first of four chapters that explains the working of major template groups. In this chapter, our focus is on the the product list templates. We will start with a sample template to see how a template works. Some basic PHP language constructs will be introduced before looking at the browse page elements and then the three different product list styles. We will look closely at each of the major templates in the group. We will guide you to customize the basic layout, the header, the navigation links, the add-to-cart form, the product list styles, and many more.

Chapter 4, *Product Details Templates*, will build upon what we have introduced in the previous chapter but shift the focus to the product details templates. We will look at the major elements that compose a product details page and then the templates that are related to each of those elements. We will look at how to customize the flypage, header, product images and files, product review, add-to-cart form, advanced attribute and custom attribute, and many more.

Chapter 5, *Changing the Look of VirtueMart*, will further our understanding of the template system by looking at peripheral stuff that is not inside a template file but are affecting the look of the site. We will look at the stylesheet, the JavaScript, the URL links, and the language element. Then we will continue our investigation in the template system by studying a few more templates that may not be considered as the core but will definitely affect the impression of the shop. Examples to customize the CSS, JavaScript, language element, manufacturer page, vendor page, ask seller form, and the VirtueMart home page are explained.

Chapter 6, From Shop Basket to Final Checkout, will walk through the latter half of the shopping life cycle, from the time that a product is added to the shop basket to the time that the customer finishes with the order. We will first explain how the shop basket data is stored in the server and look at the various elements on the shop cart page. A major part of these discussions will focus around the shop basket templates. Next, we will cross the border to the checkout templates and follow every page in the checkout process. For each of the checkout steps, there are associated templates. We will look at each of the templates and see how they can be customized to fit our needs. While working with the exercises, we will introduce further techniques that can be employed to customize VirtueMart without hacking into the core files.

Chapter 7, VirtueMart Templates and Joomla! Modules, will look at the customization of the various Joomla! modules that come with VirtueMart. We will also touch on the templates for some peripheral elements on a flypage: recent products, related products, and so on.

Chapter 8, VirtueMart Theme Anatomy, will look at the detailed structure of a VirtueMart theme. We will first look at the VirtueMart theme class and see how the whole theme system works. Then we will focus on each of the components: the images, the JavaScript, the CSS file, the theme file, and theme configuration. Finally, we will try to see how we can add new configurations to the theme configurator by hacking into the files.

Chapter 9, Theme Customizations, will look at the details of customizing or creating a VirtueMart theme. We will first see the differences between customizing and creating a theme. Then we will discuss the pros and cons of creating a new theme rather than customizing the `default` theme. We will then proceed to considering the various issues that we need to consider before creating a new theme. After that, we will demonstrate how to integrate JavaScript Utilities and Joomla! plugin to a VirtueMart theme. Finally, we will take a brief look at how to use custom VirtueMart classes to provide our own logics in VirtueMart.

Chapter 10, Additional Customization Possibilities, will look at some advanced customization possibilities for modifying the templates and theme. Most of the materials are practical stuff and each section may not be that related to the rest of the chapter. The only common thing among them may be they are all interesting customization examples. We will talk about breaking complex templates into smaller manageable ones. We will talk about sharing templates between two template groups. We will work on using images to display advanced attributes. We will use the product type template to include a file uploader. Finally, we will touch on some more exercises using custom VirtueMart class file to make various changes to the price system.

In *Appendix, VirtueMart Template Reference*, we provide a comprehensive reference for all the templates of the `default` theme, listing out the purpose and usage of the template, its parent and child parents, related page and class files. The most important part is the available fields, where you will find the fields that you can use in a template and also a brief explanation of what the field is for.

 This appendix is not present in the book but is available as a free download from `http://www.packtpub.com/sites/default/files/downloads/Appendix.pdf`.

What you need for this book

There are various possibilities for customizing and extending VirtueMart. So what you actually need will depend on how you want to modify VirtueMart.

To change the default images, you certainly need the knowledge of how to use a graphic manipulation software such as Adobe Photoshop. If you want to customize the CSS styles or change the HTML coding, you can use a web design program such as Dreamweaver. However, to be proficient in changing the PHP or JavaScript, a decent text editor is a must.

There are lots of choices for the text editor; many of them are free to download through the Internet. My favorite editor is SciTE, a text editor based on the scintilla project. All the exercises in this book are prepared using this little yet versatile text-editing tool. You can try this out by downloading a copy from `http://www.scintilla.org`. SciTE may not be the best editor but is sufficient for our purpose. If you already have your own favorite other than SciTE, you can stick with that.

Another important tool you will need is an FTP client program. FTP is a protocol to transfer files to and from your web server. Unless you plan to use your customization only on your local computer, FTP client is almost a must. You probably already have one you are using. In that case, you should stick with it unless you want to change for a better one. My favorite is FileZilla, another open source project and a free download is available at `http://filezilla-project.org`. Theoretically, you can use Firefox or Internet Explorer as an FTP client and many people are using them. However, to be a professional, you cannot do without a dedicated FTP client.

Joomla! VirtueMart versions

You probably already have a Joomla! VirtueMart website. But chances are your installation may not be the latest version. Actually, during the course of writing this book, Joomla! has already gone through several updates and VirtueMart jumped from Version 1.1.4 to 1.1.8. So you need to be sure of the version that this book is based on and whether it will be compatible with your installation, and if not, how many differences there will be.

As I wrote this book, I prepared and tested my code in a web server running Linux and Apache. The Joomla! version is 1.5.20 and the VirtueMart version is 1.1.5. The current version for Joomla! at the time of writing this introduction is 1.5.23 and VirtueMart 1.1.8. So this is not too much different from the one I have been using. Actually, the Joomla! version should not matter so long as it is 1.5.x. If by any chance you are still working with 1.0.x versions, you may encounter some problems in working with some of the exercises. But the problems are not insurmountable if your VirtueMart version is up to date.

On the other hand, most of the discussions in this book will apply to VirtueMart 1.1.x. So even if you are using VirtueMart 1.1.3 or older, this book is still useful. You will find the line numbers indicated here significantly differ from your copy but you should still be able to locate the code. VirtueMart introduced a theme class system as from version 1.1.4. So if you are using earlier versions, you will not be able to benefit from the theme class customization which slowly becomes an important aspect in developing a custom theme.

In case you are still using VirtueMart 1.0.x, the main principles of customizing templates presented in this book may still apply. But there are already lots of changes. Even the directory structure has been revised and so you may have a hard time locating the file you need. Also, VirtueMart theme is a brand new concept in version 1.1 onwards. So unless you are a seasoned developer, you may not find much use of the material in this book for 1.0.x version.

Finally, I should mention this in case your VirtueMart is installed over a mambo CMS system. VirtueMart 1.1 can run in mambo. So you will be able to run many of the exercises in this book. But there are still times when you will find the code does not work in mambo.

Basic Joomla! VirtueMart concepts you will need to know

In order to follow the discussion in this book, you should be familiar with some basic Joomla! and VirtueMart concepts. Other than the basic concepts of menu, pathway, products, categories, shopcart, checkout, order e-mail, and so on, there are a few concepts that we need to emphasize as they may be new to some readers.

Joomla! components, modules, plugins, and templates

Joomla! is a modularized content management system. That means each web page displayed by Joomla! is made up of several blocks. All except the main block are called modules. The main block is called the component (which normally will occupy the major proportion of a web page). The layout of the modules and component is determined by the template. (The template will divide the web page into positions. The concept of position is not related to the major subject of this book and so we will not go into its detail here.) Joomla! plugins are small programs that help to modify the text or behavior of Joomla!.

VirtueMart modules, themes, and templates

As we all know, VirtueMart is a webstore application that lives within the Joomla! framework. VirtueMart itself contains several packages. The major package is of course the VirtueMart component which will display content in the main area of a Joomla! site. Most of the time when we use the term VirtueMart, we are referring to this VirtueMart component. However, there are also other smaller packages in VirtueMart that will display the shop content as Joomla! modules. The `vm_product_categories` module, for example, will display all the categories of VirtueMart in a sidebar. This Joomla! module can display in a VirtueMart page (that is, a page with the VirtueMart component showing in the main area) or any other pages, though the content can differ.

VirtueMart itself is a very complex application. It has its own display engine, layout variations to cater for different site needs, and language element system that supports multiple languages. Unfortunately, VirtueMart used the term modules and templates differently from Joomla!. And we must be careful not to confuse VirtueMart modules with Joomla! modules and VirtueMart templates and Joomla! templates.

The content displayed by VirtueMart in the component area has many different possibilities. Each possibility is called a page. To make them easier to manage, VirtueMart organized these pages into modules. There are only three frontend modules: shop, checkout, and account. The shop module controls the display of the product catalog. The checkout module controls the checkout process and the account module provides management functions for logged in users. In addition to these frontend modules, there are many other backend modules. However, backend modules are not the major concern in this book as themes and templates only relate to the frontend display. As you can see, VirtueMart modules are very different from Joomla! modules. So you must be careful to distinguish them.

VirtueMart groups the display style of the frontend in themes. Each theme contains a set of templates, Javascript, CSS stylesheets, and other building blocks. The most prominent building block of a theme is certainly the templates. The VirtueMart templates are used to control the display and layout of individual frontend pages such as the product listing page. Please note that a VirtueMart template will only control the component area of a Joomla! page (and sometimes a Joomla! module that displays VirtueMart content, as we shall see in *Chapter 7, VirtueMart Templates and Joomla! Modules*). A Joomla! template is a whole set of files that control the display and layout of all Joomla! pages. A VirtueMart template, in contrast, is a single file that controls the display and layout of the VirtueMart component area or often just part of that area. So again, do not confuse Joomla! templates and VirtueMart templates.

Child products, advanced attribute, custom attribute, and product type

VirtueMart has several advanced features that you may or may not have used before. However, as we work along theme and template customization, these features will come up from time to time. So you must at least have a rough idea of what they are and whether you will need to use them.

Many products can have varieties such as color, size, or other options. Depending on the actual requirements, there can be a number of ways to implement that in VirtueMart. Child products, advanced attribute, custom attribute, and product type are different ways to provide for this kind of function. In case you are not sure what they are and what the differences between them are, you need to do some research on this before you can understand the exercises that work with them. The knowledge of those features will be assumed for the purpose of this book.

Who this book is for

This book is written for anyone who wants to learn the working of VirtueMart and try extending its capabilities. You may be the owner of a Joomla! VirtueMart web store or a designer working with Joomla! VirtueMart. If you want to customize VirtueMart to unleash its enormous potential and elevate your store to the next level, this book is for you. You must have some experience with VirtueMart and understand its basic features. You also need to know HTML, basic CSS styles, and should be comfortable taking up some challenges in PHP and JavaScript programming.

The book is especially useful to web designers who are comfortable working with graphics, HTML, CSS, and have some ideas of what JavaScript and PHP are all about. To get the most from this book, you should be familiar with administering a VirtueMart web store, well-versed with the basic features, and have a basic understanding of its advanced features such as child products, advanced attribute, custom attribute, and product type. You will find that many interesting extensions will be based on these advanced features.

You must be able to read and write clean HTML and probably know the basic CSS styles. You may not know anything about programming yet but must have a drive to learn. Hacking into VirtueMart can sometimes be simple. But for any extensive and functional hack, it probably will take some effort and time. So you should be prepared for some hard work and endure the dark valleys of testing and debugging. We will introduce ways to help you spot errors along the way. But testing and debugging is still inevitable.

While this book is useful for web designers, we have tried to make the book easy and practical for readers of diverse backgrounds. As Joomla! and VirtueMart are constantly evolving, any customization projects have to bear in mind future compatibility. While there is no absolute way to guarantee 100 percent compatibility with the next version, the examples within this book have been designed to reduce upgrade impact. Throughout the book, we have demonstrated various techniques that help to make the hack upward compatible. Within the exercises, there is no hacking into any VirtueMart core files. We also tried to restrict our changes to as few files and as few places as possible. In order to achieve that, sometimes we may not adhere to the standards that professional developers and designers will follow. For example, we may use inline CSS styles in place of an external stylesheet just to make our changes easier to manage. We will put database logic inside the template file to avoid changes to the core files. All these are not considered best practice by professionals. In these cases, you are definitely free to apply your own expertise to improve the code.

Conventions

In this book, you will find a number of styles of text that distinguish between different kinds of information. Here are some examples of these styles, and an explanation of their meaning.

Code words in text are shown as follows: "echo is used to send the value of a string to the output buffer."

A block of code is set as follows:

```
<?php if (!defined(VM_CUSTOM_CSS)) {
  define ('VM_CUSTOM_CSS',1);
?>
  <style>
    .browseProductContainer {border:1px solid #999;padding:5px;backgro
und:#eee;margin:5px;}
  </style>
<?php } ?>
```

New terms and **important words** are shown in bold. Words that you see on the screen, in menus or dialog boxes for example, appear in the text like this: "Click on the **View** button against any order you have made before."

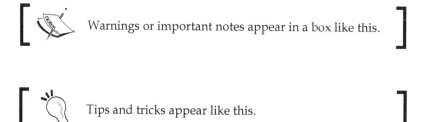

Warnings or important notes appear in a box like this.

Tips and tricks appear like this.

Reader feedback

Feedback from our readers is always welcome. Let us know what you think about this book—what you liked or may have disliked. Reader feedback is important for us to develop titles that you really get the most out of.

To send us general feedback, simply send an e-mail to feedback@packtpub.com, and mention the book title via the subject of your message.

If there is a book that you need and would like to see us publish, please send us a note in the **SUGGEST A TITLE** form on www.packtpub.com or e-mail suggest@packtpub.com.

If there is a topic that you have expertise in and you are interested in either writing or contributing to a book, see our author guide on www.packtpub.com/authors.

Customer support

Now that you are the proud owner of a Packt book, we have a number of things to help you to get the most from your purchase.

Downloading the example code for this book

You can download the example code files for all Packt books you have purchased from your account at http://www.PacktPub.com. If you purchased this book elsewhere, you can visit http://www.PacktPub.com/support and register to have the files e-mailed directly to you.

Errata

Although we have taken every care to ensure the accuracy of our content, mistakes do happen. If you find a mistake in one of our books—maybe a mistake in the text or the code—we would be grateful if you would report this to us. By doing so, you can save other readers from frustration and help us improve subsequent versions of this book. If you find any errata, please report them by visiting http://www.packtpub.com/support, selecting your book, clicking on the **errata submission form** link, and entering the details of your errata. Once your errata are verified, your submission will be accepted and the errata will be uploaded on our website, or added to any list of existing errata, under the Errata section of that title. Any existing errata can be viewed by selecting your title from http://www.packtpub.com/support.

Piracy

Piracy of copyright material on the Internet is an ongoing problem across all media. At Packt, we take the protection of our copyright and licenses very seriously. If you come across any illegal copies of our works, in any form, on the Internet, please provide us with the location address or website name immediately so that we can pursue a remedy.

Please contact us at copyright@packtpub.com with a link to the suspected pirated material.

We appreciate your help in protecting our authors, and our ability to bring you valuable content.

Questions

You can contact us at questions@packtpub.com if you are having a problem with any aspect of the book, and we will do our best to address it.

The VirtueMart Engine

1

In this chapter, we will briefly review the Joomla!/VirtueMart file structure. We will then continue to explain the presentation framework of Joomla! and VirtueMart. A high-level view of the VirtueMart engine will be presented and we will see how the VirtueMart theme and template fits in the whole system. After that, we will be able to understand the various ways to customize the VirtueMart shop and provide a list of items we need to consider before heading on a customization project.

Briefly, in this chapter, we will cover:

- Navigating through the Joomla!/VirtueMart directories
- Structure of the Joomla! URL path
- Joomla! presentation framework
- VirtueMart presentation framework
- Roles of VirtueMart themes and templates
- Ways to customize VirtueMart

Navigating through the Joomla!/ VirtueMart directories

You should have a Joomla! and VirtueMart e-commerce site installed somewhere to follow through the rest of the book. If not, you should now install one first before reading on. From this point onward, we will assume that you can access a Joomla! VirtueMart site and can freely browse its content, either on your local computer using the file manager of your operating system or in a web server somewhere using an FTP client program. To work on the exercises, you should also be able to edit each of the files.

OK. Let's start our study by navigating through the Joomla! directories. If you look at the root of your Joomla! site, you will be amazed how large the Joomla! project is. There are totally close to 5,000 files under some 350 directories! It would be difficult to find your way through this vast structure of files, if there are no hints at all. Fortunately, Joomla! has a very good directory structure and will be easy to follow once you know its basic organization. Knowing your way through this vast structure is very important when embarking on any VirtueMart customization project of considerable size. The good news is that usually we only need to know a very small fraction of those 350 directories and 5,000 files, in particular, within the scope of this little book.

Name ↓	Size	Last Modified	
administrator		28/07/2010	12:37:00 AM
cache		27/07/2010	10:50:00 PM
cgi-bin		28/07/2010	12:22:00 AM
components		28/07/2010	12:58:00 AM
images		27/07/2010	10:51:00 PM
includes		27/07/2010	10:52:00 PM
language		27/07/2010	10:53:00 PM
libraries		27/07/2010	10:56:00 PM
logs		27/07/2010	10:56:00 PM
media		27/07/2010	10:56:00 PM
modules		29/07/2010	10:45:00 PM
plugins		27/07/2010	11:00:00 PM
templates		27/07/2010	11:01:00 PM

In the Joomla! root, the most important directories we need to know are the administrator, components, modules, and plugins directories (This does not mean that the other directories are not important. We highlight these few directories just because they are the directories we will reference from time–to-time in this book) You will probably recognize that the last three of these shortlisted directories correspond to the three major extension types of Joomla! So within these directories, we will expect to see a series of subdirectories, each of which corresponds to an extension installed in the Joomla! framework. This is exactly the case, except for the plugins where the directories are arranged in terms of their type instead of their source.

Let's take a closer look at one of the most important components that comes with Joomla!. Navigate to the components directory and open the subdirectory com_ content. The com_content component is the one that manages articles we created in Joomla!. You have probably been using a lot of this component. Within this directory, you will find a number of files and a few subdirectories. We notice there is a file named controller.php and two subdirectories named models and views. We will have more to say on these in a moment.

Let's move back to the root directory and take a look at the last important directory mentioned above. This `administrator` directory mimics the root directory in many respects. We see that most of the subdirectories we found in the root have a corresponding subdirectory within the `administrator` directory. For example, we find subdirectories named `components` and `modules` within the `administrator` as well. As we know, there are two main sections of a Joomla! website, also known as the frontend and the backend. The root directory and `administrator` directory are respectively the location where the frontend and backend files are located. While this dividing line is not rigid, we can use this as a guide when we want to locate a frontend or backend file. Since both the root and the `administrator` directories contain a subdirectory called `components`, to avoid ambiguity, we will refer to them as the root components and administrator components directory, respectively.

Now, let's work our way a little bit down the directory tree to see how VirtueMart fits into this framework. Within the root components directory, you will see a subdirectory called `com_virtuemart`. Yes, this is the location where you can find all the files used by VirtueMart for the frontend. Under the `com_virtuemart` directory, among some other files and subdirectories, you will notice a `themes` subdirectory. You will find each of the VirtueMart themes you have installed there. The `themes` directory is the major work area throughout this book. From now on, we will refer to the `com_virtuemart` directory under the root components directory as the `root VirtueMart` directory or the `frontend VirtueMart` directory.

Within the administrator components directory, there is also a subdirectory called com_virtuemart where the backend VirtueMart files are located. Under this main directory, there are four subdirectories named as classes, html, languages, and sql. Obviously, these directories will contain, respectively, the class files, HTML files, language files, and SQL (also known as database) files. Actually, the classes and html directories have a deeper meaning than their names suggest, as we shall see in a moment.

Structure of the Joomla! URL path

Before leaving our high-level exploration of the Joomla! tree structure, let's digress a little bit to study how a Joomla! URL is built up. While the Joomla! directory structure is so complicated, the URL used to access the site is much simpler. Most of the time, the URL just starts with index.php?. (If you have a Search Engine Friendly or SEF system enabled, you should turn it off during the development and testing of your customization, or at least turn it off mentally while we are talking about the URL. You can turn off SEF in the Joomla! Configuration page.) For example, if we want to access the VirtueMart (frontend) home page, we can use the following URL:

```
http://your_joomla_live_site/index.php?option=com_virtuemart
```

Similarly, the URL

```
http://your_joomla_live_site/administrator/index.php?option=com_
virtuemart
```

will bring up the VirtueMart backend control panel, if you're already logged in. All other Joomla! URL, in fact, work in the same way, although many times you see some additional parameters as well. (Don't forget to replace your_joomla_live_ site in the above URL with your domain name and the Joomla! root directory, in case the site is not installed in the root.)

Actually, the index.php script is the main entry into your Joomla! site. All major requests to the frontend start from here (major requests only since there are some other entry points as well, but they don't bother us at this point). Similarly, all major requests to the backend start from the file administrator/index.php. Restricting the entry point to the site makes it very easy to control authorized and unauthorized accesses. For example, if we want to put the site offline, we can simply change a configuration in Joomla! and all components will be offline as well. We don't need to change each page or even each component one-by-one.

Understanding the structure of the Joomla! URL is pretty useful during the development and debugging process. Sometimes we may need to work on a partly live site in which the Joomla! site is already working, but the VirtueMart shop is still under construction. In such cases, it is common to unpublish the menu items for the shop so that the shop is still hidden from the public. The fact that the menu item is hidden actually means the shop is less accessible but not inaccessible. If we want to test the VirtueMart shop, we can still type the URL on the browser by ourselves. Using the URL

```
http://your_joomla_live_site/index.php?option=com_virtuemart
```

we can bring up the VirtueMart home page. We will learn some more tricks in testing individual shop pages along the way of our study of VirtueMart themes and templates in this book.

One simple application of what we learnt about the URL can be used when customizing Joomla!. When working with VirtueMart projects, we will need to go to the VirtueMart backend from time-to-time to modify the VirtueMart settings. As we all know, after logging in, what we have on the browser window is the control panel page. We will need to point to the **components/virtuemart** menu before we can open the VirtueMart backend home. This is not a complicated task, but will be very tedious if repeated every time we log back into the site. Can we make Joomla! smarter, to open the VirtueMart home by default when we log on? Yes, we can. The trick actually relates to what we talked about so far. If you want to customize Joomla! to open the VirtueMart backend by default, you can stay with me for the following warm-up exercise. I understand some of you may not want to change the default login page. Feel free to skip to the next section directly if you want to, as this exercise does not relate directly to the rest of this book.

Exercise 1.1: Making the Joomla! backend default to VirtueMart

1. Open your favorite text editor. Navigate to the Joomla! site root.

2. Open the file `administrator/includes/helper.php`.

3. At around line 44 (the actual line may vary from version-to-version), change the code `$option = 'com_cpanel';` to `$option = 'com_virtuemart';`

4. Save the file.

Open your browser and log in to your Joomla! site. Alas, you should see the VirtueMart control panel instead of the Joomla! control panel.

This simple exercise demonstrated that sometimes a useful change does not need complex coding. What we need is a little knowledge of how things work. I bet you probably understand what we have done above without explanation. After login, Joomla! will automatically go to the default component, hardcoded in the file `helper.php`. For standard Joomla!, this will be the `com_cpanel` component. In *Exercise 1.1*, we have changed this default backend component from `com_cpanel` to `com_virtuemart`. Instead of VirtueMart, we can certainly change the default to other components such as **community builder** or **MOSET**.

Joomla! 1.5 presentation framework

Since VirtueMart is a Joomla! component, it cannot exist outside Joomla!. So before diving into the detail of the VirtueMart engine, it pays to take a brief look at how Joomla! actually works. While an understanding of the presentation framework of Joomla! and VirtueMart may be useful for themes and templates development, it is not essential for the actual customization design. In case you don't want to bother with the detail of Joomla!/VirtueMart engine, feel free to skip to the section *Roles of VirtueMart themes and templates*. (For those more practically oriented readers, you can even skip directly to *Chapter 3, Product List Templates*, as you can always come back to these theoretical discussions afterwards.)

Joomla! emerged from version 1.0 and later developed into 1.5. In this upgrade, Joomla! has been basically rewritten from the ground up. A presentation structure called Model-View-Controller or MVC has been adopted in Joomla! 1.5. While a detailed explanation of the MVC structure is out of the scope of this book, a basic understanding of its working will help us understand why and how VirtueMart 1.1 behaves in the way it is right now.

Joomla! is a web application. Each page of Joomla! is in fact a text file consisting of HTML code. Depending on the detail parameters of a web request, Joomla! will generate a dynamic HTML page by combining data stored in the database and site configuration data stored in various PHP files. In the early history of dynamic web pages, program code were written in a way that HTML tags are mixed with presentation logic in one place. The spaghetti code, as it is sometimes called, makes maintenance and extension of the coding very difficult. As the basic structure of a dynamic web page is better understood, more and more new coding patterns emerge to make the life of a web developer easier. The MVC presentation framework is one of those patterns that have been proposed to build computer applications. This framework has gradually become the standard pattern for building web applications and has been adopted by many open source web projects.

Models

In the MVC presentation framework, the job of building a web page is divided into three main tiers. The backend tier is the data that is stored in the database (strictly speaking, there is no prescribed data storage format though a database is a natural way to manage the data). We need to grab data needed to build the web page. This tier of the job is done by the Model, which describes how data is stored and how data can be retrieved from the data server.

Views

The frontend tier determines what and how data is presented on the browser. This is the job of the View. For a given dataset from a Model, there can be many different ways to present the data. Let's say, we have a set of statistical data, for example. We can present this data as a bar graph or a pie chart. Each of these presentations is called a View of the same Model.

Controllers

Now statistical data is just a set of numbers. How can we convert them into a bar graph or a pie chart? That is exactly how the Controller comes into place. A Controller is a routine specifying how to convert the Model into various Views. One major advantage of this separation of data (Model) and presentation (View) makes changes to the application much easier. We can change the presentation independent of the underlying data and vice versa.

So, in the Joomla! 1.5 world, we will have a set of Models which interface with the database, a set of Views to tell the browser how to present the data, and a set of Controllers that control how to convert the Model into the View. According to the best practice, all Joomla! 1.5 components should follow this same structure. Thus, each Joomla! 1.5 component should have two subdirectories called `models` and `views`. Also, the root directory will contain a `controller.php` which extends the Joomla! controller's capability. This structure is revealed as we look at the contents of a Joomla! component which we had done previously. However, because of historical reasons and others, not all components follow this best practice. VirtueMart is one of those exceptions.

VirtueMart presentation framework

VirtueMart 1.1 was conceived during the time of Joomla! 1.0.x when the MVC structure was a new introduction to the computing world and was not yet widely adopted. In particular, why Joomla! ultimately decided to pick the MVC as its presentation framework is not clear at the time. However, the VirtueMart development team already understands the importance of structuring the web page building process, especially on the separation of data and presentation. Actually, this concept has been used in VirtueMart 1.0.x, although it is not implemented as fully as in version 1.1. Without a standard framework by then, they chose a very similar structure with three data, presentation, and controlling tiers but different nomenclature. Of course, the detailed working of the structure has many differences from the MVC framework, especially from a theoretical point of view. Nevertheless, this presentation structure works on the three-tier structure without a well-defined name for each of the tiers. So, you may not find these tiers named explicitly in the official VirtueMart developer documentation. However, the presentation framework still adheres to a close pattern as a Joomla! 1.5 component.

The class files – Data tier

In the VirtueMart world, data manipulation is the responsibility of **class** files located in the `classes` subdirectory, which we looked at briefly while navigating through the Joomla! file structure. The class file starts with a prefix `ps_` (probably derived from the historical name phpShop) followed by the data name. Let's go back to the VirtueMart file structure we've been looking at in the first section of this chapter. Navigate to the `classes` subdirectory under the VirtueMart `administrator` directory. You can see a lot of files starting with the `ps_` prefix. Most of these files define a class in the data tier of VirtueMart. So you will expect the `ps_product.php` file to handle the product data, `ps_shopper.php` to handle the shopper data, and so on.

The templates files – Presentation tier

On the other end of the framework is the presentation tier, which is responsible to send back the HTML to the browser for display. VirtueMart 1.1 adopted a very flexible template structure where the major HTML code is separated from the data and processing logic. These template files are placed in the `frontend VirtueMart` directory and have been grouped into sets under the structure called theme. A **VirtueMart theme** is basically a collection of template files which control the frontend look of a VirtueMart shop. Thus, you can compare template files to a similar structure like a Joomla! view. Different template files will present VirtueMart data in different ways. For example, you can change the product listing page of the shop from a vertical list of items to a tabular view of items by simply changing one of the templates. For an example of how this can be done, you can refer to *Chapter 3, Exercises 3.7* and *3.8*.

The page files – Business logic tier

So far, we haven't touched on the processing logic where data is converted into the presentation. In VirtueMart, we do not have controllers. Instead, the processing is done in the page files located within the `html` subdirectory under the VirtueMart `administrator` directory. All the page files are named in the pattern of `{module}.{page}.php` where module is a section of functions in VirtueMart, as we explained in the introduction.

Before we carry this similarity too far, it should be noted that VirtueMart is not actually implementing the MVC framework. So it deviates from this separation of data and presentation principle from time-to-time, as we shall see. Many times, the output of HTML code mingles with the data processing logic in the class file, making customization very difficult.

Let's look again at the real VirtueMart `administrator` directory for more insight. By navigating to the **html** subdirectory under the VirtueMart `administrator` directory, we can see a lot of files named in the pattern `{module}.{page}.php`. We see, for example, files such as `shop.cart.php`, `shop.browser.php`, `checkout.index.php`, `admin.show_cfg.php`, and so on. `.php` of course is the file extension which tells us (and also the operating system) that this is a PHP script file. `{module}` is the name of a VirtueMart module. `{page}` is the page name within the VirtueMart module. From the name `shop.cart.php`, we know this page belongs to the `shop` module and has a page name `cart`. Actually, this is the PHP script responsible for the processing of the shopcart page. Similarly, `shop.browse.php` will control the processing of the browse page, also part of the shop module. On the other hand, `checkout.index.php` will control the major logic of checking out. `checkout` is another module in VirtueMart and the name `index` suggests this is the starting page for the checkout process.

With all the background information, we will be able to appreciate the importance of themes and templates in the VirtueMart engine. When you type a VirtueMart URL on the browser (that is, URL that consists of `index.php?option=com_virtuemart`), the browser will send the request to the Joomla! site. After some initialization and routing code, the Joomla! engine will feed the request to VirtueMart for rendering the main part of the page.

The first thing VirtueMart will do is the section of initialization, including loading some basic classes, setting up the session, checking the permissions of the user, and so on. It will then check whether the request includes a pending function that needs to be done. If there is any, it will invoke the function before processing the page.

After the function is complete, VirtueMart will pass the processing to the HTML page (for example, `shop.cart`) requested. The page will load the relevant data using the appropriate class file, combining it with the session and/or configuration data already loaded. All necessary data will then be fed into the relevant template file to generate the HTML code that needs to be passed back to Joomla!. After a further filtering process by Joomla!, the HTML code will be sent as a response back to the browser for display.

Roles of VirtueMart themes and templates

It should be clear by now that template files control the HTML display on the browser. So the color, font style, font size, data field arrangement, and layout are the major jobs of a template. By invoking a different template file, the browser display will look very different. Depending on the nature of an HTML page, the final HTML code may be generated by one or more template files. The product detail page (usually referred to as the flypage), for example, makes use of several template files and its appearance will change when any one of the templates change. We will work on the details of this in *Chapter 4, Product Details Templates*.

Since the final look of a page may vary with a group of template files, it is important that the templates are consistent with each other. Mix and match of various template files may work sometimes, but will definitely seem not so well-organized and professional. Furthermore, the output of a template also depends on various configuration settings of VirtueMart. So there is a need to group the template files into a full unit. Each of these full units is named as a theme in VirtueMart.

The original intention of the template system is to separate processing logic from the final presentation. So you will find that most of the templates only take care of presentation, that is, the look of the final browser page. However, as highly diversified customization demands come up, more and more processing logic is introduced into the template. Initially, the processing logic is added by amateur developers into the template because they are not aware of the importance of separating the data from presentation. However, soon even professionals will find it necessary to place some processing logic into the template file when they do customizations.

There are two major reasons to introduce logic into templates. The first one is to restrict the changes made to the core files. Often, when processing logic changes, the presentation will need to be changed to make use of the new logic. So each change will involve both the processing logic in the HTML file as well as the presentation code in the template file. Putting the processing logic in the template will avoid the changes in the HTML file and thus reduce the number of modified files.

The second reason for putting processing logic into a template is for backward compatibility during version upgrade. As the major role of template files is for presentation, essential changes to the template are less frequent than the HTML pages. This is especially true for security upgrades. Template files are less prone to security problems and compelling changes are usually not needed. Restricting changes just to template files will affect customization less during version upgrade.

Due to the need for restricting changes to within the template file, VirtueMart even introduces a new way to extend the core functions using theme starting from version 1.1.4 onwards. In the previous section, we explained that the ps_ class files in VirtueMart handle most of the data logic. From version 1.1.4, all the ps_ class files can be overridden using a custom-built class file by putting that custom-built file in the theme directory. A new configuration item is added to VirtueMart to enable the new feature. This means that in case we need to modify or introduce new logic to the data model, the modifications can be done through a custom file in the theme. Since these custom files are not core files, they will not be modified during version upgrade. The new feature thus helps to reduce the impact of version upgrade on customization. Unfortunately, this feature only applies to class files, but not to HTML files. So, in case you need to change the processing logic, you cannot override the HTML file using a theme. Instead, you will either need to overwrite the HTML file with your changes or place the logic in the template file, if that is an option.

Ways to customize VirtueMart

Basically, there is an infinite number of ways to customize VirtueMart. This is in fact the beauty of using an open source shopcart system like VirtueMart. As we have seen, extensions to VirtueMart are welcome by the development team themselves. That's why VirtueMart has been built in a way to enable easier customization. Nevertheless, there is a range of complexity in customizing VirtueMart. While there may not be a definite limit on the customization possibilities, whether a VirtueMart customization project is advisable will be tightly coupled to the cost of its implementation. If the cost of customization is more than building a brand new shopcart, for example, there is no point in pursuing the customization.

That being said, there are still lots of customization possibilities that are worthwhile and is within the reach of an average designer who may not be comfortable working with PHP code initially. So let us have a look at the ways we can extend VirtueMart.

Textual changes

Sometimes you just want to change the text that is displayed on a certain page. This is especially the case when you are using VirtueMart in a different language environment. VirtueMart does come with several language files, but the translation may not suit you. And even when your site is totally English, you may still want to replace a text or two to fit your client's or your own shop's specific needs. There are two ways you can do this.

On one hand, you can modify the language file that comes with VirtueMart. This will involve finding the appropriate language file that contains that specific language element you want to change. VirtueMart language files are placed in the `languages` subdirectory of the VirtueMart `administrator` directory. The language files are further subdivided into modules, with each language having its own `.php` file. You should first look into the `common` subdirectory where language elements used in more than one module are placed. Open the language file in an editor and search for the text you want to change. If you cannot find it in the `common` subdirectory, you need to look in the individual module directory. For example, if you need to change text on the browse page, then you will look into the `shop` subdirectory to see if you can locate that language element, since the browse page is controlled by the `shop.browse.php` file and so it belongs to the `shop` module. We will demonstrate how this can be done in *Exercise 1.2*. Customizing language elements is discussed in detail in *Chapter 5, Changing the Look of VirtueMart*.

Exercise 1.2: Customizing a language element

In this exercise, we are going to customize two language elements found on the Product Listing page, as shown in the following screenshot:

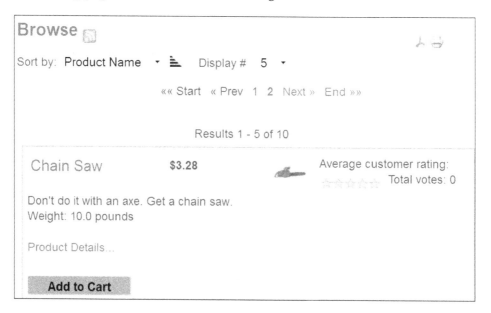

As an example, we are going to change the text for **Browse** and **Sort by**. As we shall see, the Product Listing page is actually processed by the module page shop.browse. So we will expect these language elements to be found in either the shop language file or the common language file. These are the two files we are going to search for these two elements.

Steps

1. Open your favorite text editor. Navigate to the VirtueMart administrator root.

2. Open the file languages/shop/english.php.

3. Open the search dialog of the editor and search for the text Browse and Sort by. You will find the text Browse in line 21 with an element name PHPSHOP_BROWSE_LBL. Change the text from Browse to Product List. The text Sort by, however, is not found.

4. Save the file and upload it to your server.

5. Open the file languages/common/english.php.

6. Open the search dialog of the editor and search for the text `Sort by`. You will find the text in line 405 with an element name `PHPSHOP_ORDERBY`. Change `Sort by` to `Order by`.

7. Save the file and upload it to your server.

8. Go to the frontend of your site. Browse to any Product Category Listing, and you will see the text changes.

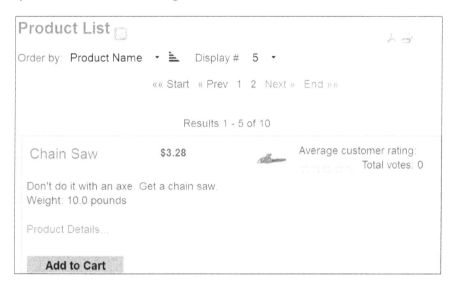

Notes

1. In this exercise, we changed the language elements in the `shop` module. You can apply similar techniques to any other module.

2. Sometimes you may have more than one language element that contain the search text. Make sure the element value matches exactly with the search text and is not a substring. Also, the case of the two text elements must also match. In case of doubt, you can test it by trial and error.

If your site is just with a single language, you don't need to bother changing the language file. You can go to the template file and change the element directly. We will be doing this from time-to-time in the exercises that will be presented in later chapters. (See, for example, *Chapter 3*, *Exercise 3.1* and *Exercise 3.6*)

Sometimes, you may want to add static text somewhere on a certain page. You will be able to do that by determining where the appropriate place is. There are probably various areas where you can insert the text. To maintain backward compatibility, it is advisable to insert the text in a *template* instead of the VirtueMart *page* or *class* file as far as possible. This may not be possible, but it is something worth considering before making any changes.

Sometimes, the text you want to add is dynamic, meaning that the text may be different depending on the specific situation. For example, you want to add a certain text to the browse page depending on the shopper group. Then you will need a PHP if construct to achieve this. We will be doing this in some of our exercises (See, for example, *Exercise 3.5* for use of the if construct).

Layout changes

Layout changes are those that involve moving elements around on the page or changing the style of an element. For example, you may want to make the product name look bigger. Or you want to display the price before the product SKU and so on. These are all layout changes that can be easily done once you locate the template file that needs to be modified.

For styling changes, you can either add the CSS style in the template file or modify the theme CSS file. Sometimes you can even change the style by modifying the Joomla! template CSS. Obviously, there are pros and cons for each of these approaches. While considering what to change, you should also think of future compatibility. It may be better to restrict the number of modified files to a minimal, but that also depends on other requirements as well.

Layout changes can also be dynamic. You may want to use one layout under a certain condition and another layout if a different condition applies. You may, for example, want to use one CSS style for products in a certain category and a different CSS style for products in another category. This again will involve PHP coding. We will also be doing some exercises of this kind in later chapters (See, for example, *Exercise 3.6*).

Frontend behavior changes

Frontend behavior changes are changes that involve JavaScript running on user's computer. You may come across a JavaScript that can create a reflection effect for the product image. Adding this kind of behavior is actually pretty straightforward. Usually this is accomplished by putting the JavaScript in the template file and modifying one or two HTML elements. The JavaScript can also be added to the theme.js file or included by other means (See *Chapter 5*, *Changing the Look of VirtueMart*, and *Chapter 9*, *Theme Customizations*, for details of using JavaScript when making behavior changes).

Another example of behavior changes is changing the Ajax add-to-cart pop-up. Some people find the time that the pop-up appears too short or too long. This can be adjusted in the `theme.js` file or in the `template` file (See how this can be done in *Exercise 8.2.*).

Modifying available template fields

Each of the templates will have a set of available fields that you can use. Sometimes you may want to display the same information in a different format. Examples of this kind of change are the `product_availability` and `product_thumb_image` fields. Many magic touches can be done in the template itself without involving changes to the VirtueMart class or page file.

Adding data fields

From time to time, you may want to add a data field to your shop. If you sell books, for example, you may want to add fields such as publisher and author. Adding data fields like this is not as simple as it may seem. First, you need to modify the database table, usually through a phpMyAdmin session. Then you will need to modify the class file to accommodate the new fields. You also need to modify the product form used in the backend so that the fields can be displayed and edited there. You will need to add this to the VirtueMart *page* file to pass it to the template. Finally, you will need to modify the template to actually display the field.

On the other hand, it will be much easier to add a new user field since VirtueMart allows adding/customizing user fields used in the frontend or backend. You should use the **Admin/Manage User Fields** menu option to update the user fields. (For a detailed discussion about customizing user fields, please see *Login/Registration and Shipping Information* in *Chapter 6, From Shop Basket to Final Checkout.*) If you need some detailed control on the user field behavior, this can be accomplished by modifying the class file or page file. In case the user field will need to be included in the order e-mail, the corresponding e-mail template will need to be modified as well.

Adding data fields to other data tables such as product category or order is also possible. The complexity of such kind of customizations will depend on the exact requirements.

Due to the complexity and technical skills needed in adding data, discussion of this type of customization will need to be done in a different book.

Modifying processing logic

The processing logic in a comprehensive shopcart like VirtueMart is definitely very complex. While VirtueMart is already very versatile and can cater for many actual applications, there are still areas that may not fit your specific needs. In that case, you may want to modify the processing logic to make VirtueMart work for you.

For situations like this, the best strategy would be to restrict your modifications to one single module. For example, if you just need changes in payments, you can probably develop your own payment methods. Anyhow, you should note that most processing logic resides in the page file and cannot be changed in a template. And the undertaking may involve complicated programming. So, the most part of this type of customization will be outside the scope of this small book. However, you may still find a few exercises that will involve modification of the page file, especially in *Chapter 10, Additional Customization Possibilities*. But those modifications definitely will be brief.

Creating a new theme

Sometimes you may want to develop your own theme, providing very different functionalities and style. Or you could even plan to sell your final design. To make it less intrusive to your user, creating a new theme is probably a good idea. This type of customization is the subject of *Chapter 8, VirtueMart Theme Anatomy,* and *Chapter 9, Theme Customizations*.

Integrating with an external system

VirtueMart is an online web store application. It does not provide accounting and customer management functions. Many users wish to make VirtueMart work together with their existing data system seamlessly. In that case, an integration system will need to be built. VirtueMart was intended to have an import/export system for that purpose. But unfortunately, the module is not well-developed and will need lots of effort to make it work.

Other customizations

There are many other types of VirtueMart customizations. We can create new VirtueMart page files to display what we want. For example, we could have created a new page for displaying manufacturers called `shop.manufacturer`. We can also create a new VirtueMart module called `wholesaler` to display pages only for a special group of shoppers. We can create new pages like `wholesaler.browse`, `wholesaler.product_detail`, and so on under this module. We can create new templates for the new page files and modules according to our needs and imagination.

How to create and integrate these pages with the bigger VirtueMart system, however, will be totally on our own.

Certainly, many real-world projects will be a combination of several of the customization types outlined previously. If you plan to customize VirtueMart involving a few of these areas, you need to have a thorough plan before you start. Otherwise, you may soon find the project becomes too big and is unmanageable.

Before starting your project

This brings us to the last section of this chapter. Before starting your project, you need to sit down and do some thinking and planning. You will find that the following steps can help to clarify your project needs and steps to meet those needs.

Determining the scope of project

First of all, you need to think about the scope of your project. Is it just a simple change of language elements or layout? Is all of the data already available? Do you need to modify the database or the class file? Do you need to change the processing logic? What modules will be involved? Will the change be done on a VirtueMart core or on a Joomla! module or even on Joomla! itself?

Sometimes a seemingly simple task may involve many modules of VirtueMart and can become very complex. The tax system, for example, involves several important areas of VirtueMart from the product list up to checkout. Any changes to the tax will thus not be a straightforward thing.

Locating file that needs modifications

When you are aware of the modules that may need change, you should drill down to the files that needs changes. Are modifications restricted solely to template files? Which template file contains the code that needs changes? There are close to 80 template files in the default theme. Locating the file to change may not be easy. If case of doubt, you can refer to the *Appendix, VirtueMart Template Reference* which contains a reference to all the template files. You can also use the technique described in testing and debugging to locate the page file that you will need to look at.

Assessing your skills – determine whether to do it in-house or outsource

Now you have an idea of the scope and the files that may need changes. But how are you going to make the modifications? Many modifications will be straightforward, especially if you are already comfortable working with HTML code. However, for more complex coding, it is better to leave it to the professional. If you have a team, probably someone in the team can be able to help. Otherwise, you will need to consider outsourcing. Professional help for small jobs are actually very affordable. You can consider using freelancers in the many online freelancer agents. Just be careful not to base your choice only on the lowest bid. Just like building a home, you won't want to compromise your safety by paying less.

Back up data and files

No matter how you are doing the job, whether in-house or outsourcing, it is always a good idea to back up your site before starting any modifications. For very small projects, such as changing the layout of a page where a database is not involved, you can just create a backup of the files that will need to be modified. You can even delay the backing up process to a time after the development has started. For projects of considerable size, however, you will need to have a full backup of the site.

Assessing impact on the site

As not all servers are created the same, it is not unusual to develop, test, and debug your customizations on your actual server. In that way, you can be sure the server configuration will be the same when you go live. If your site is already live, there is a lot more consideration. During development and testing, the site may be affected. So you need to assess the impact on the site. By carefully planning for the modifications, it is possible to restrict your changes to files that are not in use, at least in the initial stage. You can also do the development and testing at a time when there is less traffic.

Doing development and tests on a live site is not always advisable. In such cases or if you want to reduce the effect on your live site to a minimum, you should consider making a clone of the site. Cloning a site is not difficult. It just takes time. Many hosting packages will allow you to create subdomains from your main domain. Say your live site has a domain `www.yourdomain.com`. You can create a subdomain like `test.yourdomain.com`. You can then copy all the files from the live site to this subdomain site and do development and tests there.

If you cannot create your own subdomain, you can also create a subdirectory under the main domain. If the subdirectory is called test, then you can access the development site using the URL `http://www.yourdomain.com/test`. While the subdirectory site may look less professional than a subdomain site, the working is basically very similar. In both cases, you need to remember to change the site URL in the VirtueMart configuration.

Consider future upgrade compatibility

Another important point you need to consider is future compatibility. If Joomla! or VirtueMart issues an upgrade, how will that affect your customizations? Joomla! upgrade usually does not affect your changes, unless it is a major version change (such as from version 1.5 to 1.6). If it does, most probably it will affect the whole VirtueMart community and you should be able to find some help from the VirtueMart forum. More often than not, VirtueMart development team will issue a new version to support any new Joomla! version that will impact VirtueMart. But of course, there will be a time lag between the issues of the two upgrades.

The concern regarding version upgrade is very different, if there is a new version for VirtueMart. If it is a major version change (say from 1.1 to 1.5) where no patch is available, your customizations will probably be severely affected. A complete revision will then be mandatory. If this is just a minor version change, VirtueMart will usually provide a patch for each of its previous versions. You can then compare the list of files in the patch and the list of files you have modified. You are safe if none of the files overlap. Otherwise, you will need to merge the lines of code by hand.

To reduce the impact of version upgrade, you should try to limit the number of file changes as much as possible. The smaller the number, the less probable you will be impacted by a version upgrade. Usually, VirtueMart does not upgrade template files. So if your changes are all in templates, your customization will less likely be affected by a version upgrade. You can also further decrease the impact by creating a new theme for your customizations.

Implement design

We don't have much to say about implementation at this point. The principles of implementation is too big a subject to deal with in detail here. As we work on the exercises, we will mention some general principles here and there though. However, our emphasis will remain on the specific design detail instead of the general principles. The only thing we need to mention is making a comment. You should mark the area of modifications in the file clearly, making comments as appropriate. This will be useful later when you want to do further modifications or a version upgrade is needed. For large projects, you should make a log of all changes or even keep a bugtrack. Of course, each of these extra steps will cost additional time and money.

Testing and debugging

After the coding is complete, you can start testing and debugging. Testing and debugging is also a big subject in itself and cannot be covered in detail here. We will note by passing a few suggestions specifically for VirtueMart debugging.

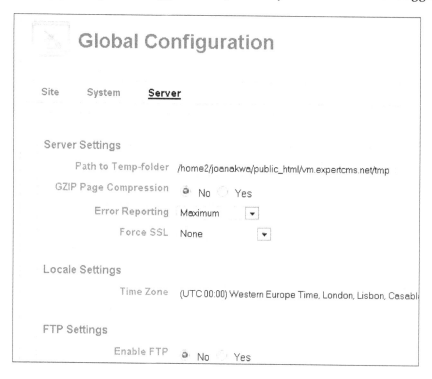

First of all, you should have PHP error reporting turned on during development, if that is possible. For an operating site, many web hosts prefer to turn off error reporting. This is in fact a best practice for live sites to avoid exposing site detail when an error occurs. However, testing without error reporting will be difficult and more time consuming. So if possible, turn error reporting to maximum. There is a Joomla! configuration that is supposed to control this. However, if your PHP configuration does not allow such kind of configuration change, the Joomla! configuration may not work. You may need to have your web host help to turn it on or, if your hosting allows, modify the `php.ini` file to allow this.

You can turn on VirtueMart debugging in the backend configuration to show some basic debug data. The debug checkbox is on the **Global** tab, in the **Core Settings** section. A similar setting is also available in Joomla! **Global Configuration**. The debug data can sometimes help you determine what's wrong with the code, but not always. Even with all this information, often the error cannot be identified until you print out some critical variables. So be prepared to make lots of use of the `print` statement to help debugging. We will give some further guidance on this as we work on the exercises.

One useful feature of the VirtueMart debug information is the filename that is involved in the data logic of a browser page. When debug is turned on, VirtueMart will print out the filename of the PHP script that controls the processing logic. This will help to locate the file that you will need to modify in case that information is not easy to guess.

Going live

Going live does not need any explanation. You just upload your code to the live site and things should work. Otherwise, you may need to remove the code from the live site and go back to the development site for testing.

Summary

In this chapter, we have navigated around the Joomla! directory and looked at the file structure of VirtueMart. We then explained the working of Joomla! through the model-view-controller model and compared this to the VirtueMart presentation framework. The roles of templates and themes in the VirtueMart pages were discussed. We then presented a list of possibilities for VirtueMart customizations and things that need to be considered before starting a VirtueMart customization project.

In the next chapter, we will take a look at the default VirtueMart theme and see how to configure it to change the look of your VirtueMart shop.

2
The VirtueMart Default Theme

In this chapter, our major focus will be on the `default` theme and its accompanied template structure. We will start with the shopping life cycle in VirtueMart, the backbone of the theme and template system. We will then give a general description of the VirtueMart configuration settings with a closer look at the **Site** configurations that relate closely to the frontend presentation. After that, we will concentrate on exploring the `default` theme. We will see the options that are available in the `default` theme configuration. Finally, we will give a brief introduction to the seven template groups under the `default` theme and understand their basic usage. The template groups will be elaborated further in the rest of the book.

Briefly, in this chapter, we will cover:

- The shopping life cycle
- VirtueMart layout configuration
- The `default` theme
- Theme configurations
- VirtueMart template groups

The shopping life cycle

VirtueMart is a Joomla! component that provides web store functions. Its purpose is to help store owner to put products online for sale. While the component itself can be used in various application settings, such as an online catalog that does not need any shop cart functions, shopping remains the major focus of the system. The theme and the whole template system also revolve around this major focus. So, an understanding of the theme system should come after the understanding of the shopping life cycle.

Landing page

Imagine when a shopper comes to the shop, the first thing he/she sees is the front door. For a web store, this is what we call the landing page or home page of the store. This landing page usually shows the major categories of what the shop is selling. However, that may not be the only items that the shop owner will want to show. Sometimes the history and background of the shop is important. Sometimes, the background of the owner is important. Sometimes, it shows special items on sale or featured products. Sometimes, it provides ideas or advice for a better shopping experience. In short, the nature of the content is not definite. But still, the landing page is there as the main entry to the shop. While the landing page of VirtueMart can be configured to any VirtueMart page, the default is `shop.index.php`. The URL for this default landing page is `http://your_joomla_live_site/index.php?option=com_virtuemart&page=shop.index`.

The product listing

Depending on the nature of the shop, there is usually a range of products of similar nature that a shopper can choose from. So products are usually arranged in categories for easier reference and selection. It is customary for a web store to display a list of products within each category that a shopper selected, either from the landing page or in a Joomla! module (for example, `mod_virtuemart`). Certainly, it is possible to list details of all the products on a single page. This may be a wise choice if there are only one or two products for sale on the site. However, most of the time there are so many products in a shop that listing each detail on a single page is not a good approach; there will be too much information and it will take too much time for the shopper to digest.

Instead, the product listing is usually just a summary list of the products giving sufficient detail to attract a shopper's attention. Shoppers who want to know more about a product can click through to the product detail page for information. While the exact detail of the listing may differ from store-to-store, the product listing is usually the starting point of direct shopping experience. The product listing page is usually referred to as the browse page in VirtueMart. The page file for the browse page is `shop.browse.php` and the URL is `http://your_joomla_live_site/index.php?option=com_virtuemart&page=shop.browse`.

The product detail

After a general view of the summary information provided by the product listing, a shopper will get an idea of which product or products will be worth the time to explore further. He/she will then be interested to know more about these products. So next comes the page showing all the details of the product. This is the Product Detail page or more commonly referred to as the flypage in VirtueMart. Again, the exact detail of the page may vary. However, this is the place where the major details of the product are shown. Usually, only one product is listed on one page. The page file for product detail is `shop.product_details.php` and the URL is `http://your_joomla_live_site/index.php?option=com_virtuemart&page=shop.product_details&product_id=id&flypage=flypage.tpl`.

Here, `id` is an identification number assigned to the product and `flypage.tpl` is the selected flypage template.

The shop cart

When the shopper decides to buy a product, there should be some way to help him/her to indicate this intention. Customarily, the system that helps shoppers to do this is called a shopcart system. There can be a number of ways to implement and show the shop cart. VirtueMart uses an **add-to-cart** button to help shoppers do this. After adding to cart, the product information will be stored in a php session variable.

If the shopper so wishes, he/she can go to the shop cart page at any time to look at the details of the items chosen and make adjustments as appropriate. The page file for the shop cart page is `shop.cart.php` and the URL is `http://your_joomla_live_site/index.php?option=com_virtuemart&page=shop.cart`.

Checkout

When the shopper is done choosing the products, and if he/she has something in the shop cart, he/she needs to pass through the checkout to create a formal order. In doing so, he/she may need to provide information for billing, shipping, choose additional options such as shipping method, payment method, and so on.

In the VirtueMart world, the shopper will need to have a Joomla! account before he/she can come back to check the order. VirtueMart also allows a shopper to check out without registering. In such a case, VirtueMart will create a temporary shopper account for checking out. The number of steps in the checkout will vary from store-to-store and VirtueMart provides configuration for defining the steps. After the shopper confirms an order, it will be created and stored in the database. An invoice e-mail will then be sent to both the store admin and the shopper.

The major checkout presentation logic is done in the page file `checkout.index.php`. The URL for checking out is `http://your_joomla_live_site/index.php?option=com_virtuemart&page=checkout.index`.

Account maintenance

The shopping system is not done with checking out if the shop allows a shopper to register. The shopper can come back to log in to Joomla! to check his/her order. The shopper can also change the registration data he/she provided after logon. VirtueMart account maintenance is done through the `account` module. The landing page is `account.index.php`. The URL is `http://your_joomla_live_site/index.php?option=com_virtuemart&page=account.index`.

Shopping digression

While shopping, a shopper may encounter a number of scenarios where a digression from the normal shopping life cycle is needed.

- **Product review**: The shopper had bought a certain item in a previous visit and would like to make a review of the product. VirtueMart will allow shoppers to enter their reviews if so permitted by the store administrator. The product review is processed by the product detail page.

- **Ask question**: The shopper has a question after seeing a product. VirtueMart allows a shopper to send his/her question to the store administrator. The page file for processing questions is `shop.ask.php`.

- **Out of stock**: The shopper tried to add a product to the shopcart, but it is out of stock. VirtueMart allows a shopper to register for notification when the product is back in stock again. The page file for processing restocking notification is `shop.waiting_list.php`.

- **Send to friend**: The shopper is interested in a certain product and feels a friend may be interested as well. He/she can choose to send a note to the friend. The page file for processing this request is `shop.recommendation.php`.

- **Vendor page**: The shopper is interested in knowing information about the vendor. The page file for processing this request is `shop.infopage.php`.

- **Manufacturer page**: The shopper is interested to know information about the manufacturer. The page file for processing this request is `shop.manufactuser.php`. The URL to access this page will also need to specify the `manufactuer_id` to identify the manufacturer.

VirtueMart configuration

VirtueMart has a wealth of configuration settings where you can customize its behavior. There are well over 100 different configurable settings. They are grouped into seven different tabs. We will not go over each of the tabs here. What concerns us most are the settings that will affect the behavior of VirtueMart in the frontend presentation.

The main purpose of looking at the configuration here is to familiarize ourselves with the settings that may be changed easily. It would be an unpleasant experience to do tons of work with the templates and find out later that what we need is just simply a configurable setting in the **Site** tab. So it is good to know what configuration is available under our fingertips before embarking on any project to customize VirtueMart.

OK. Let's log into VirtueMart and click **Admin/Configuration** on the left. You will see the seven tabs named **Global**, **Security**, **Site**, **Shipping**, **Checkout**, **Downloads**, and **Feed Configuration**. While you may be able to figure out what's in each of the tabs, it is still worthwhile to have a glance over each of the tabs to see what settings are available.

Global

The **Global** tab contains the most configurable items among the tabs. It is there to control the behavior of the shop. The settings are further subdivided into subsections.

The **Global** subsection controls whether the site is offline, the offline message, as well as whether the site is used as a catalog site where no add-to-cart function is provided.

The **Price** subsection controls whether to show the price, which Joomla! group of users can see the price, whether to show the **including XX% tax** text, and whether to show the packaging unit in the price.

The **Frontend Features** subsection basically controls the customer review features. There is also a checkbox to control whether to enable a content plugin in the product description and whether to use the coupon feature. The content plugin feature deserves a little bit more attention here. Content plugins are Joomla! extensions that are supposed to work with Joomla! content component when some specialized tags need to be replaced with dynamic text before sending out to the browser. The plugin does not replace tags in a VirtueMart page normally. However, if you placed some tags in the product description that you want the plugin to process, you can enable this feature in the configuration. Note that the feature only works with the product description, but not with tags placed in the template. We will need additional modifications to the code, if you need the content plugins to parse your tags in the template. We will work on an exercise like that in *Chapter 4, Product Details Templates* when we add a tab feature on the flypage.

The **Tax Configuration** subsection controls the tax-related features of VirtueMart.

The **User Registration Settings** subsection controls the registration type of VirtueMart and also the various settings regarding the **Terms of Service** and **Return Policy** of the site.

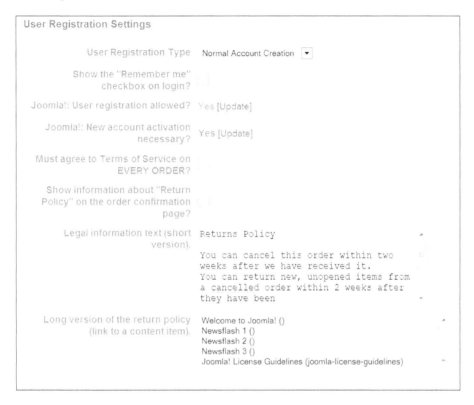

The **Core Settings** subsection is probably a misnomer. It would be better named as Miscellaneous Settings. Here, you can control whether VirtueMart will check stock, whether to check cookies, which currency converter to use, whether to use HTML format in the order e-mail, and whether to enable debug information. Regarding debug, you can configure whether the debug information will be limited to a certain IP.

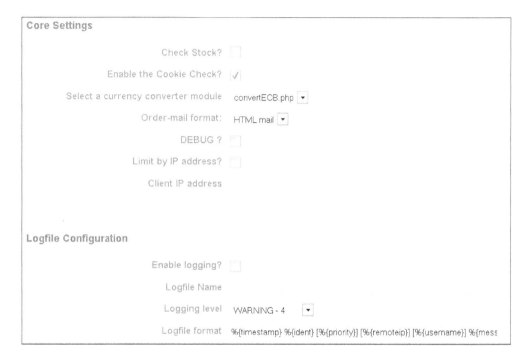

The **Logfile Configuration** subsection concerns the recording of the logfile. If you enable this feature, details of debug information will be put into the logfile you specified here.

Security

The **Security** tab comprises three subsections.

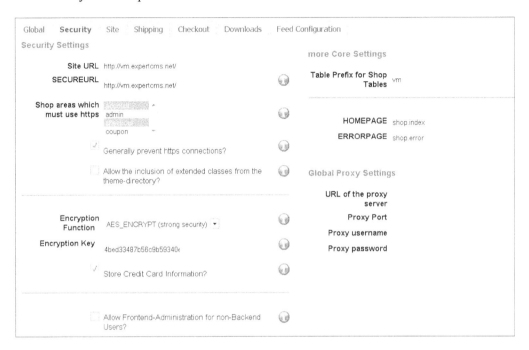

The **Security Settings** subsection controls those settings that relate to the security of the site. First, there are settings that control the root URL of the site, both for HTTP and HTTPS access. You can also control which modules to use HTTPS. You can change the encryption scheme and encryption key for storing sensitive information. You can control whether to store the credit card information in the database.

The **more Core Settings** subsection defines the prefix for VirtueMart database tables and also the page for the ViruteMart home and error page. The home page definition is not actually related to the security, but is defined here for some unknown reason.

The **Global Proxy Settings** define the values to be used, in case a proxy is needed for outward Internet access from the server. Some web hosts restrict outward Internet access for security concerns and will only allow them through a proxy. Depending on your Shipping or Payment providers, you may need Internet access from the code to the provider sites such as UPS or Authorize.net. In those cases, you will need to provide the proxy access data here.

Site

The **Site** tab contains two major subgroups. As these settings will interfere with the theme and template behavior, we will leave the discussion of this tab for a separate section.

Shipping

The **Shipping** tab controls which shipping method you will be using for checkout. You can enable or disable any of the methods installed independent of each other.

Checkout

The **Checkout** tab controls two things: whether you want to show the checkout bar and the steps that need to be used during checkout.

Downloads

The **Downloads** tab configures how VirtueMart behaves when selling downloadable products.

Feed Configuration

The **Feed Configuration** tab configures how VirtueMart behaves when providing the RSS feed. You can safely ignore this, if you are not using RSS feed or not sure what an RSS feed is.

VirtueMart site configuration

Let's go back to the **Site** tab to see how this will interact with the **default** theme. Here, you will find two major subsections: the **Display** and the **Layout**.

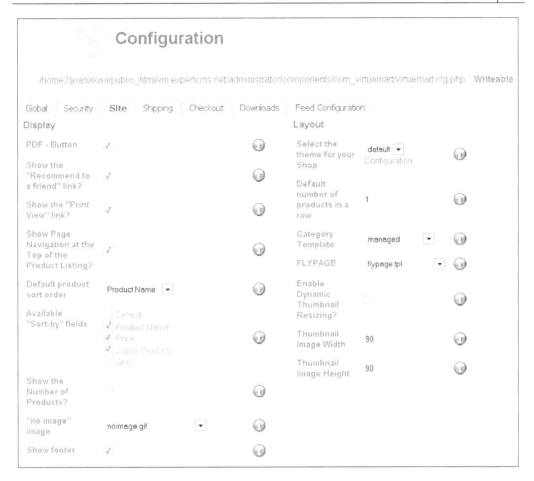

Display subsection

The settings on the left are related to the display of shop pages.

- **PDF, Recommend to a friend, Print:** The first three items in the **Display** subsection are self-explanatory. They control whether to show the **PDF**, the **Recommend to a friend**, and the **Print** link, respectively.

- **Navigation and sorting:** Next come the controls for the navigation and sorting settings on the browse page. By default, VirtueMart will show the navigation section at the bottom of the page. If you need an additional navigation section at the top, you can enable this here. Actually, the navigation is something that relates to the template and should be set as a theme setting instead. Anyhow, you know that it is here when you need it. The next controls are the default sort order and the sorting options available from the frontend.

- **Number of products in category:** The next item controls whether to show the number of products after the category link in the child category list. This concerns only the product listing page and those categories that have child categories only.

- **No image and footer:** The last two items of the **Display** subsection are again self-explanatory.

Layout subsection

The **Layout** subsection determines some of the major presentation options and is more intimately related to the themes and templates. Actually, some of the settings here would be better placed in the Theme configuration instead of the VirtueMart configuration, as we shall see.

- **Theme and Configure Link:** The first item in the configuration is the theme. Here you should see a drop-down with all the themes you have installed in the site. Usually, installation simply means uploading the theme directory to the directory `components/com_virtuemart/themes`. Each theme has a unique name, the same as the directory name. Under the theme drop-down, there is a link labeled **Configuration**. Depending on the theme, there are more configurable settings you can control by going to the theme configuration. We will go into the details of the theme configuration of the `default` theme in the next section.

- **Default number of products:** The second item is the default number of products in each row of the browse page. You can define this number for each individual category in the new/edit category page. If the category, manufacturer, and search product listing do not have a predefined number, the default number defined in this setting will be used.

- **Default templates:** The next two items are the default template for the browse page and flypage, respectively. As the available templates for selection vary with the theme, the drop-down selection options will change when the theme is changed. This sometimes gives rise to mysterious problems relating to your browse page and flypage. So whenever you need to change the theme, check the default templates to make sure they exist for your theme. Otherwise, you may find the browse page or flypage empty.

  In the default browse template drop-down, there is a mysterious template called **managed**. Actually, this is not a physical template. When you select the managed template, VirtueMart will select the appropriate template for you, depending on the choice of the number of products per row, either defined for the category or as defined in the default number in the setting above. If the number is 1, then browse_1 will be used, if the number is 2, browse_2 will be used, and so on.

  We will have more to say about the other template options when we study the browse and flypage templates in detail in the next two chapters.

- **Image thumbnail:** The last three items in the **Layout** tab concern the product image thumbnail. VirtueMart has an automatic system that will generate the thumbnail dynamically. You can turn this feature on and off at any time and VirtueMart will work accordingly. The thumbnail width and height can also be configured here. Note that the thumbnail size is the same for both the browse page and the flypage. You can customize the flypage template to use a different thumbnail size. This will be one of our exercises in *Chapter 4, Product Details Templates*.

The default theme configuration

As mentioned in the previous section, each of the themes can have its own configuration page. If you are still on the **Site** tab, you can click on the **Configuration** link to bring up the configuration page for the default theme. If not, please go back to the VirtueMart **Configuration**, **Site** tab to reach the **Configuration** link. Make sure the default theme is selected in the drop-down above before you click on the **Configuration** link.

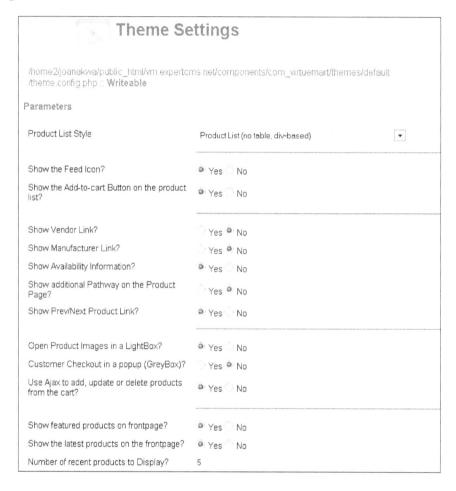

Most of the configurable items within the default theme settings are related to the flypage (also known as the product page). You can, therefore, assume this is true unless otherwise stated.

- **Product List Style:** The first item, which determines the product list style, obviously applies only to the browse page. You can choose whether to display the list in table style, list style using HTML tables, or list style without using the HTML table (div-based). The default is to use the div-based list style without using the table.

- **Show the Feed Icon:** The next item controls whether to show the Feed icon. The Feed icon is supposed to open the page for the RSS feed. If you don't need this, you can turn this off here.

- **Show the Add-to-cart Button on Product List:** The next item controls whether to show the **add-to-cart** button on the browse page (also known as product list page). For all the flypage templates in the `default` theme, the **Add-to-cart** button will be shown on the flypage to allow a shopper to add a product to the shop cart, unless you have set the site to use as a product catalog (see **Global Configuration** in the *VirtueMart configuration* section). The option to also show this button on the browse page is a useful shortcut to let the shopper add a product to the cart directly without going through the flypage. However, if this is not what you need, you can turn it off here.

Note that the **Add-to-cart** button will not be shown even if this option is turned on when the product contains child products, advanced attributes, or custom attributes. The existence of these additional attributes will complicate the processing logic on the add-to-cart function and so is not allowed.

- **Vendor Link, Manufacturer Link**, and **Availability Information:** The next three items control whether to show the Vendor Link, the Manufacturer Link, and the Availability Information, respectively. These options are self-explanatory and do not need further explanation.

- **Additional Pathway on Flypage:** The next item controls whether to show the additional pathway on the flypage. The pathway shows the path through which the shopper has to browse through to reach the current page. The pathway is also called the breadcrumbs in some systems. If you need this feature you can turn this on.

- **Previous and Next Product** link: The next item controls whether to show the **Previous and Next Product** link on the flypage. The Previous and Next Product refers to the order of the products in the latest or the default category of the product. This is a useful feature to allow a shopper to browse through the products in a category sequentially without going back to the product list page.

- **Full image LightBox effect**: The next item controls whether to show the product's full image in a lightbox effect. The lightbox effect is used only on the flypage templates. If you need the same effect for the browse page, you can customize the browse template for this.

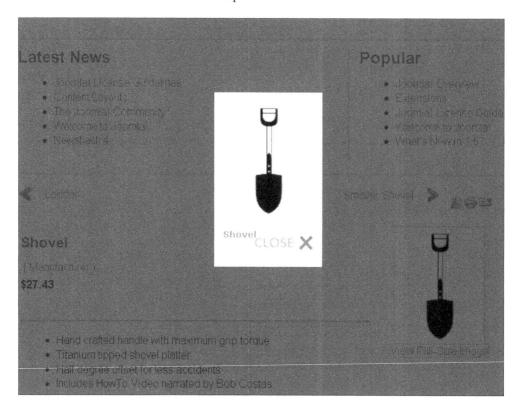

- **Checkout GreyBox effect:** The next item controls whether to use the greybox effect during checkout. If this option is on, the checkout pages will be shown in a greybox instead. The greybox size is hardcoded to 500 x 600 in the template. If you need to change this, you can customize the template.

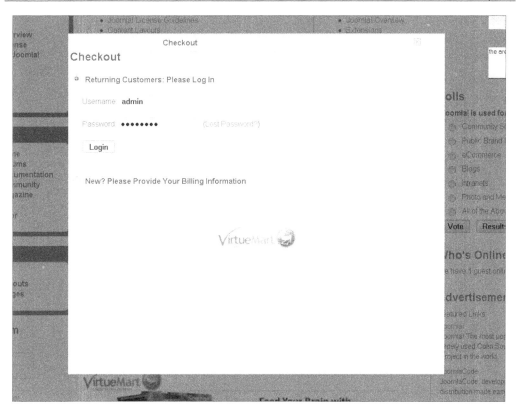

- **Ajax add-to-cart:** The next item controls whether to use Ajax to add-to-cart. In case you aren't familiar with this, Ajax is the acronym for asynchronous JavaScript XML. This is a technology to send an HTML request back to the server without refreshing a page. When this option is on, the add-to-cart request will be sent through Ajax to the server when the add-to-cart button is clicked. After the response is received from the server, the shopper will briefly see a pop up telling them whether the update is successful, and if yes, give them the option to go to the shop cart page or continue on the current page. While the option says VirtueMart will add, update, and delete products in the cart through Ajax, actually Ajax is used only with the **add-to-cart** button on the flypage and browse page. This does not apply to the shopcart page where most update and deletions are done. The **add-to-cart** button can delete or update a shop cart only when used with a child product in the listing style.

- **Featured products, latest products**: The next two items control whether to show featured Products and the latest Products on the VirtueMart front page (also known as VirtueMart home page). The number of products to show for both is hardcoded to 10 in the default templates. If you wish to change that number, you need to change it in the template. While both options say specifically that they apply to the front page, actually the Featured Products setting is also used in the flypage and browse page. So, if you want to show featured products only on the VirtueMart home page, you will need to modify the flypage.

- **Recent products:** The last item controls the number of recent products to show on the browse page and flypage. Recent products actually refer to the products that the shopper has browsed through during the session. Setting the number of recent products to 0 is equivalent to turning off the recent products feature. We note in passing that this setting is actually used by VirtueMart globally independent of the theme, and therefore is more logical to be placed back in the VirtueMart configuration instead.

VirtueMart template groups

There are well over 80 different templates in the default theme. They are placed into seven directories. While VirtueMart does not have a specific term for these template groupings, we shall refer to each directory as a template group to facilitate easier discussion. In this section, we will only give a brief overview of the groups and templates. Details of the templates can be found in *Appendix, VirtueMart Template Reference*. We will also discuss most, if not all, of the major templates in the chapters to come.

Name ↓	Size	Last Modified	
basket		28/07/2010	12:58:00 AM
browse		28/07/2010	12:58:00 AM
checkout		28/07/2010	12:58:00 AM
common		28/07/2010	12:58:00 AM
order_emails		28/07/2010	12:58:00 AM
pages		28/07/2010	12:58:00 AM
product_details		28/07/2010	12:58:00 AM
index.html		20/05/2010	1:34:00 PM

browse

The `browse` template group is one of the largest template groups in VirtueMart. It controls the layout of the product listing page for categories, manufacturers, and search results. The browse templates actually comprise two different types: the browse template proper and the templates for various elements on the browse page.

The browse page has a number of elements on it including the header, the navigation, the sort order, additional information such as featured products, latest products, related products, and so on. Also, it has the product summary list which is what we referred to as the browse template proper above.

Each category can have its own browse and product detail template which can be changed in the category edit page. This so called "browse" template is actually the browse template proper. There are quite a number of browse templates to choose from. This is the template that controls the layout of the product summary for each individual product. If there is no category template defined, the default template, as defined in the theme configuration, is used. The default template also applies to the case of the manufacturer product listing and search result listing.

For the other elements on the browse page, there is only one template within the same theme. That means, if you want to show a different view of the navigation depending on the category, there is no way that you can achieve this by writing a different template. You can do so only by customizing the template, however, as we shall see.

While we have no control over most of the elements on the browse page without hacking into the templates, there is one exception to this rule. VirtueMart does allow users to change the style of the browse page, based on the site's needs. Specifically, you can change the browse page style to table style, list style without using HTML table, or list style without HTML table, as we have explained in the *VirtueMart configuration* section above. Each of those styles has a corresponding template in the `includes` subdirectory under the `browse` directory. If you want to use a different style based on a user or category, you will need to hack into the template.

We will have more to say about the `browse` templates in *Chapter 3*, *Product List Templates*.

product_details

Just like the `browse` template group, the `product_details` group comprises two types of templates: the flypage template proper and the flypage elements template.

You can specify the flypage template proper based on the category in the category edit page. If no flypage template is selected, the default template, as defined in the VirtueMart configuration, will be used. In addition to this, you can override the flypage template through the URL request parameter. Let's assume you have two templates in the theme named as `flypage.tpl.php` and `special.tpl.php` and the default template is `flypage.tpl.php`. The URL

`http://your_joomla_live_site/index.php?option=com_ virtuemart&page=shop.product_detail&product_id=1&flypage=special. tpl` will display the flypage using the `special.tpl` template instead of the default template or even the category template, if one has been defined.

The flypage template proper is probably the most commonly customized VirtueMart template. There is a lot of stuff that you can customize here. You have all the product fields in the data table at your fingertips. You can choose to show or not show any of those fields. You can also control whether to show product type parameters, the price, the add-to-cart button, the product review, product review form, related products, more images, recent products, and so on.

Many of the elements on the flypage have their own template. The addtocart element templates are found in the `includes` subdirectory. You can change the way the advanced attribute or the custom attribute are displayed. If you don't want to use a drop-down for your advanced attribute, for example, you can use a radio button instead by customizing the `addtocart_advanced_attribute.tpl.php` template. The same will apply to the custom attribute. We will work on an exercise of this type in *Chapter 4, Product Details Templates*. The display of child products is also determined by the addtocart templates. By default, child products are displayed as a drop-down. However, you can choose a different style for individual products on the product edit page.

Other than the addtocart templates, some flypage element templates are placed in the `common` template group instead.

basket

The basket templates will control the layout of the cart contents on the shopcart page as well as the cart section throughout the checkout pages. There are four templates in this group, two for the case where the cart contents will be editable and two for the case when the cart contents are read only. The read-only templates are used in the final confirmation page. Otherwise, the cart will be editable. The read-only template files have a prefix of ro_ (stands for read only) in their names.

In each of the two cases, the template labeled as b2c (that is, business to consumer) will show tax information, if the shopper is logged in when the tax rate can be calculated. The template b2b (business to business) will not show tax information until the very end.

As from version 1.1.5, VirtueMart introduces a new template in the basket group for PayPal express checkout. This template will show PayPal features to enable a shopper to checkout through the PayPal express module instead of the normal VirtueMart checkout path.

checkout

Checkout is actually a different VirtueMart module for handling all stuff during the whole checkout process. There are a number of pages related to this and most of the related templates are placed in the checkout template group.

First, there is a login/registration page where shoppers will need to provide billing information to the system. The login form has its own template and is placed under the common template group. However, the layout of the login/registration form is controlled by the template login_registration.tpl.php in the checkout group. Actually, the display of user data is done mostly in the ps_userfield class. So, if you want to change the user field display, do not look at this template. You will need to customize ps_userfield.php instead. However, if you have a problem with the accordion effects for the login and registration form, this is the right template to look into.

After billing information is available, either through login or input through the registration section, the shopper may be required to enter the shipping information. This brings up the get shipping address page. There is a template get_shipping_ address.tpl.php to control the layout of this page. VirtueMart also has a template customer_info.tpl.php to control the layout of the shopper information and a template list_shipto_addresses.tpl.php to list the shipping addresses.

Similarly, there is a template for getting the shipping method and for getting the payment method. As shipping requirement varies greatly among the providers, it may not be wise to dictate the final format of the detailed display. Thus, you will find that the template `list_shipping_methods.tpl.php` basically does nothing. The detail of the shipping method display is the responsibility of each individual shipping method. In case you need to customize the display of the shipping rates, you may need to hack into the shipping method code instead of the templates.

The display of the payment method is pretty much similar. VirtueMart thus controls the display tightly through its own template `list_payment_methods.tpl.php` and its own code in the `ps_checkout` class. In case you have a custom need, you can modify the template. However, you will need to hack into the class file for any detailed changes.

After the payment method is selected, all the information for the order is pretty much available. VirtueMart will show a confirmation page to get confirmation from the shopper before committing the order. The page layout is controlled by the template `get_final_confirmation.tpl.php`. There is a lot of processing logic included in this template, so customizing this template is not easy for novice coders. Perhaps, what you can modify is moving around the different sections of coding on the script to lay out the elements differently.

The last template we need to mention in the checkout group is the template `checkout_bar.tpl.php`, which controls the checkout bar showing up during the course of checkout.

order_emails

`order_emails` is the simplest template group in VirtueMart. There are only two templates within this group. The template `confirmation_email.tpl.php` controls the layout of the order e-mail or otherwise known as the invoice to the shopper and administrator. There is a wealth of data passed to the template and there are lots of customization possibilities. We will go into the detail of this template in *Chapter 10, Additional Customization Possibilities*.

The other template `enquiry_email.tpl.php` in this group concerns the reply to a shopper when he/she sends a question to the store admin. This is a very raw e-mail. If you constantly have enquiries of this sort, you will definitely want to customize this template to make the reply look better.

common

The common template group contains templates that are shared among different pages or even different modules. Thus, the nature of the templates varies greatly.

- availability.tpl.php
- buttons.tpl.php
- categoryChildlist.tpl.php
- couponField.tpl.php
- featuredProducts.tpl.php
- login_form.tpl.php
- minicart.tpl.php
- moreImages.tpl.php
- pathway.tpl.php
- price.tpl.php
- product_type.tpl.php
- productsnapshot.tpl.php
- recent.tpl.php
- relatedProducts.tpl.php
- reviewform.tpl.php
- reviews.tpl.php
- shopIndex.tpl.php
- voteform.tpl.php
- votes_allvotes.tpl.php

Basically, you can guess the function of the template by looking at the filename. Some of these templates will be referred to throughout the book. We will give some explanations on them when they are used, especially for those more complicated templates. Otherwise, you can check the details in the *Appendix, VirtueMart Template Reference.*

pages

The pages template group controls the layout of the VirtueMart page that has the same name. Not all pages have a corresponding template. However, if a page does, you will have some fine control over its layout. The pages that have a template are:

- account.billing.tpl.php
- account.index.tpl.php
- account.order_details.tpl.php

- `account.orders.tpl.php`
- `account.shipping.tpl.php`
- `account.shipto.tpl.php`
- `checkout.thankyou.tpl.php`
- `shop.ask.tpl.php`
- `shop.cart.tpl.php`
- `shop.infopage.tpl.php`
- `shop.manufacturer.tpl.php`
- `shop.savedcart.tpl.php`
- `shop.waiting_list.tpl.php`
- `shop.waiting_thanks.tpl.php`

Again, we won't go into the detail of each template here. Explanation will be given for those more complicated ones when they are referred to throughout the book. Otherwise, you can check the *Appendix*, *VirtueMart Template Reference* for details on each template.

Summary

In this chapter, we looked at the shopping life cycle in VirtueMart. We then explored the various settings that are available on the VirtueMart **Global Configuration** and also took a closer look at the **Site** tab, which relates intimately with the frontend presentation. We went on to see how the `default` theme can be further configured. Finally, we looked at the seven template groups available in the `default` theme.

In the next chapter, we will look at the `browse` template group in detail and start doing some actual customizations.

3
Product List Templates

This chapter is the first of four chapters that explain the working of the major template groups in VirtueMart. In this first chapter, our focus will be on the `browse` (product list) template group. We will start with a sample template to see how a template works. Some basic PHP language constructs will be introduced before looking at the browse page elements and then the three different product list styles. Then we will look closely at each of the major templates in the group. We will guide you to customize the basic layout, the header, the navigation links, the add-to-cart form, the product list styles, and many more.

Briefly, in this chapter, we will cover:

- The product list page
- Looking at our first template
- Core browse templates
- Header templates
- Navigation templates
- Add-to-cart form template
- Addendum templates
- Product list style templates

The product list page

Product list page is the most important starting page for the shopping life cycle. While the landing page will give some general information regarding the shop, the list of items for sale in the shop is the major job of the product list page. Some shop owners even prefer to use product list page as their home page. Product list page is in singular, but actually the product list page is a series of pages. The total number of pages in the series varies from store-to-store and typically depends on the number of categories you have in the site. Each category will have its own page or even pages, if the category contains many products. Furthermore, the product list page is also used to list the products that relate to a particular manufacturer. It is also used for the keyword search and advanced search, if you enable the product search and advanced search Joomla! modules or the product search Joomla! plugin.

To simplify our discussion, we will first restrict ourselves to the study of category listing. The manufacturer listing and search listing are very similar. We will go back to the differences later in the chapter. Let's take a look at a typical category listing.

Garden Tools

PAGE HEADER

Garden Tools

Sort by: Product Name ▾ ≞ Display # 5 ▾

NAVIGATION   «« Start « Prev 1 2 3 Next » End »»

Results 1 - 2 of 6

Chain Saw   **$164.61**   Average customer rating:
Total votes: 0

Don't do it with an axe. Get a chain saw.
Product Details...

Quantity: 1   ▲ ▼   PRODUCT LISTING

Add to Cart

Circular Saw   **$242.44**   Average customer rating:
Total votes: 0

Cut rings around wood. This saw can handle the most delicate projects.
Product Details...

«« Start « Prev 1 2 3 Next » End »»

PAGE FOOTER

Display # 5 ▾
Results 1 - 2 of 6

Featured Products

Hand Shovel   **Circular Saw**

$5.48 $242.44

ADDENDUM ELEMENTS

Nice hand shovel to dig with in the yard.   Cut rings around wood. This saw can handle the

From the preceding screenshot, we can identify a number of important elements on a product list page:

- **Page header**: This includes the category name, category description, the PDF, and print icons. The layout of the page header will depend on the page header templates.

- **Navigation**: This includes the order by form, the order by direction button (toggle between ascending and descending), number per page drop-down box, and the page navigation links. Note that the page navigation links can appear both at the top and the bottom. The navigation layout is controlled by the navigation templates.

- **Product listing**: This is the major item of the page, where the products are listed in a way defined by the product listing style and the number of products per row settings. Each of the products displayed within the listing is controlled by the core browse template (the core browse template is explained in the section *Core browse templates*).

- **Addendum elements**: This includes the recent products, latest products, featured products, and so on. Each of the addenda may have its own template.

- **Page footer**: This is the element placed at the end of the listing. Right now, there is only one element within the page footer, the page navigation.

As we shall see, the layout of each of these elements is controlled by one or more templates. By customizing any one of these templates, we may be able to change the look of the page completely.

We need to distinguish the usage between the terms browse templates and core browse templates. For the purpose of making things clear, we retain the term "browse templates" to refer to all templates within the browse template group. Within this broad template group, there are two subgroups: those which control the layout detail of each individual product (each product in the product listing section) and those which control all the other elements. We refer to them as core and non-core templates, respectively. The core browse templates reside directly under the templates/browse subdirectory. All the non-core templates reside under the subdirectory templates/browse/includes. The difference between the core and non-core templates will become clear in the following explanation.

Looking at our first template

While VirtueMart templates are different from each other, they actually follow a definite pattern. To understand how the template is structured, probably the best way is to look at a sample.

Let's take a look at the file `browse_1.tpl.php` as an example. This is one of the core browse templates. The full text of this file is as follows (with line numbers added):

```
1.   <?php if( !defined( '_VALID_MOS' ) && !defined( '_JEXEC' ) )
die( 'Direct Access to '.basename(__FILE__).' is not allowed.' );
2.   mm_showMyFileName(__FILE__);
3.   ?>
4.   <div class="browseProductContainer">
5.           <h3 class="browseProductTitle"><a title="<?php echo
$product_name ?>" href="<?php echo $product_flypage ?>">
6.               <?php echo $product_name ?></a>
7.           </h3>
8.
9.           <div class="browsePriceContainer">
10.          <?php echo $product_price ?>
11.          </div>
12.
13.          <div class="browseProductImageContainer">
14.              <script type="text/javascript">//<![CDATA[
15.              document.write('<a href="javascript:void window.
open(\'<?php echo $product_full_image ?>\', \'win2\', \'status=no
,toolbar=no,scrollbars=yes,titlebar=no,menubar=no,resizable=yes,wi
dth=<?php echo $full_image_width ?>,height=<?php echo $full_image_
height ?>,directories=no,location=no\');">');
16.              document.write( '<?php echo ps_product::image_
tag( $product_thumb_image, 'class="browseProductImage" border="0"
title="'.$product_name.'" alt="'.$product_name .'"' ) ?></a>' );
17.              //]]>
18.              </script>
19.              <noscript>
20.                  <a href="<?php echo $product_full_image ?>"
target="_blank" title="<?php echo $product_name ?>">
21.                  <?php echo ps_product::image_tag(
$product_thumb_image, 'class="browseProductImage" border="0"
title="'.$product_name.'" alt="'.$product_name .'"' ) ?>
22.                  </a>
23.              </noscript>
24.          </div>
25.
26.          <div class="browseRatingContainer">
27.          <?php echo $product_rating ?>
28.          </div>
```

```
29.          <div class="browseProductDescription">
30.              <?php echo $product_s_desc ?> 
31.              <a href="<?php echo $product_flypage ?>"
title="<?php echo $product_details ?>"><br />
32.                  <?php echo $product_details ?>...</a>
33.          </div>
34.          <br />
35.          <span class="browseAddToCartContainer">
36.          <?php echo $form_addtocart ?>
37.          </span>
38.
39. </div>
```

HTML fragments

The coding is pretty typical of a VirtueMart template file. You can see that the template is basically an HTML fragment embedded with PHP coding. All PHP code is enclosed within the tag <?php ... ?>. In most cases, the PHP code uses the statement echo $field_name to add the field value to the HTML code. We will be looking at those PHP constructs in the next subsection. After parsing the template, the output should be a well-formed HTML code.

You should note that the template is just an HTML fragment, meaning no <html>, <head>, and <body> tags are needed. As you can recall, VirtueMart is just a Joomla! component that will handle the main content. So the HTML fragment produced by the template (together with other code, if any, built up by the page file) will be returned to the Joomla! engine for further processing. Typically, the Joomla! engine will pass this HTML fragment into the Joomla! template which, in turn, will insert the HTML into a location designated by the template. The final output of the Joomla! template will then be a valid HTML document. The <html>, <head>, and <body> tags will therefore be the responsibility of the Joomla! template.

Let's look at the code to see how these 39 lines of code work. Remarks will only be needed for lines with the PHP tag. All the rest are HTML code that you should be familiar with.

- Lines 1 to 3 are actually some housekeeping code following the Joomla!/VirtueMart pattern. They will restrict direct access to the code and print out the template filename when debugging.

- Line 5 will output the product title with the product name embedded inside a hot link pointing to the product detail page.

- Line 10 will output the product price.

- Lines 14 to 23 contain a lengthy JavaScript code. The purpose is to output the image thumbnail embedded inside a hot link to open the full image. We need JavaScript here because we want to ensure the pop-up window size fits the full image size. (Otherwise, the pop-up window size will depend on the default size of the browser.) The window size cannot be controlled by HTML and so we need JavaScript help. If JavaScript is not enabled in a client browser, we will fall back to HTML code to handle the pop-up.

- Line 27 outputs the product rating, as reviewed by the user.

- Line 30 outputs the product's short description.

- Lines 31 to 33 outputs the text of **product details** within a hot link pointing to the product details page.

- Line 36 outputs the add-to-cart form, which includes the **add-to-cart** button, the quantity box, and so on.

PHP crash course

While we are not going to present all the complex program structure of PHP, it will be useful if we have a basic understanding of some of its major constructs. You may not fully understand what exactly each line of code does at first, but stick with us for a little while. You will soon grasp the concept as the pattern appears repeatedly in the exercise we will work on. In the preceding sample template, the PHP coding is pretty simple. (The most complex structure is actually the JavaScript that tries to spit out some HTML on the client browser, not PHP!) We can identify a few basic PHP constructs among the sample code:

- **Variables**: Just like any other programming language, a variable is a basic element in PHP. All PHP variables start with the dollar sign $. A variable name consists of alphanumeric characters and the underscore _ character. The first character must be either alphabetical or _, while numerals can also be used after the first character. It should be noted that the space character, together with most punctuation characters, are not allowed in a variable name. Alphabetic characters can be either uppercase or lowercase. Conventionally, VirtueMart will use only lowercase letters for variable names. While both uppercase and lowercase letters can be used without restrictions, variable names are case sensitive, meaning that $Product and $product will be treated as two different variables.

The variable name chosen usually reflects the actual usage of the variable. In the sample template, `$product_name` and `$product_flypage`, for example, are typical variables and they will represent the value of a product name and product flypage, respectively. VirtueMart uses _ to separate words within a variable name to make the variable name more readable. Actually, many of the variables are passed into the template by the VirtueMart page file. These variables are called available fields. We will have more to say about that in the next subsection.

- **Constants**: Variables are changing values. You can assign a new value to it at any time and it will take up the new value. There are times when you want to keep the value unchanged. You can use a constant for that purpose. A constant name is pretty much the same as a variable name, but you don't need the $ character. In line 1 of the sample template, both `_VALID_MOS` and `_JEXEC` are constants. You probably recognize that they both use capital letters. This is conventional for Joomla! and VirtueMart so that constants stand out within the code.

  Constants are values that cannot be changed. If you try to give it another value, PHP will complain and fail.

- **Data type**: Any variable will have a data type associated with it. Data type can be a number, a string (that is, a series of characters or text), or other possibilities. Since the major purpose of a VirtueMart template is to produce HTML code, we will find that most of the variables we deal with are strings.

  Often, we will need to write out a literal string in our coding. To distinguish our string from the rest of the coding, we need to enclose the literal string with quotes. We can use single or double quotes. Single and double quotes actually have subtle differences, but we won't go into the detail for the time being. According to the VirtueMart program standard, a literal string should be enclosed in single quotes such as `'product name'`. Note that `'product name'` is a literal string containing the text `product name`. It is different from `$product_name`, which is a variable and may contain characters like `'circular saw'` instead.

- **Operators**: You learnt addition and subtraction at school. They are mathematical operations to combine numbers. In PHP, we also have other operations to combine two or more variables. The most important one in our exercises is probably string concatenation, symbolized by . (the dot character). String concatenation combines two or more strings together to form a single string. The operation `'hello'.'world'` will give a new string `'helloworld'`. Note that there is no space character between the words. To make sure the words are separated by a space, we will need to use two concatenations such as `'hello'.' '.'world'`, which will give you the new string `'hello world'`.

- **Functions**: Often, we will find that the same pattern of program code is used repeatedly to produce a given result. In PHP, we can group those code together to form a function. Each function will have a name and can be invoked using the following syntax:

  function_name (*parameters*)

  Here, *parameters* are values that will need to be passed into the function to evaluate the result. In PHP, we have lots of functions that deal with strings. The function `strlen($product_name)`, for example, will return the number of characters in the string variable `$product_name`. If `$product_name` contains the string `'circular saw'`, `strlen($product_name)` will return 12. (You probably recognize that `strlen` is just a short form for string length.) We will learn some more functions along the way.

- **echo statements**: This is the most common statement in the template. `echo` is used to send the value of a string to the output buffer. So `echo $product_name` literally means "print out the value of the variable `$product_name` to the output buffer".

  Sometimes, the `echo` statement is mistaken to be a function. So you may try to write something like `echo($product_name)`, instead of `echo $product_name`. While this is acceptable in PHP most of the time, the braces are actually not needed. (You may be aware that sometimes the command `print` function is used to send data to the output buffer in the place of `echo`. While `print` and `echo` seem interchangeable, `echo` runs faster than `print` and so should be the preferred choice to output data.)

- **if statements**: The `if` statement is a construct to test a condition before taking a certain action. The action will be taken only if the condition evaluates to true. The syntax of an `if` statement is as follows:

  `if (condition) action`

  where the *condition* is an expression for testing and *action* is a statement or a series of statements to be performed, if the expression evaluates to true. The expression can be a true-false type condition (such as `$i>0`), a mathematical expression (such as `$i+$j`), or some kind of complex operation involving functions. In any case, it will be considered as true, if it evaluates to a non-zero number or a non-empty string.

- **Statement separator**: One important PHP construct we usually overlook is the statement separator `;` (the semicolon). We need this to separate two or more statements, even if they are on new lines of their own. In the preceding sample code, we have a "`;`" at the end of line 1 and 2. This `;` is very important. Without that, the PHP parser will be confused and will probably refuse to execute and will give you a fatal error.

These are just a few constructs in PHP for the time being. We will have more to say about PHP as we encounter more constructs along the way.

Available fields

Since many of the variables in our template code are passed down from the VirtueMart page file, one natural question to ask is "What variables can we use in our code?". Variables that we can use in a template are known as available fields.

The available fields we have inside a template will vary with the template itself. A field which is available in the flypage template may not be available in a browse template. Even among the browse templates, there may be differences. To maximize our customization effort on a template, it is essential to be aware of the available fields in each template.

However, there are so many available fields in a template that it may not be wise to list them all here. We will dedicate that job to the *Appendix, VirtueMart Template Reference,* where you can find a template reference, detailing the available field and its usage. For now, it will be useful to distinguish four different types of available fields:

- **Database fields**: Most of the data we have comes from the database. Often, the VirtueMart page file just passes those fields directly to the template without changing anything. They are called database fields. The same data you put into the database from the backend will be at your fingertips. Examples are `$product_id` and `$product_sku`.

- **Formatted database fields**: Sometimes the data you stored in the database is raw data. You will need a different format in the presentation. VirtueMart will do some formatting on the data before passing it to the template. An example is `$product_available_date`, which is stored in the database as an integer. However, you need to display it in a form that is appropriate to your culture such as `yyyy-mm-dd`, `mm-dd-yyyy`, and so on.

- **Processed data**: Sometimes there may be complex logic before you can produce data that is useful in the template. A typical example is the `$product_price`. Do not expect this to be a simple number or a formatted number with the currency symbol added. Actually, the product price will depend on a number of factors such as whether the user has logged in, the shopper group, discount, tax, and so on. So the `$product_price` in the frontend may be different from the value you entered in the backend. Sometimes it is a formatted number and sometimes it is a message such as **call for price**. Another example is `$product_thumb_image`. You may expect this to be just the file location you see in the backend, but its value will depend on whether it is an out of site image, whether the image exists, and whether you want the image to be resized from the full image.

- **VirtueMart class object**: In certain cases, VirtueMart developers may think there are too many possibilities for the use of a piece of data. So they decided to let the template designer control what to do with the data. In those cases, VirtueMart will simply pass a class object to the template. An example of this is `$ps_product`. There are lots of opportunities to make good use of these class objects. However, you will need to understand how this can be properly used and bear all the complexities to make it work.

Core browse templates

Product listing is unarguably the most important element on the product list page. There are two major factors that will affect the product listing: the product listing style, and the core browse template.

Core browse templates are used to define the layout and styles for each product in the product list. There are actually six different core browse templates in the `default` theme. We can define a default core browse template for general use and also a specific template for each of the product categories, as discussed in *Chapter 2*, *The VirtueMart Defualt Theme*. If you take a closer look at the templates, you will find that they are pretty much the same, except the last one which is for creating a PDF file.

We already saw the detail coding in the `browse_1.php`. We don't need to repeat it here again. So, let's start on some exercises with the `browse_1` template right away.

Exercise 3.1: Adding an Ask-Seller link to the browse page

We know that in the product detail page, there is an **Ask-Seller** link which will bring up a form so that a shopper can ask a question about the product. This link is not available on the product list page. In this exercise, we will add a similar link to the browse page. The link we add is not as generic as the one created by VirtueMart. While we can use the exact same link here, we purposely use a simpler way to do it to make it easier to understand.

Steps

1. Open your favorite text editor. Navigate to the VirtueMart frontend root.

2. Open the file `themes/default/templates/browse/browse_1.php`.

3. Insert the following line of code after line 5:

```
<a href="index.php?option=com_virtuemart&page=shop.ask&
product_id=<?php echo $product_id ?>">Ask a question about this
product</a><br />
```

4. Save the file and upload it to your server.

5. Point your browser to any VirtueMart browse page that uses the `browse_1.php` template, you should see the **Ask-Seller** link added to every product. (This exercise is done on the `browse_1` template only. If you browse to the product list of an individual category, the new styles will show only if the category is using the `browse_1` template. The same applies to most of the following exercises.)

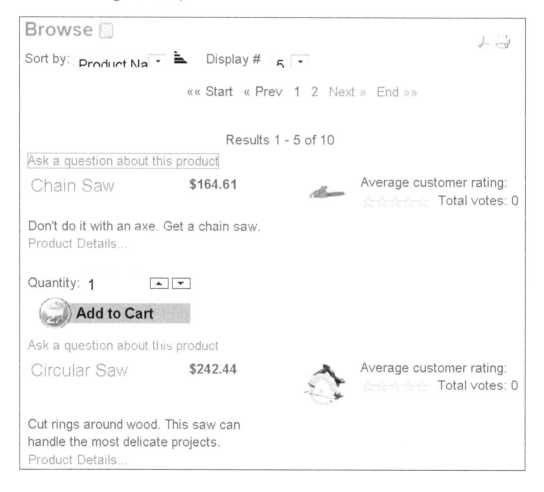

Notes

1. The **Ask-Seller** link is an `<a>` tag with the `href` pointing to the Ask Seller page.

2. The `href` is built using three parameters:

   ○ `option=com_virtuemart` points to the VirtueMart component.

   ○ `page=shop.ask` points to the actual Ask Seller page. By changing the `page` parameter, we can point the shopper to any of the VirtueMart pages.

   ○ `product_id=<? echo $product_id ?>` provides the product ID to the Ask Seller page so that it knows which product the shopper has questions on. We need to use a variable because the `product_id` will vary from product to product.

3. In the previous code, we purposely hardcoded the link as a relative URL to make the code simpler. This works unless SEF is enabled. To cater for SEF, a more generic way to create the link will be needed. We will learn to create a generic link in a later exercise.

4. The text **Ask a question about this product** is static text. Feel free to change it to anything you think appropriate. This will not affect the function of the link.

5. `<br />` is needed to insert a line break after the link.

Exercise 3.1 demonstrates the basic technique to modify a template. You can add static text to a template in whatever way you want. If you need variable data, simply insert the appropriate `echo` statement at the required place.

Exercise 3.2: Changing core browse template CSS

One major task of customizing a template is changing the style of HTML elements. In this exercise, we are going to add some CSS styles to the core browse template.

Preparation

This exercise is built upon the `browse_1.php` file we modified in *Exercise 3.1*. If you start from the original template file, the exact line number may differ.

Steps

1. Open your favorite text editor. Navigate to the VirtueMart frontend root.

2. Open the file `themes/default/templates/browse/browse_1.php`.

3. At line 4 (that is, the top of the file), insert the following lines of code:

```
<?php if (!defined(VM_CUSTOM_CSS)) {
  define ('VM_CUSTOM_CSS',1);
?>
  <style>
    .browseProductContainer {border:1px solid #999;padding:5px;bac
kground:#eee;margin:5px;}
  </style>
<?php } ?>
```

4. Save the file and upload it to your server.

5. Point your browser to any VirtueMart browse page that uses the `browse_1.php` template. You should see the product list now with the border, margin, and padding added.

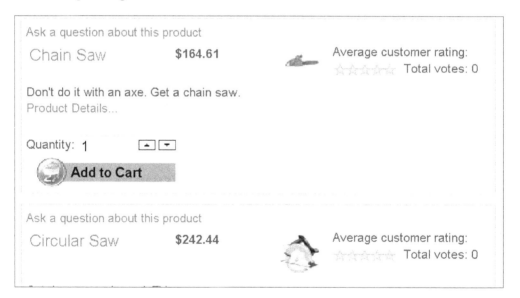

Notes

1. We added a stylesheet for the class `browseProductContainer` in the template file. The stylesheet will be included as part of the HTML output to the browser.

2. The core browse template will be applied for each product. So any coding added to it will be repeated for each product. To ensure that the stylesheet is included only once in the HTML, we define a constant named `VM_CUSTOM_CSS` the first time the stylesheet is included.

3. The `if` condition at the start of the coding tests for the existence of the constant `VM_CUSTOM_CSS`. When the code is executed a second time, `VM_CUSTOM_CSS` is already defined and so the statements within the braces will be skipped.

Exercise 3.2 demonstrates another basic technique to modify a template. The technique applies not only to a CSS stylesheet, but to all coding in general. It can be used for JavaScript inclusion, and for other coding that you only need to appear once in the HTML.

Exercise 3.3: Moving and modifying data

In this exercise, we are going to experiment with moving data around and adding some new data fields that are available for the template.

Preparation

This exercise is built upon the `browse_1.php` file we modified in *Exercise 3.2*. If you start from the original template file, the exact line numbers may differ.

Steps

1. Open your favorite text editor. Navigate to the VirtueMart frontend root.

2. Open the file `themes/default/templates/browse/browse_1.php`.

3. At line 40, insert the following line of code:

```
<br />Weight: <?php echo number_format($product_weight,1) .
' ' . $product_weight_uom ?><br />
```

4. Move the **Ask-Seller** link from line 13 to line 47, that is, after the closing `</span>` tag for `form_addtocart`.

5. Move the `<br />` tag from the end of line 47 to the beginning of the line, that is, the line will become:

```
<br /><a href="index.php?option=com_virtuemart&page=shop.ask&
product_id=<?php echo $product_id ?>">Ask a question about this
product</a>
```

6. Save the file and upload it to your server.

7. Point your browser to any VirtueMart browse page that uses the `browse_1.php` template and you should see that the **Ask-Seller** link has moved to the end of the display, and the product weight and unit has been added to every product.

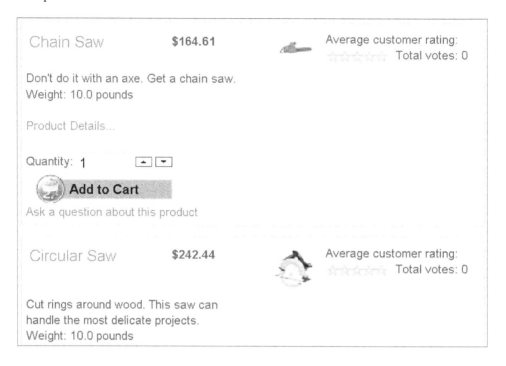

Notes

In this exercise, we have performed two modifications. We moved the **Ask-Seller** link to the bottom instead of the top and added the `product_weight` field to the browse template.

Actually, the order of appearance of the product fields can be changed at will. You can move it around to fit your requirement similar way.

To add new data to the display, you first need to determine what you want to show and whether the data is within the list of available fields. Since we know `$product_weight` and `$product_weight_uom` (uom stands for unit of measure) are available, we can simply use concatenation to build the final text for the output.

The weight is rounded off to 1 decimal place using the `number_format()` function to make it look nicer. You can change the number of decimal places by changing the second parameter to the `number_format()` function.

Header templates

Page header is the next important element on the product list page. The page header varies with the type of product list page. So the category product listing, manufacturer product listing, and the keyword product listing have their respective header templates. There is an additional header template for the all product listing which lists out all the products in the VirtueMart shop. All these header templates are found within the browse/includes subdirectory of the VirtueMart templates directory. They are named as browse_header_category.tpl.php, browse_header_manufacturer.tpl.php, browse_header_keyword.tpl.php, and browse_header_all.tpl.php, respectively.

The browse_header_category template is used when the listing requested belongs to a certain category, identified by category_id in the URL request parameters. For the standard VirtueMart install, the category_id=1 corresponds to the **Hand Tools** category. The URL for this category is http://your_site_domain/index.php?option=com_virtuemart&page=shop.browse&category_id=1.

The category header template consists of four major subelements (in addition to the print, e-mail, and PDF buttons): the category name, the RSS feed button, the child category list, and the category description. The child category list may or may not exist. This is the list of child categories that belong to the category of the given category_id.

The browse_header_manufacturer template is used when there is a manufacturer_id specified in the URL. The template just contains two subelements: the manufacturer name and the manufacturer description.

The `browse_header_keyword` template is used for product searches. The template has just a single element: the search text.

The `browse_header_all` template is used just for the all product list. The link for the all product list is found in the `mod_virtuemart` module. You can also create your own all product list link by setting `page=shop.browse` in the URL. The full URL is `http://your_site_domain/index.php?option=com_virtuemart&page=shop.browse`.

The `browse_header_all` template consists of two sub elements: the browse page label and the RSS feed button.

Exercise 3.4: Adding a category banner

In this exercise, we are going to add a category banner to the category browse header. Here we will use a simple JPEG file. However, you can replace them with a flash slide or even an HTML page.

Preparation

Create category banners `category_banner_1.jpg`, `category_banner_2.jpg`, `category_banner_3.jpg`, and `category_banner_4.jpg` for the four categories with a standard VirtueMart install. You can use Photoshop or any other graphic editing program for this. The files should be placed under the subdirectory `shop_image` of the frontend VirtueMart directory.

Steps

1. Open your favorite text editor. Navigate to the VirtueMart frontend root.

2. Open the file `themes/default/templates/browse/includes/browse_header_category.tpl.php`.

3. At line 4, insert the following line of code:

   ```
   <img src="components/com_virtuemart/shop_image/category_
   banner_<?php echo $category_id ?>.jpg" /> <br />
   ```

4. Save the file and upload it to your server.

5. Point your browser to the VirtueMart browse page for each of the categories. You should see a different category banner for each category.

Notes

1. In this exercise, we demonstrated one way to show a different image file for a different category.

2. The technique is not limited to JPG files. You can replace the `img` tag with an `object` tag to show a flash file. You just need to find some way to map the category to the file. In this example, we use `$category_id`. You can use `$category_name` or some other available fields.

Navigation templates

The navigation section is controlled by the template `browse_orderbyform.tpl.php`. There are two major elements in the navigation: the page navigation list and the sort order form, each of them has its own template. Both navigation templates are found in the `includes` subdirectory of the `templates/browse` directory.

The page navigation list is controlled by the template `browse_pagenav.tpl.php`. There are three subelements in the template: navigation links (including page number, previous, and next links), the limit drop-down box (to control the number of products per page), and the page counter (showing the current product numbers on the page). Actually, VirtueMart will pass a `pageNavigation.class` object to the template to show these three subelements.

The sort order form is controlled by the template `browse_orderbyfields.tpl.php`. This template will list out the order by selection with a drop-down box. The options available in the drop-down box are controlled by the VirtueMart configuration on the **Site** tab. You can refer to *Chapter 2*, *The VirtueMart Defualt Theme,* to set this drop-down box.

Exercise 3.5: Using a custom sort order form

In this exercise, we are going to replace the sort order form drop-down with a list of hyperlinks.

Steps

1. Open your favorite text editor. Navigate to the VirtueMart frontend root.

2. Open the file `themes/default/templates/browse/includes/browse_orderbyfields.tpl.php`.

3. Replace lines 10 to 43 with the following lines of code:

```php
<script language="javascript" type="text/javascript">
  function submit_orderby(option) {
    var frm = document.forms["order"];
    frm.orderby.value=option;
    frm.submit();
  }
</script>
<style type="text/css">
  #orderby_options {display:inline;}
  #orderby_options a {padding:1px 3px;}
</style>
<div id="orderby_options">
  <input type="hidden" name="orderby" value="" />
<?php
// SORT BY PRODUCT LIST
if( in_array( 'product_list', $VM_BROWSE_ORDERBY_FIELDS)) { ?>
    <a href="javascript:void(0)" onclick="submit_orderby('product_list')">
    <?php echo $VM_LANG->_('PHPSHOP_DEFAULT') ?></a>
<?php
}
// SORT BY PRODUCT NAME
if( in_array( 'product_name', $VM_BROWSE_ORDERBY_FIELDS)) { ?>
    <a href="javascript:void(0)" onclick="submit_orderby('product_name')">
    <?php echo $VM_LANG->_('PHPSHOP_PRODUCT_NAME_TITLE') ?></a>
<?php
}
// SORT BY PRODUCT SKU
if( in_array( 'product_sku', $VM_BROWSE_ORDERBY_FIELDS)) { ?>
    <a href="javascript:void(0)" onclick="submit_orderby('product_sku')">
    <?php echo $VM_LANG->_('PHPSHOP_CART_SKU') ?></a>
<?php}
// SORT BY PRODUCT PRICE
if (_SHOW_PRICES == '1' && $auth['show_prices'] && in_array('product_price', $VM_BROWSE_ORDERBY_FIELDS)) { ?>
    <a href="javascript:void(0)" onclick="submit_orderby('product_price')">
    <?php echo $VM_LANG->_('PHPSHOP_PRODUCT_PRICE_TITLE') ?></a>
<?php
}
// SORT BY PRODUCT CREATION DATE
```

```
if( in_array( 'product_cdate', $VM_BROWSE_ORDERBY_FIELDS)) { ?>
    <a href="javascript:void(0)" onclick="submit_orderby('product_
cdate')">
    <?php echo $VM_LANG->_('PHPSHOP_LATEST') ?></a>
<?php
}
?>
</div>
```

4. Save the file and upload it to your server.

5. Point your browser to the VirtueMart browse page. You should see the sort by text link instead of the drop-down box.

Notes

1. There are different ways to present the sort order options to the shopper without changing anything in the server coding. This is the beauty of separating the presentation from the data and, for that matter, using the template.

2. The variable $VM_BROWSE_ORDERBY_FIELDS is an array containing the different options set in the VirtueMart configuration. An array is a PHP construct used to hold several values within one single variable. Each value or element will have an index which is either a number or a string. In the default VirtueMart configuration, the array $VM_BROWSE_ORDERBY_FIELDS contains three values:

```
{0:product_name,1:product_price,2:product_cdate}
```

This actually means

```
$VM_BROWSE_ORDERBY_FIELDS[0]='product_name';
$VM_BROWSE_ORDERBY_FIELDS[1]='product_price';
$VM_BROWSE_ORDERBY_FIELDS[2]='product_cdate';
```

3. The five possible options for sorting are product_list, product_name, product_sku, product_price, and product_cdate. They are pretty much self explanatory. The only two options that may need explanation are product_list and product_cdate. Sort by `product_list` means sorting in order of adding the product to the category. This doesn't seem to be controlled by any backend function and can probably only be changed at the database level. Sort by `product_cdate` means sorting by the creation date of the product.

4. In this exercise, we replace the drop-down with a list of links. Basically, we retain the original logic that the link will show as set by the $VM_BROWSE_ORDERBY_FIELDS.

5. Because we are using an `<a>` tag, we need to use JavaScript to control when to submit the form. The JavaScript function `submit_orderby` does exactly that. It first sets the `orderby` field of the form (named `order`) and submits the form.

6. We also added some basic CSS styles to format the links in a nicer way. You can change the styles without affecting the basic function.

Add-to-cart form template

Whether the **add-to-cart** button will show in the product list page or not will depend on the settings in the VirtueMart configuration and also on the product. If the product is a parent product and/or has advanced/custom attributes, the shopper will need to select additional options before the product can be added to the shop cart. In those cases, the add-to-cart form will not show in the product list. Instead, the shopper will need to go to the product detail page to order that product. (The add-to-cart will not show if VirtueMart is just used for a catalog or if there is no price set for the product as well.)

If the add-to-cart shows in the product list, its layout will be determined by the template `addtocart_form.tpl.php`. This is not a complicated template and there is not much to customize. But you can still change it if the need arises.

Exercise 3.6: Showing the add-to-cart button in all cases

As explained previously, there are situations where the **add-to-cart** button will not show. This is certainly appropriate if the site is used just as a catalog or when there is no price set. However, it may appear puzzling to the shopper if just a few products on the product list do not have the **add-to-cart** button. They may think that the products are not for sale.

However, you should bear in mind that when a product needs additional parameters before it can be placed in the shopcart, the only way to do that is on the product details page. (You may be tempted to show the attribute drop-down on the product list, but VirtueMart does not have a provision for that. Adding that feature will need substantial changes in several core VirtueMart files.)

Can we still show an **add-to-cart** button for those products that need additional selection? Maybe we could just redirect the shopper to the product details page to make the additional selection. This is exactly what this exercise tries to accomplish. However, we will need to modify the core browse template instead of the add-to-cart form template to make this work.

Preparation

This exercise is built upon the `browse_1.php` file we modified in *Exercise 3.3*. If you start from the original template file, the exact line numbers may differ.

Steps

1. Open your favorite text editor. Navigate to the VirtueMart frontend root.

2. Open the file `themes/default/templates/browse/browse_1.php`.

3. Replace lines 45 with the following lines of code:

```php
<?php
     if ($form_addtocart)
       echo $form_addtocart;
     else {
       $button_lbl = $VM_LANG->_('PHPSHOP_CART_ADD_TO');
       $button_cls = 'addtocart_button';
     ?>
       <input type="button" class="<?php echo $button_cls ?>"
value="<?php echo $button_lbl    ?>" title="<?php echo $button_lbl
?>" onclick="location='<?php echo $product_flypage ?>'" />
     <?php
     }
  ?>
```

4. Save the file and upload it to your server.

5. Point your browser to the VirtueMart browse page. You should see the **add-to-cart** button showing for all products. (For example, the **add-to-cart** button will show up for **Circular Saw** as well.)

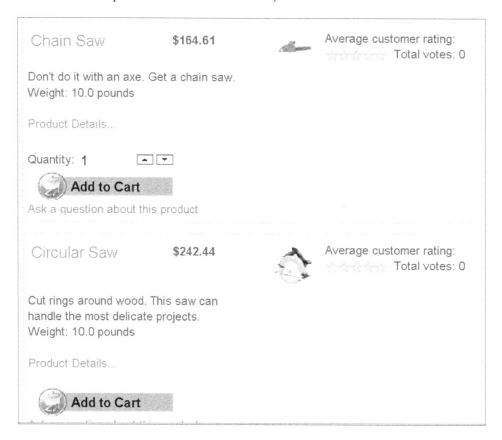

Notes

1. Since our goal is to change the **add-to-cart** button, it seems the work should be done on the addtocart_form template. But actually, customizing the addtocart_form template does not help. This is because the template will not be invoked at all when there are attributes that need to be selected.

2. In the original coding, the VirtueMart page file shop.browse.php will check whether the product should have an **add-to-cart** button. If yes, it will invoke the addtocart_form template and pass its value to the core browse template (in this case, browse_1.php) through the variable $form_addtocart. For those products that do not match the prescribed conditions, the addtocart_form will not be called at all. In those cases, shop.browse.php will simply pass an empty string to the core browse template.

3. We can certainly modify the `shop.browse.php` logic to enable the `addtocart_form` template to be parsed for all products. However, there are two problems with this approach:

   ° `shop.browse.php` is a core file. Customization will be lost after upgrade.

   ° We will need to modify two files instead of one.

4. In the preceding modifications, the magic is solely done in the core browse template. Instead of using `echo $form_addtocart` unconditionally, we replace it with an `if` condition. If `$form_addtocart` is not empty, the `if` condition will evaluate to true, the original **add-to-cart** button will still be sent as before.

5. If `$form_addtocart` is an empty string (meaning the VirtueMart prescribed conditions do not apply), we need to create the button ourselves. The coding is actually a clone from that in the `addtocart_form` template. We need to change the `input type` from `submit` to `button` to change the click behavior. We also added an `onclick` event handler to open the product flypage instead of adding the product to the shopcart.

6. Previously, we used `add to cart` as the button label. You can change the label to whatever text you deem appropriate (such as `Select Additional Attributes`). You don't need the function call `$VM_LANG->_()` unless multilanguage is needed. Simply replace the line with the following line of code:

   `$button_lbl = 'your text';`

7. Otherwise, you will need to add another language element to the language file. We will work on customizing language elements in a later exercise.

8. We also assumed that it is appropriate to show an **add-to-cart** button for all the products. Actually, this is not correct if the product does not have a price or the product is not in stock. To cater for these cases, additional checking will need to be added.

Addendum element templates

There are a few addendum elements that can be shown on the product list page. These include the recent products that the shopper has visited, featured products, and the latest products. Each of these elements has its own template in the `common` template group. We will leave the discussion of these templates to *Chapter 7, VirtueMart Templates and Joomla! Modules.*

Product list style templates

So far, all our examples have been based on a div-based product list style. There are actually three different product list styles, each of which has its own template. The `browse_notables.tpl.php` template is used for div-based list style. The `browse_layouttable.tpl.php` is used for table-based list style. The `browse_listtable.tpl.php` template is used for showing the products in a table.

The div-based and table-based product lists aren't too different in the frontend. However, the table style product list is very different, with a header row at the top and a table row for each product.

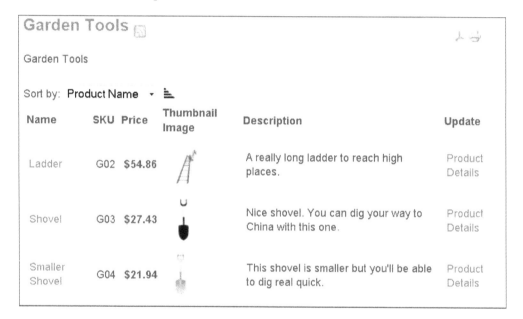

Exercise 3.7: Adding a new column to the table style product list

The table style product list does not use the core browse template to show the product properties. Instead, the entire layout is done in one single template: `browse_listtable.tpl.php`. If you need to add a column or change any CSS style, you have to modify this template. In this exercise, we will explore how to add a new column to the table style product list.

Preparation

We can see the effect of changing the table style product list only when the product list style has been set to table style. So we need to go to the theme configuration page to set this first. Go to the VirtueMart backend of you site. Click **Admin/ Configuration** on the left menu. On the right-hand side of the **Site** tab, just under the theme drop-down, click on the **Configuration** link. On the page that comes up, change the **Product List Style** to **Flat Product List**.

Steps

1. Open your favorite text editor. Navigate to the VirtueMart frontend root.

2. Open the file `themes/default/templates/browse/includes/browse_ listtable.tpl.php`.

3. Insert the following line of code before line 16:

   ```
   $tableheader[] = 'Weight';
   ```

4. Insert the following line of code before line 42:

   ```
   $data[$row][] = number_format($product['product_weight'],1) .
   ' ' . $product['product_weight_uom'];
   ```

5. Save the file and upload it to your server.

6. Point your browser to the VirtueMart browse page. You should see the new **Weight** column after the **SKU** column.

Notes

1. In order to add a column in the table style product list, we need to add both the header text as well as the new value for subsequent data rows.

2. In step 3, we add a new table cell to the header row.

3. In step 4, we add the data cell for the additional column. You can probably see that this is of the same form we used in *Exercise 3.3*, where we added a new data field to the core browse template.

Exercise 3.8: Changing the product list style based on category

In core VirtueMart, the product list style setting applies to all product lists, including category, manufacturer, keyword search, as well as the all list. Sometimes you may want to use a different style for a certain category. In this exercise, we will guide you and help you make this happen.

Preparation

This exercise will be based on `browse_notables.tpl.php`. We need to change the **Product List Style** back to div-based product list style. Go to the VirtueMart backend of your site. Click **Admin/Configuration** on the left menu. On the right-hand side of the **Site** tab, just under the theme drop-down, click on the **Configuration** link. On the page that comes up, change the **Product List Style** to **Product List (no table, div-based)**.

Steps

1. Open your favorite text editor. Navigate to the VirtueMart frontend root.

2. Open the file `themes/default/templates/browse/browse_notables.tpl.php`.

3. Insert the following lines of code before line 4:

```php
<?php
  if ($category_id==1 || $category_id==3) {
    echo $this->fetch( 'browse/includes/browse_listtable.tpl.php'
);
    return;
  }
?>
```

4. Save the file and upload it to your server.

5. Point your browser to the VirtueMart browse page. You should see the div-based product style. Point your browser to either `http://your_site/index.php?option=com_virtuemart&page=shop.browse&category_id=1` (**Hand Tools**) or `http://your_site/index.php?option=com_virtuemart&page=shop.browse&category_id=3` (Garden Tools). You will see the table style product list instead.

Hand Tools

Hand Tools

Sort by: Product Name Price Latest Products

Name	SKU	Weight	Price	Thumbnail Image	Description	Update
Hammer	H02	10.0 pounds	$1.10		A great hammer to hammer away with.	Product Details
Hand Shovel	G01	10.0 pounds	$5.48		Nice hand shovel to dig with in the yard.	Product Details
Nice Saw	H01	10.0 pounds	$27.43 $25.43 You Save: $2.00		This saw is great for getting cutting through downed limbs.	Product Details

Notes

1. You may probably be amazed by how simple this customization can be. There are only three lines of code (the last closing brace } is actually a part of the `if` statement) and yet we can change the layout completely. Thanks to the wonderful framework of VirtueMart itself.

2. The first line of code is an `if` condition checking the value of `category_id`. Note that when comparing equality, PHP uses `==` instead of `=`. Also, the symbol `||` (two pipe characters) is the PHP symbol for or. So `$category_id==1 || $category_id==3` checks whether `$category_id` is 1 or 3 and if it is, the following two lines of code will be executed. Otherwise, it will fall back to the normal code after the closing brace `}`.

3. The second line of code is a function call to `$this->fetch()`. This function will parse the template file given (relative to the `templates` directory) and return the result as a string. Obviously, we are feeding the template `browse_listtable.tpl.php` to the parsing engine.

4. The third line of code is a `return` statement. This is used within a function to go back to the caller. The template is actually included as a function by the VirtueMart template engine, and so `return` means going back to the original caller that calls the template.

5. The interesting thing regarding this exercise is that you can actually execute any template to return HTML as needed, so long as all the available fields needed in the template are passed into it. In our case, the templates `browse_notables.tpl.php` and `browse_listtable.tpl.php` are of the same type and so we can be sure that all the available fields are there.

Summary

In this chapter, we have seen the structure of the product list page. We also looked through all the templates related to the product list and worked through several exercises to customize the browse templates. The technique we learnt here is not specific to the browse templates. You can apply them to other VirtueMart templates or even to Joomla! or non-Joomla! PHP code. In the next chapter, we will continue our study with the next important set of pages in VirtueMart, the product details pages.

4
Product Details Templates

In this chapter, we will build upon what we introduced in the last chapter, but shift the focus to the product details templates. We will look at the major elements that compose a product details page and then the templates that are related to each of those elements. We will look at ways to customize the flypage, header, product images and files, product review, add-to-cart form, advanced attribute and custom attribute, and much more.

Briefly, in this chapter, we will cover:

- The product details page
- Looking at a sample flypage template
- Flypage templates
- Header templates
- Product images and files
- Product review templates
- Add-to-cart form templates
- Other product details templates

The product details page

The product details template group is the other major template group in VirtueMart other than the product list templates. While the two template groups share many common characteristics, the product details templates are more complicated as there are many details that will vary from product-to-product.

From the previous screenshot, we can recognize several elements:

- Header – including the buttons and navigation links
- Product fields
- Product price
- Product images and files
- Product availability
- Product reviews
- Add-to-cart form
- Miscellaneous links, such as ask-seller link, vendor link, and manufacturer link
- Footer – including the PayPal logo, recent products, related products, child categories, and so on

Many of these elements are the end product of a complicated processing routine and may have a template of their own. We will be looking at each of these elements and related templates one-by-one.

The layout of the product details page is actually determined by a set of flypage templates, as it is usually called. You can set a different flypage template for each product category, if you want to. Otherwise, the default flypage template in the VirtueMart configuration will be used. All the flypage templates reside directly under the `templates/product_details` subdirectory. The templates for individual elements, on the other hand, reside under the subdirectory `templates/product_details/includes` and also in the subdirectory `templates/common`. This is because they are shared by more than one VirtueMart page.

Looking at a sample flypage template

The flypage template resembles the core browse template in many respects. There are also some features that are particular to the flypage template itself.

Let's take a look at the file `flypage.tpl.php` as an example. The full text of this file is shown below (with the line numbers added):

```
1. <?php if( !defined( '_VALID_MOS' ) && !defined( '_JEXEC' ) ) die(
'Direct Access to '.basename( __FILE__ ).' is not allowed.' );
2. mm_showMyFileName ( __FILE__ );
3. ?>
4.
5. <?php echo $buttons_header // The PDF, Email and Print buttons ?>
```

```
6.
7.  <?php
8.  if( $this->get_cfg( 'showPathway' )) {
9.  echo "<div class=\"pathway\">$navigation_pathway</div>";
10. }
11. if( $this->get_cfg( 'product_navigation', 1 )) {
12. if( !empty( $previous_product )) {
13. echo '<a class="previous_page" href="'.$previous_product_url.'">'.
shopMakeHtmlSafe($previous_product['product_name']).'</a>';
14. }
15. if( !empty( $next_product )) {
16. echo '<a class="next_page" href="'.$next_product_url.'">'.
shopMakeHtmlSafe($next_product['product_name']).'</a>';
17. }
18. }
19. ?>
20. <br style="clear:both;" />
21. <table border="0" style="width: 100%;">
22. <tbody>
23. <tr>
24. <?php  if( $this->get_cfg('showManufacturerLink') ) { $rowspan =
5; } else { $rowspan = 4; } ?>
25. <td width="33%" rowspan="<?php echo $rowspan; ?>"
valign="top"><br/>
26. <?php echo $product_image ?><br/><br/><?php echo $this-
>vmlistAdditionalImages( $product_id, $images ) ?></td>
27. <td rowspan="1" colspan="2">
28. <h1><?php echo $product_name ?><?php echo $edit_link ?></h1>
29. </td>
30. </tr>
31. <?php if( $this->get_cfg('showManufacturerLink')) { ?>
32. <tr>
33. <td rowspan="1" colspan="2"><?php echo $manufacturer_link ?><br
/></td>
34. </tr>
35. <?php } ?>
36. <tr>
37. <td width="33%" valign="top" align="left">
38. <?php echo $product_price_lbl ?>
39. <?php echo $product_price ?><br /></td>
40. <td valign="top"><?php echo $product_packaging ?><br /></td>
41. </tr>
42. <tr>
43. <td colspan="2"><?php echo $ask_seller ?></td>
44. </tr>
```

```
45. <tr>
46. <td rowspan="1" colspan="2"><hr />
47. <?php echo $product_description ?><br/>
48. <span style="font-style: italic;"><?php echo $file_list ?></span>
49. </td>
50. </tr>
51. <tr>
52. <td><?php
53. if( $this->get_cfg( 'showAvailability' )) {
54. echo $product_availability;
55. }
56. ?><br />
57. </td>
58. <td colspan="2"><br /><?php echo $addtocart ?></td>
59. </tr>
60. <tr>
61. <td colspan="3"><?php echo $product_type ?></td>
62. </tr>
63. <tr>
64. <td colspan="3"><hr /><?php echo $product_reviews ?></td>
65. </tr>
66. <tr>
67. <td colspan="3"><?php echo $product_reviewform ?><br /></td>
68. </tr>
69. <tr>
70. <td colspan="3"><?php echo $related_products ?><br />
71. </td>
72. </tr>
73. <?php if( $this->get_cfg('showVendorLink')) { ?>
74. <tr>
75. <td colspan="3"><div style="text-align: center;"><?php echo
$vendor_link ?><br /></div><br /></td>
76. </tr>
77. <?php   } ?>
78. <?php if( isset($paypalLogo)) : ?>
79. <tr>
80. <td colspan="3" align="center">
81. <?php echo $paypalLogo ?>
82. </td>
83. </tr>
84. <?php endif;?>
85. </tbody>
86. </table>
87. <?php
```

```
88. if( !empty( $recent_products )) { ?>
89. <div class="vmRecent">
90. <?php echo $recent_products; ?>
91. </div>
92. <?php
93. }
94. if( !empty( $navigation_childlist )) { ?>
95. <?php echo $VM_LANG->_('PHPSHOP_MORE_CATEGORIES') ?><br />
96. <?php echo $navigation_childlist ?><br style="clear:both"/>
97. <?php
98. } ?>
```

While the code is different from the core browse template, the pattern is pretty similar. There are lots of echo() function calls embedded inside an HTML fragment. Most of the echo statements will send out the value of some available fields. Just like the browse template, you can check out all the available fields in the *Appendix*, *VirtueMart Template reference*. We will also discuss some of the fields while working through the exercises. We also noted a couple of special constructs in the template:

- The function $this->get_cfg() is called several times in the template. $this is a special variable in PHP. From the point of view of the PHP parser, the template is a PHP class. We will not deal with the details of class concept here, but we just want to mention in passing that each class has its own functions and variables. We access the function and variable of a class using the symbol ->. Here, get_cfg() is a template function that will get the setting in the template configuration file. (We will talk more about get_cfg() in *Chapter 8*, *VirtueMart Theme Anatomy* and *Chapter 9*, *Theme Customizations*). If you can still recall from *Chapter 2*, *The VirtueMart Default Theme*, there are a number of settings in the default template configuration. One of them is **Show Manufacturer Link**. The function call $this->get_cfg('showManufacturerLink') will get this value from the template configuration file and act accordingly. If the value is yes, the manufacturer link will be sent and not otherwise.

- Another template function that has been used in this template is $this->vmlistAdditionalImages. This is a function used to list out all additional images for the product. We will have more to say on this later in the section *Product images* below.

- Another class used in the template is the $VM_LANG. This class is the VirtueMart language manager. The most important function of this class is $VM_LANG->_. It will retrieve the appropriate language element from the language file. $VM_LANG->_('PHPSHOP_MORE_CATEGORIES'), for example, will retrieve the language element PHPSHOP_MORE_CATEGORIES.

Flypage templates

There are six flypage templates in the default theme:

- `flypage-ask.tpl.php`
- `flypage.tpl.php`
- `flypage_images.tpl.php`
- `flypage_lite_pdf.tpl.php`
- `flypage_new.tpl.php`
- `garden_flypage.tpl.php`

Most of the templates are very similar, except `flypage_lite_pdf.tpl.php` which is aimed for PDF output. These templates are there just as examples. The name of the template file actually does not reflect its content. For example, `flypage_new.tpl.php` does not mean it is a newer template than `flypage.tpl.php`. Also, both `flypage.tpl.php` and `flypage_images.tpl.php` show the image and additional images. So, don't be misled by the filename itself.

You can, of course, set a different template for a different product category. For example, if you have a category of products such as training courses that does not have an image, you can create a `flypage_no_image.tpl.php` by simply removing the `$product_image` variable from this template and setting the category flypage to this template.

Exercise 4.1: Adding product fields to the flypage

There are actually around 60 available fields for a flypage template. However, the default flypage templates do not make use of most of them, especially those database fields. In this exercise, we are going to show some of the fields.

Steps

1. Open your favorite text editor. Navigate to the VirtueMart frontend root.

2. Open the file `themes/default/templates/product_details/flypage.tpl.php`.

3. At line 38, insert the following lines of code

   ```
       Weight: <?php echo number_format($product_weight,1) . ' ' .
   $product_weight_uom ?><br />
       Size: <?php echo number_format($product_length,2) . ' ' .
   $product_lwh_uom ?><br />
   ```

```
Stock: <?php echo $product_in_stock ?><br />
```

4. Save the file and upload it to your server.

5. Point your browser to the **Circular Saw** page (the URL is `index.php?page=shop.product_details&flypage=flypage.tpl&product_id=8&category_id=2&option=com_virtuemart`). You should see the **Weight**, **Size**, and **Stock** lines added.

Circular Saw

Weight: 10.0 pounds
Size: 0.00 inches
Stock: 33
Price: $242.44

View Full-Size Image   Ask a question about this product

- Patented Sightline; Window provides maximu
  for straight cuts
- Adjustable dust chute for cleaner work area
- Bail handle for controlled cutting in 90° to 45°

Notes

1. We have added three product fields to the flypage. Using database fields is straightforward. You just need to use the `echo()` function and the variable name.

2. We purposely use a different label **Size** for the `product_length`. While the field name should normally reflect the usage of the value, you don't need to use it that way. Circular saws come in a certain size, but the VirtueMart product datatable does not have such a field. To cater for this need, you can either create a new field in the datatable or use an existing field for that purpose. Adding a field to the database is not as simple as it seems. Other than doing it in the database (that calls for using `phpmyadmin` if your web host provides such a function), you will need to add the field to the backend edit form and also add codes to insert and update the field to the database. Moreover, since the core files have been modified, you will have concerns on version upgrade as well. Your changes to the code will be lost when you upgrade your VirtueMart. Changing the meaning of the database field is much simpler. In our case, we are using `product_length` as **Size**. You can then go to the backend and change the product length of the Circular Saw to 7.25. In your frontend, you will see the length displayed as **Size** using this modified template.

3. You don't need to use the same flypage template for all products. That is, using `product_length` as **Size** just applies to a certain category; take Saws, for example, you can set that category flypage to this modified template. In this way, `product_length` can be used as **Size** in some products, **Diameter** in some products, and **Length** for the rest.

4. The `product_in_stock` field is used by the core VirtueMart file to calculate product availability. However, there is no reason why we cannot show its raw value in the frontend as well. And, in case you are short of product fields to use, `product_in_stock` can also be used to represent some data that is normally not supported by VirtueMart.

Header templates

The header of the product details page does not need a separate template. All the header elements are placed in the flypage template directly. How you reach the product details does not matter. Whether you come from a category product list, manufacturer product list, or keyword search result list will not affect the page.

There are three elements in the product details header:

buttons header

This includes three buttons, the PDF button, print button, and e-mail button. If you don't need the buttons, you can simply remove the `echo $buttons_header` line in the flypage template. In case you need to modify the buttons or add other buttons, you can do so by modifying the template `buttons.tpl.php` in the `common` template group.

pathway

The pathway is the series of links at the top of the page that shows the hierarchy of pages that lead to the current page. Joomla! has its own pathway and many Joomla! templates already have a pathway. But if you need the pathway for the product details page, you can enable this in the theme configuration.

The VirtueMart pathway has its own template in the `common` template group. The name of the template is `pathway.tpl.php`.

Navigation links

There are two navigation links for each product. One links to the previous product and the other links to the next product in the same category. These links are placed here for the sake of convenience. A shopper can use them to navigate through all products in the same category without going back to the browse page. If there are no more products in either direction, the links will not show.

Exercise 4.2: Adding a category banner

In this exercise, we are going to add a category banner to the product details page as well. Here we will use a simple JPEG file. However, you can replace them with a flash slide or even an HTML page. This is actually very similar to *Exercise 3.4*, discussed in *Chapter 3, Product List Templates*.

Preparation

This exercise is built upon the flypage template created in *Exercise 4.1*. If you start from the default template, the line number may be different.

If you have the banners created in *Exercise 3.4*, you can skip the following preparation.

Create category banners `category_banner_1.jpg`, `category_banner_2.jpg`, `category_banner_3.jpg`, and `category_banner_4.jpg` for the four categories with the standard VirtueMart install. You can use Photoshop or any other graphic editing program for this. The files should be placed under the subdirectory `shop_image` of the frontend VirtueMart directory.

Steps

1. Open your favorite text editor. Navigate to the VirtueMart frontend root.

2. Open the file `themes/default/templates/product_details/flypage.tpl.php`.

3. At line 5, insert the following line of code:

   ```
   <img src="components/com_virtuemart/shop_image/category_
   banner_<?php echo $category_id ?>.jpg" /> <br />
   ```

4. Save the file and upload it to your server.

5. Point your browser to various product pages. You should see a different category banner for each product.

Product images and files

The product image is an important element in a product catalog and is certainly an indispensable way to show a product on an online store. VirtueMart has very good support for using product images. Two product fields have been dedicated to record the product full image and the product thumbnail image. In addition, it also has a dynamic thumbnail generation mechanism. This means you only need to provide the full image and have VirtueMart do the downsizing for you.

For some products, you may want to show several images for the same product. In those cases, you can use the VirtueMart media manager to upload additional images to the site. VirtueMart also has provision for showing the additional images in the flypage template. We already saw in the sample template that the template uses the function `$this->vmListAdditionalImages()` to list out the additional images. If you don't like the way the images are listed, you can certainly customize the template and use your own.

VirtueMart media manager does not only handle image files, but it can also manage downloadable products and other file types. VirtueMart handles downloadable products very well. It can also list out all additional files in the flypage. However, as there are so many possibilities, the file list by VirtueMart is very basic and is not very attractive. If you want to display the files in fancier ways, you need to customize the template to provide support for the additional requirements.

Exercise 4.3: Using a different thumbnail size in flypage

By default, the product flypage will use the same thumbnail as in the browse page. However, the dynamic thumbnail generation mechanism in VirtueMart can provide for an infinite number of thumbnail sizes. To make use of this, you need to make a little tweak in the flypage.

Preparation

We are going to use the dynamic thumbnail generation in VirtueMart to help us to create a second thumbnail for the flypage. So we will need to activate dynamic thumbnail creation. If you don't have dynamic thumbnail resizing enabled in the VirtueMart configuration, you need to do this before doing this exercise. Please go to the VirtueMart backend, click **Configuration** on the left, and then click the **Site** tab. The dynamic thumbnail resizing setting is on the **Layout** section on the right. (Dynamic thumbnail resizing requires GD2 in your PHP system. If you do not have this set up, you cannot follow this exercise. In case of doubt, you can contact your web host.)

This exercise will build upon the flypage template, as created in *Exercise 4.1* and *Exercise 4.2*. If you start from the default template, the line number may vary.

Steps

1. Open your favorite text editor. Navigate to the VirtueMart frontend root.

2. Open the file `themes/default/templates/product_details/flypage.tpl.php`.

3. Replace line 27 with the following lines of code:

```php
<?php
  $thumb_width=100;
  $thumb_height=100;
  $thumb='<img src="components/com_virtuemart/show_image_in_
imgtag.php?filename='.$product_full_image
    .'&newxsize='.$thumb_width.'&newysize='.$thumb_height.'" />';
  $product_thumb = preg_replace('/<img [^>]+>/',$thumb,$product_
image);
  echo $product_thumb;
?>
<br/><br/><?php echo $this->vmListAdditionalImages( $product_id,
$images ) ?></td>
```

4. Save the file and upload it to your server.

5. Point your browser to the **Hammer** page (URL is `index.php?page=shop.product_details&flypage=flypage.tpl&product_id=6&category_id=1&option=com_virtuemart&Itemid=1`). You should see the larger thumbnail.

Hammer

Weight: 10.0 pounds
Size: 0.00 inches
Stock: 500
Price: $1.10

Ask a question about this product

View Full-Size Image

Notes

1. Normally, the variable `$product_image` contains the HTML for displaying the thumbnail and the link to open the full image. However, VirtueMart only allows one thumbnail image and the `$product_image` will display this thumbnail instead of a dynamic resized thumbnail. In the preceding code, we add lines of code to rebuild the product thumb image link to make use of the dynamic resize mechanism.

2. The first two lines of code are to set the thumbnail size. You can change the width and height independently to any value you desire. The VirtueMart thumbnail generation mechanism will keep the aspect ratio automatically.

3. The third line creates the `$thumb` URL using the `$product_full_image`. `$product_full_image` is raw data from the database and contains the filename of the full image. The VirtueMart image regeneration code is located at `components/com_virtuemart/show_image_in_imgtag.php`. To create a dynamically resized thumb image, we need to provide three parameters in the query string: the `filename`, the `newxsize` (thumb width), and the `newysize` (thumb height).

4. For simplicity, we used a relative link in the above coding. This may not work if you use a SEF. We will learn to generate a generic link in a later chapter.

5. In the fourth line, we use the `preg_replace()` function to replace the `img` tag inside the `$product_image` variable with the `img` tag we created above in line 3. `preg_replace()` is a very powerful function that builds on regular expressions. A thorough discussion of regular expressions is outside the scope of this book.

Exercise 4.4: Creating a custom file list

In the VirtueMart media manager, you are not limited to uploading image files. You can upload additional files of another type, such as a PDF file. In this exercise, we are going to modify the flypage template so as to display a PDF icon for PDF files.

Preparation

Before we can follow the exercise, we must have a product which has an associated PDF file on the server. So, the preparation will involve uploading a PDF file to the server using the VirtueMart media manager.

1. Log in to the VirtueMart backend. On the left menu, click **Product** and then **List Product**.

2. In the **Product List**, click on the media icon (in the media column) for the product **Hammer**.

#		Product Name	Media	SKU	Price	Category	Manu
1	☐	Chain Saw	(2)	P01	149.99 USD	Outdoor Tools Garden Tools	Manu
2	☐	Circular Saw	(2)	P02	220.90 USD	Power Tools Garden Tools	Manu
3	☐	Drill	(2)	P03	48.12 USD	Indoor Tools	Manu
4	☐	Hammer	(2)	H02	1.00 USD	Hand Tools	Manu
5	☐	Hand Shovel [Item Information]	(2)	G01	4.99 USD	Hand Tools Garden Tools	Manu

3. In the media manager pop-up, click **New** on the top toolbar.

4. In the **Upload a File** pop-up, select your PDF by clicking the **Browse** button. Change the **File Type** drop-down to **Additional File**. Then click **Save** in the top toolbar.

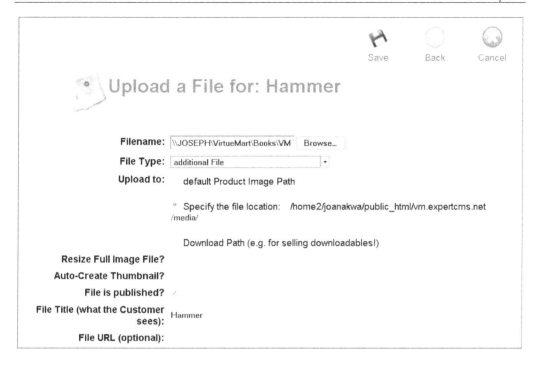

5. If everything works without any problems, you should see the PDF file in the media manager file list.

6. And in the frontend, you will see a new link **Hammer** (or whatever text you have placed for the **File Title** above).

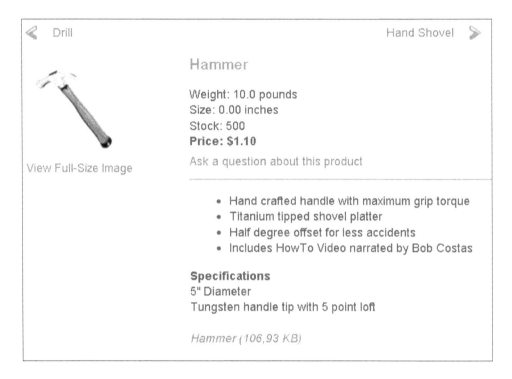

7. You are now ready to start the exercise. This exercise is built upon the flypage template created in the previous exercises. If you start from the default flypage template, the line number may differ.

Steps

1. Open your favorite text editor. Navigate to the VirtueMart frontend root.

2. Open the file `themes/default/templates/product_details/flypage.tpl.php`.

3. Replace line 60 with the following lines of code:

```php
<?php
  foreach ($files as $file) {
    if ($file->file_extension=='pdf') {
      echo '<a href="'.$file->filename.'"><img src="images/M_
images/pdf_button.png" />'.$file->file_title.'</a>';
    }
  }
?>
```

4. Save the file and upload it to your server.

5. Point your browser to the **Hammer** page (URL is index.php?page=shop.
product_details&flypage=flypage.tpl&product_id=6&category_
id=1&option=com_virtuemart&Itemid=1). You should see the PDF icon
before the Hammer file.

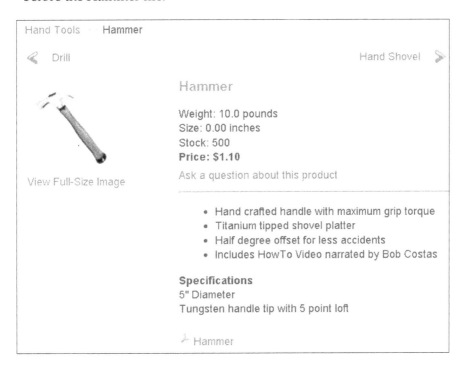

Hand Tools Hammer	
≪ Drill	Hand Shovel ≫

Hammer

Weight: 10.0 pounds
Size: 0.00 inches
Stock: 500
Price: $1.10

View Full-Size Image

Ask a question about this product

- Hand crafted handle with maximum grip torque
- Titanium tipped shovel platter
- Half degree offset for less accidents
- Includes HowTo Video narrated by Bob Costas

Specifications
5" Diameter
Tungsten handle tip with 5 point loft

⊁ Hammer

Notes

1. Normally, the variable $file_list contains the HTML for displaying the list
of additional files. In this exercise, we only want to show PDF files and also
the PDF icon. So we need to rebuild the list from the variable $files.

2. $files is an array containing a list of file objects. Each file object has the
following properties:

```
file_id => Identifier of the file
file_product_id => product_id
file_name => path of the file relative to site root
file_title => title specified when creating the file
file_description => description specified when creating
file_extension => file extension
file_mimetype => mime type of the file
file_url => URL to download the file
file_published => whether the file is available to the
```

```
public
        file_is_image => whether the file is an image
        file_image_height => height of the image
        file_image_width => width of the image
        file_image_thumb_height => thumbnail height
        file_image_thumb_width => thumbnail width
```

3. We use a `foreach` loop to go through each file and we output the link only when the file extension is `pdf`.

4. The link is created from the filename. The Joomla! PDF image is used as the icon. We also display the file title to identify the link.

5. For simplicity, we used a relative link in the above coding. This may not work if you use a SEF. We will learn to generate a generic link in a later chapter.

Product review templates

Product reviews are comments and ratings supplied by shoppers or previous users. There are four templates that relate to product reviews and all of them belong to the `common` template group.

votes_allvotes.tpl.php

This template is used to show the overall rating of the product. VirtueMart has an image file for each of the ratings 1, 2, 3, 4, and 5, showing the number of stars that the product has been given. The template also prints out the number of votes that have been cast to make up the overall rating. You can certainly modify the template to give the rating a different look.

voteform.tpl.php

This template shows a form for users to rate the product. It is basically a radio button list, with one button for each of the five ratings. One possible way to customize this is to use a slider control instead of the radio button list. However, you will need to provide your own JavaScript coding to achieve this.

reviews.tpl.php

This template controls how the reviews will be displayed on the flypage. Basically, an array of review objects is passed to the template for layout. Each review object contains the following fields:

```
userid => identifier of the user
```

```
username => login name of user
name => friendly name of user
time => time when the review was done this is an unix time stamp (an
integer)
user_rating => rating from 1 to 5
comment => The comment text
```

You can use the default template to show the review or design your own layout based on this data.

reviewform.tpl.php

The review form includes both the form for the rating and a textarea for the users to write their comment. The template also contains a JavaScript function that will check the number of characters that a user has typed in. The counter will be updated as a user types. The review will be rejected if its length does not lie within these limits. The minimum and maximum number of characters that are allowed can be set in the VirtueMart configuration. Since the review form already includes the rating form, you don't need the rating form if you use the review form template.

VirtueMart only allows logged-in users to write comments and rate a product. So if you want to see the rating and comment form, you will need to log in.

Exercise 4.5: Adding an overall rating to a flypage

In the default flypage template, the average customer rating is not shown. Actually, this rating is readily available in VirtueMart without much coding. In this exercise, we will add the **Average customer rating** to the flypage.

Preparation

This exercise will build upon the result of previous exercises. If you start from the default template file, the line number may differ.

Steps

1. Open your favorite text editor. Navigate to the VirtueMart frontend root.

2. Open the file `themes/default/templates/product_details/flypage.tpl.php`.

3. Insert the following lines of code before line 38:

   ```
   <?php
   ```

```
        $product_rating = ps_reviews::allvotes( $product_id );
        echo $product_rating . '<br />';
    ?>
```

4. Save the file and upload it to your server.

5. Point your browser to the **Hammer** page (URL is index.php?page=shop. product_details&flypage=flypage.tpl&product_id=6&category_ id=1&option=com_virtuemart&Itemid=1). You should see the **Average customer rating** under the product name.

Hammer

Average customer rating:

★★★★☆   Total votes: 1

Weight: 10.0 pounds
Size: 0.00 inches
Stock: 500
Price: $1.10

Ask a question about this product

Notes

The average customer rating is calculated by calling the function ps_ reviews::allvotes(). ps_reviews and is one of the core VirtueMart classes. We call the function using :: instead of -> because allvotes() is a class function and can be called without creating an object first.

Add-to-cart form templates

The add-to-cart form on the flypage is a pretty complicated template. Many advanced features of VirtueMart, such as child product, advanced attributes, and custom attributes are related to this form. You probably recall we have a template of the same name in the browse templates. The two templates are different in a number of ways. The major difference is that the product listing page will have several add-to-cart forms on the same page while there will only be one add-to-cart form in the product details page. Several forms on the same page with potentially very complex child products and attribute settings caused the VirtueMart development team to use a separate template for the product listing and the product details.

Within the includes subdirectory of the product details template group, we can see many template files with names starting with `addtocart`. Obviously, these files all relate to the add-to-cart form. The remaining two start with `quantity_box`. This suggests that they relate to the display of the quantity box, which is also part of the add-to-cart form. Thus, all the templates in this subdirectory are related to the add-to-cart form.

Quantity box templates

Let's start with the simplest templates first. There are two templates for the quantity box. This box will allow a shopper to enter the quantity of the product that will be required before adding to the shop cart. VirtueMart actually provides several options of the quantity box to cater to different shops' needs. All these options are product-specific and can be set in the product edit form, in the **Display Options** tab:

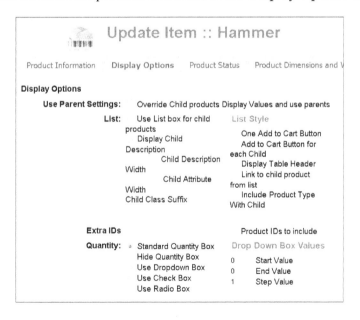

At the bottom of the tab, you will see a series of radio buttons for the various options of the quantity box:

- **Standard Quantity Box** is a textbox where a shopper can enter any quantity.

- **Hide Quantity Box** means that there will be no quantity box showing. The quantity value will default to 1 using a hidden `input` element.

- **Use Dropdown Box** means a drop-down will be used for the quantity. A shopper can choose only from the limited values in the drop-down. The **Start Value**, **End Value**, and **Step Value** can be set on the right next to the **Quantity** radio-button list. To allow only even numbers from 2 to 10, for example, the **Start**, **End**, **Step** values should be set as 2, 10, 2 respectively.

- **Use Check Box** means the quantity will be displayed as a checkbox which a shopper can check to order (the quantity will be tacitly assumed to be 1). This is useful for the child product list with only one **add-to-cart** button (see the following *Child product templates* section).

- **Use Radio Box** will probably cause some confusion with radio button. It may be better renamed as **Use Spin Button** in the North American world. However, please note VirtueMart is an international development project and so the terminology will sometimes depend on the developers' environment. Anyway, for this option, two input buttons will be shown where a user can click one to increase the quantity and the other to decrease it. This is similar to the behavior when setting the volume and channel on a television, or may be in many car radios.

Let's return back to the quantity box templates. There are two templates. The `quantity_box_general.tpl.php` template will be used in most cases, even if you have selected the **Use Radio Box** option. The `quantity_box_radio.tpl.php` template is used only for child products with radio options. We will not go into the detail of the template here as the logic is pretty straightforward.

Child product templates

A child product is also referred to as product family, where the parent product is an umbrella for a series of products which differ in certain attributes such as color, type, weight, and so on. On the flypage of the parent product, all the child products will be shown directly. How the child products will be displayed is configurable on a per product basis. You probably noticed in the previous screenshot that the **Display Options** tab contains a number of settings for child products.

There are two ways to display the child products: a **Dropdown** or a **List**. In the **Dropdown** option, child product selections are placed in a drop-down box. When you change the drop-down box, the appropriate child product will be displayed (probably in an Ajax manner without any page refresh, if you don't have Ajax disabled in the theme configuration). Shoppers can then choose the quantity they want and add it to the cart.

In the **List** option, you have several more settings. The **List** option basically displays the child products in a table. You can set whether to show the product description (which is probably very lengthy and will be difficult to have a nice display) in the table and its width. You can also set the column width for other attributes in the table. In the **List Style** options on the right, you can use the checkboxes to control whether to display the table header, to use a hot link for the child product name to link to the child product page, and to include product type information (more lengthy stuff that will distort your nice table).

You probably noticed that I did not mention the radio button at the top of the **List Style** section. We leave this to the end because they relate to our templates. There are two possible options to display the **add-to-cart** button in the child product table. You can choose whether to show one button for each child product.

Otherwise, you can use one single button for all child products:

Depending on which options you have set, one of the templates (`addtocart_drop.`
`tpl.php`, `addtocart_list_single.tpl.php`, or `addtocart_list_multi.tpl.php`)
will be used.

Exercise 4.6: Using an HTML table to display the child product list

You probably noticed that the child product list in the screenshot above does not
look good at all, with each row in various sizes and columns misaligned. This is
because the list is displayed using `div` instead of the table element. Of course, you
can tweak your CSS to make the `div` work for you. Another possibility is to use the
HTML table to lay out the list. This may be an easier option unless you definitely
need a tableless HTML page.

Preparation

We will be working with the product Hand Shovel (`product_id=1`) in this exercise.
And because we are experimenting with the child product list display, you need to
set the **Display Options** for this product in the backend first.

1. Log in to your VirtueMart administrator backend. Click **Product** and then
    List Product on the left menu. In the product list that comes up, click **Hand
    Shovel** to open the product edit form.

2. Click the **Display Options** tab to see the various options. Make sure you
    have the following settings:

    o   **Use List box for child products** - checked

    o   **Display Child Description** - checked

° **List Style One Add to Cart Button** - checked

° **Display Table Header** – checked

3. All the other options do not matter.

Steps

1. Open your favorite text editor. Navigate to the VirtueMart frontend root.

2. Open the file `themes/default/templates/product_details/includes/addtocart_list_single.tpl.php`.

3. Replace lines 30 to 91 with the following lines of code:

```php
<tr class="<?php echo $product['bgcolor'].$cls_suffix ?>">
    <td class="vmCartChildElement<?php echo $cls_suffix
>">
        <input type="hidden" name="prod_id[]" value="<?php
echo $product['product_id'] ?>" />
        <input type="hidden" name="product_id" value="<?php
echo $product['parent_id'] ?>" />
        <?php if( $child_link ) : ?>
        <label for="selItem<?php echo $product['product_id']
?>">
        <?php endif; ?>
        <span class="vmChildDetail<?php echo $cls_suffix ?>"
style="width :<?php echo $desc_width ?>" />
            <?php echo $product['product_title'] ?></span>
    <?php if( $child_link ) : ?>
    </label>
    <?php endif; ?>
</td>
        <?php // Ouput Each Attribute
    if( !empty( $product['attrib_value'] )) {
      foreach($product['attrib_value'] as $attribute) { ?>
        <td class="vmChildDetail<?php echo $cls_suffix ?>"
style="width :<?php echo $attrib_width ?>;">
        <?php echo " ".$attribute ?></td>
      <?php
      }
    }
    ?>
    <?php
        // Output Quantity Box
        if (USE_AS_CATALOGUE != '1' ) { ?>
            <td style="padding-right:5px;"><?php echo
product['quantity_box'] ?></td>
```

```php
            <?php }
            // Output Price
            if( $_SESSION['auth']['show_prices'] && _SHOW_PRICES)
{
                ?>
                <td class="vmChildDetail<?php echo $cls_suffix ?>"
style="text-align: right;padding-right:5px;" >
                <?php
                if( $product['price'] != $product ['actual_price']
) { ?>
                    <span class="product-Old-Price"><?php echo
$product['price'] ?> </span>
                <?php
        }
        ?>
                <span class="productPrice"><?php echo
$product['actual_price'] ?></span>
        </td> <!-- close the vmChildDetail -->
            <?php } ?>
        <?php
        // Out Put Product Type
        if ($display_product_type == "Y" && $product['product_
type'] != "") { ?>
            <td class="vmChildType<?php echo $cls_suffix ?>">
            <?php echo $product['product_type'] ?>
            </td>
        <?php }
        // Output Advanced & Custom Attributes
        if(USE_AS_CATALOGUE != '1' && ($product['advanced_
attribute'] != "" || $product['custom_attribute'] != "")) { ?>
            <td class="vmCartAttributes<?php echo $cls_suffix ?>">
                <?php if($product['advanced_attribute']) {
                    echo $product['advanced_attribute'];
                }
                if($product['custom_attribute']) {
                    echo $product['custom_attribute'];
                }
            ?>
            </td>
        <?php } ?>
    </tr>
<?php } ?>
</table>
```

4. Replace lines 10 to 24 with the following lines of code:

```
<table>
<?php if($display_header == "Y") { ?>
    <tr class="vmCartChildHeading<?php echo $cls_suffix ?>">
        <td style="float: left;width: <?php echo $desc_width
?>;"><?php echo $VM_LANG->_('PHPSHOP_PRODUCT_DESC_TITLE') ?></td >
        <?php //Ouput Each Attribute Heading
        foreach($headings as $key => $value) { ?>
            <td style="width: <?php echo $attrib_width ?>;"
><?php echo $headings[$key] ?></td>
        <?php } ?>
        <td style="width: 15%;"><?php echo $VM_LANG->_
('PHPSHOP_CART_QUANTITY') ?></td>
        <td style="width: 12%;"><?php echo $VM_LANG->_
('PHPSHOP_PRODUCT_INVENTORY_PRICE') ?></td>
        if ($display_product_type == "Y" && $product['product_
type'] != "") { ?>
    <td>   </td>
    <?php } ?>
    <?php if(USE_AS_CATALOGUE != '1' && ($product['advanced_
attribute'] != "" || $product['custom_attribute'] != "")) { ?>
    <td>   </td>
    <?php } ?>
    </tr>
<?php }
```

5. Save the file and upload it to your server.

6. Point your browser to the **Hammer** page (URL is `index.php?page=shop.product_details&flypage=flypage.tpl&product_id=1&category_id=1&option=com_virtuemart&Itemid=1`). You should see the new view of the child product list aligned nicely in a table.

Notes

1. In the preceding code, there are two major steps: one for the table body and one for the table head.

2. We added the `<table>` start and end tag, replaced the enclosing `<div>` with `<tr>` and subsequent `<div>` with `<td>`. There are some exceptions where we've changed the `<span>` tag to `<td>` as well. In any case, care has been taken to make sure that the number of cells in each row in the header and the body match each other.

3. We also removed all `float` attributes from the style. The `float` attribute is not needed to align the elements in an HTML table. We also removed the class `vmCartChild` from the `<tr>` tag inside the body.

4. If you want to further customize the code, note that there are several parts in the coding. You have to ensure that both the table heading and the table body match for all of these parts:

   ○ The product description column.

   ○ The child product attributes – each attribute has a column of its own.

   ○ The price column.

   ○ The quantity box column.

   ○ The product type column – in case you need to display the product type.

   ○ The advanced attribute and custom attribute column – we just use a single column for both. In case you need it, you can use two columns.

5. The coding is pretty messy and not easy to understand because of the several `if` statements for checking various conditions. You can drop the checking in case you are sure they will apply. If the condition will not apply, you can drop that section of code entirely. For example, if your child product will never have a product type, you can remove the coding that takes care of the product type.

Advanced and custom attribute templates

The templates `addtocart_advanced_attribute.tpl.php` and `addtocart_custom_attribute.tpl.php` will control respectively how the advanced and custom attributes display. Advanced and custom attributes are part of the data that need to go into the shop cart when a shopper adds the product to the shop cart. Thus they are inseparable parts of the add-to-cart form. The advanced attribute normally displays as a drop-down and the custom attribute displays as a textbox. However, there is no reason why you cannot display them in another way, so long as it fits your need. What you need to do is simply customize the templates.

Exercise 4.7: Displaying the advanced attribute as a radio button

The advanced attribute is usually displayed as a drop-down box. In this exercise, we will change it to radio buttons instead.

Steps

1. Open your favorite text editor. Navigate to the VirtueMart frontend root.

2. Open the file `themes/default/templates/product_details/includes/addtocart_advanced_attribute.php`.

3. Replace lines 9 to 17 (the line that starts with `<?php foreach ( $attribute['options_list'] as $options_item ) : ?>`) with the following lines of code:

```php
<?php
    $i=0;
    foreach ( $attribute['options_list'] as options_item ) : ?>
        <input type="radio" id="<?php echo $attribute['titlevar'].
$i ?>_field" name="<?php echo $attribute['titlevar'].$attribute['product_id'] ?>" value="<?php echo $options_item['base_var'] ?>">
        <?php if( isset( $options_item['display_price']) ) : ?>
        <?php echo $options_item['base_value'] ?> (<?php echo
$options_item['sign'].$options_item['display_price'] ?>)
        <?php else : ?>
```

```php
<?php echo $options_item['base_value'] ?>
  <?php endif; ?>
  <?php $i++;
endforeach; ?>
```

4. Add the following code to the end of the file (after line 25):

```css
<style type="text/css">
  .vmCartChild {float:none}
</style>
```

5. Save the file and upload it to your server.

6. Point your browser to the **Circular Saw** page (URL is `index. php?page=shop.product_details&flypage=flypage.tpl&product_ id=8&category_id=2&option=com_virtuemart&Itemid=1`). You should see that the advanced attribute shows in the radio button list.

Notes

1. The template is passed as an array of advanced attributes to be displayed through the variable `$attributes`. Each of the attributes will contain the following properties:

   ○ `product_id` => product identifier

   ○ `title` => name of attribute to be used as label

   ○ `titlevar` => name of the attribute to be used as a field name for the HTML form

   ○ `options_list` => an array of options for the attribute

2. Each element of the `options_list` will contain the following properties:

   ○ `base_var` => value of the option to be passed back to the server

   ○ `base_value` => value of option to be displayed to the shopper

   ○ `sign` => sign of price adjustment, can be +, -, or =

   ○ `display_price` => price to be displayed with option

3. The original template code contains two loops, first one to loop through all the attributes and the second to loop through all the options.

4. What we did is to combine the `select` and `option` tag to build the radio buttons.

5. We used a loop variable `$i` to make sure each of the radio buttons had a different `id` value.

6. At the end of the code, we inserted a section of CSS style. This is needed to ensure the `div` containing the advanced attribute will not float to the left, as defined in the VirtueMart stylesheet.

Exercise 4.8: Using textarea for a custom attribute and adding a length-checking routine

A custom attribute is usually displayed as a textbox. In this exercise, we will change it to a textarea instead and add a length-checking JavaScript.

Preparation

In this exercise, we will need to test the display of a custom attribute, so we need to create a custom attribute before we start.

1. Log in to your VirtueMart administrator backend. Click **Product** and then **List Product** on the left menu. In the product list that comes up, click **Drill** to open the product edit form.

2. Click the **Product Status** tab. At the bottom of the **Custom Attribute List** textbox, type in **Request**.

3. Click on the **Save** option in the top toolbar to save the changes.

Steps

1. Open your favorite text editor. Navigate to the VirtueMart frontend root.

2. Open the file `themes/default/templates/product_details/includes/addtocart_custom_attribute.tpl.php`.

3. Replace lines 10 to 16 (the line that starts with `<div class="vmAttribChildDetail" style="float: left;width:30%;text-align:right;margin:3px;">`) with the following lines of code:

```
    <div style="float: left;width:60px;text-align:right;margin:3px;">
```

```
         <label for="<?php echo $attribute['titlevar'] ?>_
field"><?php echo $attribute['title'] ?>
         </label>:
     </div>
     <div class="vmAttribChildDetail" style="float:left;width:60%;m
argin:3px;">
         <textarea class="inputboxattrib" id="<?php echo
$attribute['titlevar'] ?>_field" rows="5" cols=30"
         name="<?php echo $attribute['titlevar'].$attribute['produ
ct_id'] ?>">
     </textarea>
     </div>
```

4. Insert the following lines of code after line 2:

```
?>
<script language="JavaScript" type="text/JavaScript">//<![CDATA[
  var maxLength=10;
  var maxExceededMessage="Maximum length exceeded";
  var script1="if (checkForm(this)==false) return false;";
  var script2="handleAddToCart( this.id );return false;";
  var scriptAdded=false;
  function checkForm(frm) {
     for (var i=0; i<frm.elements.length; i++) {
       var el=frm.elements[i];
       if (el.tagName=="TEXTAREA" && el.value.length >
maxLength {
             alert(maxExceededMessage);
             return false;
         }
       }
     return true;
  }
  function addScript(el) {
     if (scriptAdded) return;
     var frm=el.form;
     frm.onsubmit=new Function("event",script1+script2);
     scriptAdded=true;
  }
  //]]>
  </script>
<?php
```

5. Save the file and upload it to your server.

6. Point your browser to the **Drill** page (URL is `index.php?page=shop.product_details&flypage=flypage.tpl&product_id=9&category_id=2&option=com_virtuemart&Itemid=1`). You should see the custom attribute shows in the textarea. Try typing more than 10 characters in the textarea and click **Add to cart**. You will see the **Maximum length exceeded** message.

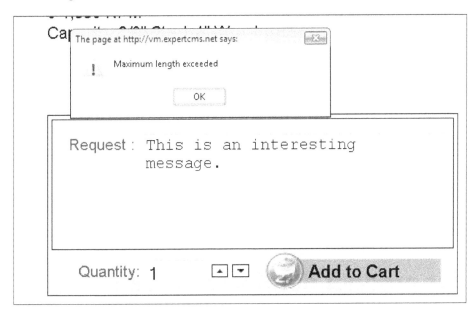

Notes

1. Changing the display from a textbox to a textarea is very simple. You just need to replace the `<input>` tag with the `<textarea>` tag.

2. We also removed some of the `float` and `width` style to make sure the `textarea` displays nicely on the page.

3. To add a length-checking routine, we added a section of JavaScript to the top of the template. There are three major parts in the JavaScript. In the first part, we set up a number of variables. (If you do not follow the JavaScript, feel free to skip it for the time being. We will give a basic introduction to JavaScript in the next chapter.)

4. `maxLength` defines the length limit of the text in the textarea. You can change this to a larger value.

5. `maxExceededMessage` is the error message to be displayed when the maximum is exceeded.

6. `script1` is the JavaScript to check the form.

7. `script2` is the JavaScript to use Ajax call to update the shop cart. If you do not use Ajax, you can simply set this variable to an empty string `""`.

8. `scriptAdded` is a true/false to make sure the JavaScript will be added only once.

9. The second part is a `checkForm` script. This JavaScript will loop through all the elements in the form. It will only check the `textarea` element and if the maximum length is exceeded, the shopper will be prompted with the error message.

10. The third part of the script is to modify the form's `onsubmit` event handler so that before the form is submitted, the `checkForm` script will be executed to make sure the text inside the `textarea` will not exceed the maximum. This `addScript` script will be executed when the first `textarea` got focus and will be executed only once.

addtocart_form template

The most important template in the add-to-cart templates is the `addtocart_form.tpl.php`. This template, in fact, just makes use of the other templates to compose the add-to-cart form.

Other product details templates

There are several other templates that are related to the product details. All these templates are located in the `common` template group. We will only briefly mention some of them. The rest will be discussed in a different chapter, and so we won't go into detail here.

price.tpl.php

This is used by both the product list page and the product details page to lay out the product price. The three major logics are:

- If there is no product price defined, display the **Call for Price** text.

- If there is a discount price for the shopper, show the original price as strike-out. If you don't want to show the original price, you can remove this section.

- If there is a discount price for the shopper, show the **You save** value for the product. Again, you can remove this section if you don't want to show this.

availability.tpl.php

This template is used to output the availability information. The availability message depends on both the quantity in stock and also the availability date. The logics are:

- If we need to check stock and there is no stock, or the availability date is later than today, show not available message.

- If availability date is later than today, show the available date.

- If there is a quantity in stock, show the in-stock value when check stock is enabled.

- If the product is not in stock, we show the not available icon. Otherwise, show the available icon as defined for the product.

featuredProducts.tpl.php

This template is used to lay out featured products. It will be discussed in *Chapter 6, From Shop Basket to Final Checkout*.

recent.tpl.php

This template is used to lay out recent products. It will be discussed in *Chapter 6, From Shop Basket to Final Checkout*.

relatedProducts.tpl.php

This template is used to lay out recent products. It will be discussed in *Chapter 6, From Shop Basket to Final Checkout*.

product_type.tpl.php

This template is used to lay out the product type. There are essentially two `for` loops to display the product type parameter in a table form. The logic for the template is:

- Loop through all the product types that the product belongs to and output the product parameter table in the inner loop below.

- Loop through all the parameters within a product type. Show the parameter label on the left cell and the parameter value on the right. The parameter description will show as a tooltip button and the parameter unit will show next to the value, in case there is one.

Summary

In this chapter, we have seen the structure of the product details page. We also looked through all the templates related to the product details and worked through several exercises in customizing the product details page. The technique we learnt here is not specific to the product details templates. You can apply them to other VirtueMart templates or even to Joomla! or non-Joomla! PHP code. In the next chapter, we will continue our study with the other templates in the shopping life cycle before products are added to the shop basket.

5
Changing the Look of VirtueMart

In the last two chapters, we went over most of the basics of the VirtueMart template. By now, you should have a basic understanding of how easy it is to customize a template, especially for the product list and product details. In this chapter, we will extend our understanding of the template system by looking at several peripheral concepts that are not inside a template file but will definitely affect the look of the site. We will look at the stylesheet, the JavaScript, the language element, and the URL links. Then, we will continue our investigation of the template system by studying a few more templates up to the stage when products are added to the shopcart.

Briefly, in this chapter, we cover:

- The structure of a web page design
- Default theme stylesheets
- Default theme JavaScript
- More on VirtueMart URLs
- The VirtueMart language system
- Manufacturer, vendor, and ask seller templates
- Home page templates

The structure of web page design

Joomla!/VirtueMart websites are a set of coherently related web pages that help to sell products to shoppers. So the structure of a VirtueMart web page is not too different from other web pages.

The most important element of a web page is definitely its content. The content includes all the text, graphics, and hyperlinks. The contents of a web page are presented using HTML tags. The order of the tags, in most cases, will determine the order and layout that the contents will be presented on the browser. In the case of VirtueMart, the contents will be determined mainly by the templates which, as we have seen in the last two chapters, consist mainly of HTML fragments. The VirtueMart templates will therefore be the main control of what and how the ViruteMart contents will be seen on the browser.

When the browser receives the HTML coding sent from a web server, it will also download a number of subordinate files from the server. These include, in particular, CSS files which will specify the styles of the HTML elements and also the JS files that will change the behavior of the page on the browser.

We need to be familiar with the standard stylesheets and JavaScript of VirtueMart before we can customize or extend them. This is what we are going to do in the next two sections.

default theme stylesheets

There are three CSS files in the `default` theme. They are named `theme.css`, `admin. css`, and `admin.styles.css`. Just from the names, we can guess that the last two files are related to the backend administration. That's indeed the case. However, since it is possible to put the administration function on the frontend (this is a setting in the VirtueMart configuration), so the admin stylesheets are also placed under the `default`, so that you can customize it to fit your frontend needs. While it is possible to use the administration modules in the frontend, they are not the norm. So we will not go into the detail of the admin stylesheets here. We will look at the `theme.css` in more detail below.

admin.css

admin.styles.css

theme.config.php

theme.css

There are close to 100 different stylesheet definitions in the `theme.css` file. Most of them are defined for class. Because of the cascading nature of a stylesheet, it is best practice to link the styles to class (or ID) instead of tags. Otherwise, the styles may overflow to other parts of the Joomla! page and produce unintended effects. The styles can be grouped into several style groups according to their usage. Some of the groupings in the CSS file, however, have been misplaced.

add-to-cart form styles

These are styles for the add-to-cart form elements. Styles in this category affect the product list pages, the product details pages, and also the Joomla! modules.

- `.addtocart_button`: This class applies to the **add-to-cart** button. In particular, it defines the button image and is usually customized to remove the VirtueMart standard look.

- `.notify_button`: Same as the `addtocart_button`, but applies to the notify button when the product is out of stock.

- `.addtocart_button_module`: Same as the `addtocart_button` class, but applies to the **add-to-cart** button in a Joomla! module. Basically, it is almost the same definition as the `addtocart_button` and only differs in text color and background image.

- `input.addtocart_button_module:hover`: Applies a color change when the input button is mouseover.

- `.addtocart_form`: Applies to the add-to-cart form.

- `.inputboxquantity`: Applies to the quantity textbox.

- `.quantity_box`: Applies to the quantity textbox label.

- `.quantity_box_button`: Applies to both the increment and decrement quantity buttons, which will change the value in the quantity box.

- `.quantity_box_button_down`: Applies to the decrement quantity button only, used mainly to define the button image.

- `.quantity_box_button_up`: Same as the `.quantity_box_button_down`, but defines the increment quantity button image.

- `.quantitycheckbox`: Applies to checkbox type quantity input.

Navigation link styles

These styles are for links that provide shortcuts for easy navigation.

- `.continue_link`: Applies to the link to continue shopping on the `shop.cart` page. Also, specifies the background image for the button.

- `.checkout_link`: Same as the `.continue_link`, but applies to the checkout link on the `shop.cart` page.

- `.next_page`: Applies to the link to go to the next product on the product details page. Again, this specifies the button image.

- `.previous_page`: Same as the `next_page`, but applies to the previous product.

Product list page styles

These styles are used in the core browse templates.

- `.browseProductContainer`: Applies to the container that holds individual product information on the product list.

- `.browseProductTitle`: Applies to the product name of the product.

- `.browseProductImageContainer`: Applies to the container that holds the product image.

- `.browseProductDetailsContainer`: Not used in the `default` theme.

- `.browseProductDescription`: Applies to the product description of the product.

- `.browsePriceContainer`: Applies to the container that holds the price. This will enable you to use a different price format for the product list page and the product details page.

- `.browseAddToCartContainer`: Applies to the container that holds the add-to-cart form. This will enable you to use a different add-to-cart style for the product list page and product details page.

- `.browseRatingContainer`: Applies to the container that holds the product rating.

Product detail page styles

There should be more classes in the flypage templates, but it is unclear why many of the styles are hardcoded in the flypage template and just one is defined in the CSS.

- `.thumbnailListContainer`: Applies to the container that holds additional images. This class is used only in the `flypage_images` template.

Checkout page styles

These styles are for the registration page and shipping info page. They are not used in any `default` theme template but are used in the `ps_userfield` class. We will discuss the `ps_userfield` in *Chapter 6, From Shop Basket to Final Checkout*, on customizing registration and shipping page.

- `.formLabel`: Applies to the label of the registration and shipping info page.

- `.formField`: Applies to the input box of the registration and shipping info page. Used together with `.formLabel`.

- `#agreed_div`: Applies specifically to the `<div>` element containing the agreed to "term of service".

- `.missing`: Applies to the required fields that are missing when the registration form or shipping address form is submitted.

Administration styles

Some of these styles are used only in administration. They should be in `admin.styles.css` instead. It is unclear why they are included in `theme.css` instead. The rest of the styles are for VirtueMart messages.

- `.adminListHeader`: From the name, it should apply to administration listing pages such as product list, order list, and so on. However, this class is only used in the store display page (`page=store.display`).

- `.labelcell, table.adminform td.labelcell, .iconcell, .vmquote, .editable`: It isn't clear why they are placed in `theme.css`. Applies to administration pages only.

- `.shop_error, .shop_warning, .shop_info, .shop_debug, .shop_critical`: Applies to VirtueMart error, warning, info, debug, and critical error messages' respectively.

- `.shop_tip`: Applies to VirtueMart tips, not sure where it is used.

add-to-cart detail styles

These styles are used in product details templates related mainly to the add-to-cart form and its supporting templates. There are two sets of similar classes. The one with suffix `_2up` are supposed to be used when the product type detail is placed side-by-side with the child product table. However, the `default` theme does not seem to be using these `_2up` classes.

- `.vmCartContainer`: Applies to the outermost container holding the add-to-cart form.

- `.vmCartChildHeading`: Applies to the child product table header.

- `.vmCartChild`: Applies to the container that holds the add-to-cart form of individual child products. This is used when each of the child products has its own **add-to-cart** button.

- `.vmCartChildElement`: Applies to the child product table.

- `.vmChildDetail`: Applies to each detail column of the child product table.

- `.vmChildDetail a, .vmChildDetail a:link, .vmChildDetail a:hover`: Used to fine-tune the anchor tag within the detail column of the child product table. Supposed to be used for the child product link that links to an individual child product page, but the `default` theme is not actually using them.

- `.vmCartAttributes`: Applies to the custom attribute and advanced attribute container inside the child product table.

- `.vmChildType`: Applies to the product type table inside the child product table.

- `.vmMultiple`: Does not seem to be used anywhere by VirtueMart.

- `.vmClearDetail, .vmClearAttribs`: Supposed to be used in the `<clr>` tag but the `default` theme is not using them.

- `.vmRowOne, .vmRowTwo`: Control the background color of the alternating rows in the child product table.

- `.vmAttribChildDetail`: Applies to the custom attribute and advanced attribute container.

- `.inputboxattrib`: Applies to the input box for each individual attribute in the custom attribute and advanced attribute.

- `.vmCartModuleList`: Supposed to be used in Joomla! cart modules. But the `default` theme does not seem to be using it.

Miscellaneous styles

Styles that are shared in various templates or do not belong to other groups.

- `.availabilityHeader`: Applies to the label of the availability used in the availability template.

- `.productPrice`: Applies to the product price used in the price template.

- `.product-Old-Price`: Applies to the original product price used in the price template. Normally, a strike over effect on the old price.

- `ul.pagination`: applies to the `<ul>` tag for page navigation.

- `.clr`: A class to specify the clear property of the `<br>` tag.
- `.legalinfo`: Applies to the terms of service container.
- `div.pathway`: Applies to the pathway.
- `div.pathway img`: Applies to the pathway images.
- `div.buttons_heading`: Applies to the heading buttons found in the product list and product detail pages. Basically contains the PDF button, the e-mail button, and the print button.

Customizing theme.css

There are a number of ways for customizing the styles of the templates:

- Used the style attribute of an HTML tag. This is the most direct method and is good, if this is the only place you need to change. However, it also means the style is hardcoded and cannot be changed by attaching other stylesheets. As we all know, this is against the general rules that we should separate the presentation from the data.

- Use the `<style>` tag in the template file. This has an advantage of keeping the modifications at one place, especially if you have modified the template file as well. There are two problems with this approach. First, if the template is a subtemplate that is used several times on a page, the style will be included several times. You will need to add an `if` statement in order to make sure it is included only once. Secondly, if the same class will be used in several places, you will need to add the tag to several templates.

- Modify the `theme.css` file. By doing this, you can maintain the separation of data and presentation and also keep styles in one place. This will enable you to attach a different CSS very easily. Also, it will be easier for future maintenance. By looking in the page source in the browser, you can find the class for the style and then edit the class in the CSS file accordingly.

In theory, the last method is the best practice and should be upheld as far as possible. However, in practice, this will be the best approach only if your changes are just limited to the `theme css`. Many times, you have done some customizations in the templates already. Making changes in the `theme.css` file will increase the number of modified files by 100 percent. While this may not be a big challenge, it will definitely add to the time and effort for doing a customization and future maintenance.

Exercise 5.1: Changing the shopcart image

VirtueMart comes with a set of shopcart images that you can use. This is a good thing as you can have your cart up and running without getting dirty with all the shop graphics. However, when people browse your site, the shopcart image itself will tell them you are using a canned package for your site. So customizing the shopcart image is always a must to give your site its own identity.

Preparation

Before you can work with this exercise, you should prepare a different shopcart image and name it as `add-to-cart_blue1.gif`. You can certainly name it something else, but make sure you modify the stylesheet with the correct name. This new shopcart image should be placed in the directory `images`, subdirectory of the `themes/default` directory of your VirtueMart frontend root.

Steps

1. Open your favorite text editor. Navigate to the VirtueMart frontend root.

2. Open the file `themes/default/templates/theme.css`.

3. Replace lines 20 to 22 (the `.addtocart_button` stylesheet) with the following CSS style definition:

   ```
   .addtocart_button {
     background: url( 'images/add-to-cart_blue1.gif' ) no-repeat
   center transparent;
   }
   ```

4. Save the file and upload it to your server.

5. Point your browser to the **Outdoor Tools** page (the URL is `index.php?page=shop.product_browse&category_id=4&option=com_virtuemart`). You should see the new shopcart image.

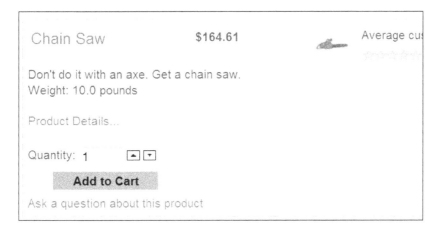

Notes

1. In the preceding example, we just chopped off the VirtueMart icon from the shopcart image. You can modify it in any way you please.

2. You may need to adjust the `width` and `height` of the stylesheet to fit your image size. Otherwise, the **Add to Cart** text will not align.

default theme JavaScript

JavaScript is a very important tool in modern web design. It is a major building block in Web 2.0 design for better user experience.

What is JavaScript?

JavaScript is a scripting language that has many different applications. All modern browsers carry with them a JavaScript engine that can execute JavaScript programs. This means you can write (actually, you don't need to write it yourself as there are so many free scripts on the Internet) a JavaScript program and link it to your HTML pages and you can have the functionality available when your web page is rendered in the client machine.

JavaScript frameworks

JavaScript is a very powerful language. It can be used to write a full-fledged desktop application just like any modern computer language. However, many advanced features of JavaScript are buried inside its simple syntax. Moreover, different browsers have their own HTML and JavaScript model, making it difficult to write cross-browser compatible JavaScript programs.

JavaScript has two major advantages that made it popular in recent years. JavaScript is very extensible and it is also an interpreted language. The extensibility of JavaScript provides opportunities to add functions to the browser engine. That JavaScript is an interpreted language pretty much means JavaScript code is open source and anyone can easily incorporate code developed by others into their own web page. In view of the need to have a cross-browser platform for writing useful JavaScript programs, quite a number of JavaScript frameworks have emerged in the last five years or so, prototype, jQuery, MooTools, and ExtJS, to name a few. These JavaScript frameworks are basically code libraries that extend the JavaScript engine of the browsers, making a JavaScript program much easier to write and much more powerful.

Unfortunately, the frameworks work somewhat differently and may not be compatible with each other. So a script written in jQuery cannot be executed in a MooTools environment and vice versa. Given a situation like this, the Joomla! development team has to make a choice among the frameworks that they will stick with. They chose MooTools as the platform to develop their JavaScript support. Along the same trend, VirtueMart's `default` theme is also based on MooTools.

The fact that VirtueMart's `default` theme used MooTools does not mean you cannot use other JavaScript frameworks. You can still use them unless there are incompatibilities. Actually, the VirtueMart backend extensively uses ExtJS. For the frontend, VirtueMart uses a number of smaller JavaScript libraries in addition to MooTools as well. You can control whether to load MooTools in the theme initialization code. We will come to that when we discuss theme structure in *Chapter 8, VirtueMart Theme Anatomy*.

JavaScript functions in the default theme

There are two JavaScript files in the `default` theme, `theme.js` and `theme.prototype.js`. The two files basically provide the same functions. `theme.js` is based on MooTools while `theme.prototype.js` is based on Prototype. Actually, `theme.prototype.js` is not referenced anywhere in the `default` theme. So probably this is some legacy code. Apparently, Prototype was used as the base during the early development of VirtueMart 1.1 and the development team later switched to MooTools.

There are five functions defined in the `theme.js` file:

- `loadNewPage`: This function will load a new page using Ajax call. There are two parameters `el` and `url`. `el` is the HTML element holding the content that needs to be replaced with the Ajax request and `url` is the site URL that needs to be called to obtain the content. This function is typically used to update the page when a child product is selected in the child product drop-down.

- `handleAddToCart`: This function is used to update the server shopcart using Ajax. When the **add-to-cart** button is clicked, this function will be invoked (unless Ajax is disabled in the `config`) to add the product to shopcart. If the update is successful, a pop-up will be shown to allow a shopper to choose to go to the shopcart page or continue with shopping on the same page. The function takes two parameters. `formId` is the ID of the add-to-cart form. The second parameter `parameters` is not used. This is probably some legacy code for backward compatibility.

- `handleGoToCart`: This function is used with the pop-up window above. If a shopper chooses to go to the shopcart page, this function will be invoked.

- `updateMiniCarts`: This function is used to update the Joomla! module content on the same page after `handleAddToCart`. (We will learn more about the Joomla! modules in *Chapter 7, VirtueMart Templates And Joomla! Modules*.) While the function name suggests it will update the mini cart, the fact is it will update all HTML elements on the page with a CSS class `vmCartModule`.

- `fancyPop`: This function is obsolete code and actually will not run.

Other than the JavaScript defined in the `theme.js` file, there are a number of scripts embedded in individual `default` theme templates. We will come across some of them in the various exercises throughout the book.

Exercise 5.2: Modifying the duration of the shopcart pop-up

If you use Ajax update shopcart function (which is the default), the server shopcart will be updated using an Ajax call. There will be a pop-up window after a successful update which will be gone after a certain time interval. In this exercise, we are going to change the duration when the pop-up will appear.

Steps

1. Open your favorite text editor. Navigate to the VirtueMart frontend root.

2. Open the file `themes/default/templates/theme.js`.

3. Replace line 50 (the line that starts with `setTimeout`) with the following line of code:

   ```
   setTimeout( 'document.boxB.close()', popUpDuration );
   ```

4. Insert the following line of code after line 27 (the line starts with `var timeoutID`):

   ```
   var popUpDuration = 10000;
   ```

5. Save the file and upload it to your server.

6. Point your browser to any of the product pages. Try adding the product to the cart and you will notice the duration of the pop-up will be longer.

Notes

1. We have added a JavaScript variable `popUpDuration` to the script and set it to 10,000. The duration unit is in millisecond. So 10,000 will be equivalent to 10 seconds. The default is 3,000. We purposely used a larger delay. You probably would like to use a smaller one like 4,000 or 5,000.

2. We modified the pop-up window code so it will use `popUpDuration` for show the pop-up instead of the hardcoded 3,000.

3. The `popUpDuration` variable is not mandatory. We can as well modify the hardcoded value 3,000 to 5,000 directly without using a variable. The additional variable makes the hardcoded number easier to understand and will allow us to add to a theme setting to control its value. We will add this setting to the theme in *Chapter 9*, *Theme Customizations*.

More on VirtueMart URLs

In *Chapter 1*, *The VirtueMart Engine*, we had a brief look at the Joomla! URL structure. We noted that the major entry point into the Joomla! site is through the page `index.php`. From that basic URL, we can add additional parameters to tell Joomla! which component should be invoked to process the page. Thus, `index.php?option=com_virtuemart` will pass the main page processing to VirtueMart.

VirtueMart URL parameters

In addition to Joomla! parameters, VirtueMart will also recognize a number of other parameters. We have seen how to tell VirtueMart which page to process by passing the `page` parameter. The `page` parameter is definitely the most important parameter for VirtueMart. There are two parts for this parameter separated by a period (.). `index.php?option=com_virtuemart&page=shop.browse` will tell VirtueMart to return the browse page within the shop module. In the frontend, VirtueMart exposes only three public modules to the public: `shop`, `checkout`, and `account`. Each of these modules contains a number of pages. You can see all these pages in the `html` subdirectory of the VirtueMart administrator root.

In addition to the `page` parameter, VirtueMart also recognizes other parameters:

- `product_id`: This is the identifier for the product telling VirtueMart the product the current page needs to reference.

- `category_id`: This is the identifier for the category telling VirtueMart the category the current page needs to reference.
- `manufacturer_id`: This is the identifier for the manufacturer telling VirtueMart the manufacturer the current page needs to reference.
- `vendor_id`: This is the identifier for the vendor telling VirtueMart the vendor the current page needs to reference. The `vendor_id` is used only for showing the vendor page (`page=shop.infopage`).
- `flypage`: The flypage template name to use. This is used only for the product details page (`page=shop.product_details`).
- `keyword`: The keyword to search for during a wild search. This is used only for the product list page (`page=shop.browse`).
- `limitstart`: The first product to show in a search. This is used only for the product list page (`page=shop.browse`).
- `limit`: The number of products to show in a search. This is used only for the product list page (`page=shop.browse`).

There are many other possibilities for the parameters, but we cannot cover all of them here. Actually, you can design your own parameters to be used in your templates. However, that's beyond the scope of this book.

Search engine friendly (SEF)

There are many search engine friendly components available for the Joomla! system. The basic idea of an SEF system is to replace the raw URL of a page with one that looks more friendly to search engines. Most of the time, if not always, the SEF system will convert the URL with parameters into a URL with directory structure. So a raw URL such as `index.php?option=com_virtuemart&page=shop.browse` may be converted into `/virtuemart/shop.browse/index.php` or something similar.

SEF URLs are not just used by search engines. They are used by browsers as well. For the raw URL, the page is located at the website root. But for the SEF URL, the apparent page location will depend on the SEF URL created. For the previous example, the browser will treat this page as coming from the directory `/virtuemart/shop.browse/`. This may not be a problem if all the URLs (such as images and JavaScripts) for the page are absolute, where the real directory information is encoded in the URL. If the URL is relative, however, the browser will wrongly interpret its actual location and a 404 Page Not Found error will result. For example, an absolute URL of the image located at `/images/stories/shop.png` will be correctly accessed. A relative URL `images/stories/shop.png` will be interpreted correctly as `/images/stories/shop.png` if the URL is `/index.php? option=com_virtuemart&page=shop.browse`. But for the SEF URL `/virtuemart/shop.browse/index.php`, the relative URL will be interpreted as `/virtuemart/shop.browse/`

`images/stories/shop.png`. Since the directory `virtuemart/shop.browse` does not exist, this URL will be doomed to produce a 404 error.

Since relative URLs are interpreted differently with an SEF system enabled, we need to be cautious in handling URLs when doing template customization. Perhaps, you may think this is not a big problem, as we can always rewrite a relative URL in its equivalent absolute URL. This is true, if we have only one website to work with. However, there are cases when we cannot be sure of the absolute URL. This is true especially when we are designing a template that will be used in different websites. Another possible scenario is we need to develop the template in a test site and migrate to a live site after testing. So, we need a way to make sure our URL will work independent of the domain and location of the Joomla! site.

VirtueMart site URLs

To make sure the URL can be written in absolute URL, VirtueMart has a configuration setting for the site URL for both non-secure and secure access. These settings are defined in the **Security** tab of the **Configuration** and the settings are named as `URL` and `SECUREURL`, respectively. You must take special care to ensure these settings are correct. Otherwise, you will encounter some peculiar results without knowing why.

With the `URL` and `SECUREURL` defined, VirtueMart will deduce from them the values for various important root URLs:

- `IMAGEURL`: {SiteUrl}`/components/com_virtuemart/shop_image/`
- `VM_THEMEURL`:{SiteUrl}`/components/com_virtuemart/themes/`{YourTheme}`/`
- `COMPONENTURL`: {SiteUrl}`/administrator/components/com_virtuemart/`

Here, `IMAGEURL` is the root location of the image. `VM_THEMEURL` is the root location of the theme and `COMPONENTURL` is the root location of the VirtueMart administrator root. {SiteUrl} can be secure or non-secure and will depend on whether the site is accessed using HTTP or HTTPS. {YourTheme} is the theme name that you set in the configuration. By default, this will be the default theme `default`.

With these root locations, we will be able to set up most static URLs as absolute URLs. Take *Exercise 3.4* Step 3 as an example, the relative image location should be rewritten as `IMAGEURL .'/category_banner_'.$category_id.'jpg'`. This is an absolute URL and so will work in both SEF and non-SEF sites. Similarly, in *Exercise 4.3* Step 3, the variable `$thumb` should be defined as:

```
$thumb='src="'.URL.'components/com_virtuemart/show_image_in_imgtag.
php?filename='.$product_full_image
    .'&newxsize='.$thumb_width.'&newysize='.$thumb_height.'" />';
```
This will ensure the code works both in SEF and non-SEF sites.

Exercise 5.3: Adding a manufacturer banner and link to the manufacturer product list

As we saw in *Chapter 3, Product List Templates*, the `default` theme manufacturer header only shows the manufacturer name and the description. We will add a manufacturer banner and a link to the manufacturer page in this exercise.

Preparation

Create a manufacturer banner `manufacturer_banner_1.jpg` for the default manufacturer. You can use Photoshop or any other graphic editing program for this. The file should be placed under the subdirectory `shop_image` of the frontend VirtueMart directory.

Steps

1. Open your favorite text editor. Navigate to the VirtueMart frontend root.

2. Open the file `themes/default/templates/browse/includes/browse_header_manufacturer.tpl.php`.

3. Replace line 4 with the following lines of code:

```php
<?php
$manufacturer_id=$_REQUEST['manufacturer_id'];
$manufacturer_link=URL.'index.php?option=com_
virtuemart&page=shop.manufacturer_page&manufacturer_
id='.$manufacturer_id;
$manufacturer_banner=IMAGEURL.'manufacturer_
banner_'.$manufacturer_id.'.png';
?>
```

```
<h3><a href="<?php echo $manufacturer_link ?>"><?php echo
$browsepage_lbl ?></a></h3>
<div><img src="<?php echo $manufacturer_banner ?>" /></div>
```

4. Save the file and upload it to your server.

5. Point your browser to the VirtueMart browse page for the manufacturer (`index.php?page=shop.browse&manufacturer_id=1&option=com_virtuemart`). You should see a manufacturer banner and the manufacturer's name is a hot link to the manufacturer's page.

Notes

1. Not sure why VirtueMart does not pass the `manufacturer_id` to the template. In this exercise, we fetch the `manufacturer_id` value directly from the `$_REQUEST` global variable. `$_REQUEST` is an array containing all the URL parameters (as well as HTML form variables and cookies) indexed by parameter names. So for the URL `index.php?page=shop.browse&manufacturer_id=1&option=com_virtuemart`. You will have the following values in the `$_REQUEST` array:

   ○ `$_REQUEST['page'] = 'shop.browse'`
   ○ `$_REQUEST['manufacturer_id] = '1'`
   ○ `$_REQUEST['option'] = 'com_virtuemart'`

 There may be additional elements in the `$_REQUEST` array as it contains all request parameters including POST, GET, and COOKIE.

2. Both the banner link and the manufacturer URL are absolute URLs, so this template works both in non-SEF and SEF sites.

VirtueMart language system

Joomla! has default support for different languages. The site can work in any language so long as the translation is available. The same is true for VirtueMart. It has a sophisticated language system of its own and is multi-language-enabled. It will display the correct translation of the language, as reported by Joomla!. You just need to ensure that the language files are in place.

All the language files are placed in the `languages` subdirectory under the VirtueMart administrator root. These language files are grouped by modules. The following screenshot shows the structure of the VirtueMart languages directory:

account	7/28/2010	12:58:00 AM
admin	7/28/2010	12:58:00 AM
checkout	7/28/2010	12:58:00 AM
common	7/28/2010	12:58:00 AM
coupon	7/28/2010	12:58:00 AM
help	7/28/2010	12:58:00 AM
manufacturer	7/28/2010	12:58:00 AM
msgs	7/28/2010	12:58:00 AM
order	7/28/2010	12:58:00 AM
product	7/28/2010	12:58:00 AM
reportbasic	7/28/2010	12:58:00 AM
shipping	7/28/2010	12:58:00 AM
shop	7/28/2010	12:58:00 AM
shopper	7/28/2010	12:58:00 AM
store	7/28/2010	12:58:00 AM
tax	7/28/2010	12:58:00 AM
vendor	7/28/2010	12:58:00 AM
zone	7/28/2010	12:58:00 AM

As you can see, all the 16 modules of VirtueMart have their own subdirectories. There are two additional subdirectories not corresponding to any module: `common` and `msgs`. The `msgs` language files are not actually used. The `common` subdirectory is used for storing common language elements, as explained further below.

This means that all language elements in the shop modules will be placed in a language file in the shop subdirectory. The name of the language file is the same as the language; so English language elements will be stored in a file called english.php and so on. You can keep more than one language file in the module to cater to a multi-language web shop.

Name	Size	Last Modified	
english.php	5 KB	11/11/2010	1:23:00 AM
english_before_JK.php	5 KB	5/20/2010	1:35:00 PM
french.php	5 KB	11/16/2009	12:24:00 AM

As there are many elements that are common to several modules, it is reasonable to keep a language file for those common elements instead of repeating the language elements in all the modules. This language file is placed in the common subdirectory. So when you want to look for a language element, you should search both in the common subdirectory as well as in the individual module subdirectory.

Within a language file, all language elements are given a name as the identifier. Each language element is stored as an element of an array indexed by the element name. For easier identification, all the language names are in capital letters. (PHP is case sensitive in regard to array indexes, so make sure you are using the correct case.) The following screenshot shows the language elements in the coupon/english.php file.

```
global $VM_LANG;
$langvars = array (
  'CHARSET' => 'ISO-8859-1',
  'PHPSHOP_COUPON_EDIT_HEADER' => 'Update Coupon',
  'PHPSHOP_COUPON_CODE_HEADER' => 'Code',
  'PHPSHOP_COUPON_PERCENT_TOTAL' => 'Percent or Total',
  'PHPSHOP_COUPON_TYPE' => 'Coupon Type',
  'PHPSHOP_COUPON_TYPE_TOOLTIP' => 'A Gift Coupon is deleted after
permanent coupon can be used as often as the customer wants to.',
  'PHPSHOP_COUPON_TYPE_GIFT' => 'Gift Coupon',
  'PHPSHOP_COUPON_TYPE_PERMANENT' => 'Permanent Coupon',
  'PHPSHOP_COUPON_VALUE_HEADER' => 'Value',
  'PHPSHOP_COUPON_PERCENT' => 'Percent',
  'PHPSHOP_COUPON_TOTAL' => 'Total'
); $VM_LANG->initModule( 'coupon', $langvars );
?>
```

VirtueMart also declared a global variable named `$VM_LANG`, which is an object of the class `vmLanguage`. You don't need to actually care about the details of this class. The only function you need to know is the function `_()`. This special function is used to get the value of a language element. To get the language element of `PHPSHOP_CART_SHOW`, for example, you will use the function call `$VM_LANG->_('PHPSHOP_CART_SHOW')`.

VirtueMart also allows you to create your own language element. This is a very simple process. First, you need to determine the module that will be using the language element. If it is used only in the shop module, you should edit the language file in the `shop` subdirectory. If it will be used in more than one module, you should edit the language file in the `common` subdirectory instead. If unsure, you should treat the element as a `common` language element and put it in the language files under the `common` subdirectory. In this way, you can make sure it is available in all the modules you will be using. You also need to make sure the element is added to all the language files that will need this element. To add the language element, simply open the language file, add the element in a form similar to other language elements, and you are done.

Exercise 5.4: Adding a language element

Creating a language element is pretty straightforward. In this exercise, we will create one and use it in the manufacturer header.

Steps

1. Open your favorite text editor. Navigate to the VirtueMart administrator root.

2. Open the file `languages/shop/english.php`.

3. Insert the following lines before line 80 (just before the closing bracket). Don't miss the comma at the beginning of the line. You will get a PHP error if this comma is missed.

   ```
   ,'VM_MANUFACTURER_HEADER' => 'Manufacturer Header'
   ```

4. Save the language file and upload it to your server.

5. Navigate to the VirtueMart frontend root and open the file `themes/default/templates/browse/includes/browse_header_manufacturer.tpl.php`.

6. Insert the following lines of code before line 4 (before the `<?php` tag):

   ```
   <div><?php echo $VM_LANG->_('VM_MANUFACTURER_HEADER') ?></div>
   ```

7. Save the file and upload it to your server.

8. Point your browser to the VirtueMart browse page for the manufacturer (`index.php?page=shop.browse&manufacturer_id=1&option=com_virtuemart`). You should see the new language element at the top of the page.

Notes

1. We gave the name `VM_MANUFACTURER_HEADER` to the language element. You can give it any name you like. The name starts with `VM_` just to make it easier to associate this with VM.

2. We put this language element in the `shop` module language file. This is because the text is only used in the shop module. If you want to use the text in some other modules as well, you should put it in the `common` subdirectory instead.

Manufacturer, vendor, and ask seller templates

Other than the product list and product details, there are a number of peripheral pages that will affect the shoppers' impressions of your site. The `default` templates for these pages are pretty basic. You should consider customizing them in case you need to use these pages. All three templates belong to the `pages` template group.

Manufacturer page

The manufacturer page is controlled by the file `shop.manufacturer_page.php` in the `html` subdirectory. The template file is called `shop.manufacturer.tpl.php`.

The available fields in the manufacturer page are the same as the fields in the data table. `$mf_desc` is HTML text where you can place HTML fragments. You can definitely add lots of information and design here.

Exercise 5.5: Adding a manufacturer logo to the manufacturer page

One missing item in the manufacturer data table is the manufacturer logo. We will add one in this exercise.

Preparation

Create a manufacturer logo named `manufacturer_logo_1.jpg` for the default manufacturer. You can use Photoshop or any other graphic editing program for this. The file should be placed under the subdirectory `shop_image` of the frontend VirtueMart directory.

Steps

1. Open your favorite text editor. Navigate to the VirtueMart administrator root.

2. Open the file `themes/default/templates/pages/shop.manufacturer.tpl.php`.

3. Replace line 29 (before the line `<?php echo " " . $mf_name . "<br />"; ?>`) with the following lines of code:

   ```
   <td align="center"colspan="2">
   <img src="<?php echo IMAGEURL ?>manufacturer_logo_<?php echo
   $db->f('manufacturer_id') ?>.png" />
   ```

4. Save the file and upload it to your server.

5. Point your browser to the manufacturer page. (`index.php?page=shop.manufacturer_page&manufacturer_id=1&option=com_virtuemart`). You should see the manufacturer logo above the manufacturer name.

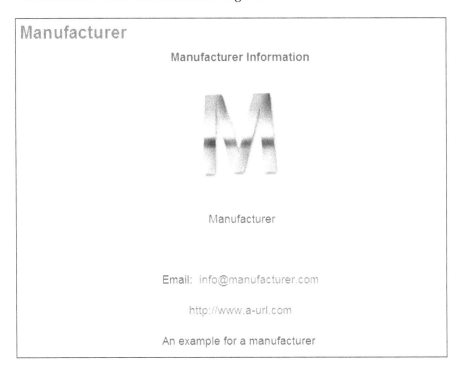

Notes

Sometimes we don't need to rely on the database to store the information we need. We can name the manufacturer logo file according to the `manufacturer_id` or `manufacturer_name`. In this way, we can easily refer to the logo file in the template.

Vendor page

The vendor page is pretty much similar to the manufacturer page. The processing is done in the file `shop.infopage.php` and the template is `shop.infopage.tpl.php`. The file name `infopage` may not be so intuitive, especially when you have more than one vendor in the same shop. Anyway, this is the template that you should look at, if you want to customize your vendor page.

Exercise 5.6: Using tableless HTML for the vendor page

The processing of the ask seller page is done in the file `shop.ask.php` and the template is `shop.ask.tpl.php`.

Steps

1. Open your favorite text editor. Navigate to the VirtueMart administrator root.

2. Open the file `themes/default/templates/pages/shop.infopage.tpl.php`.

3. Replace lines 21 to 55 (that is, all of the HTML code) with the following lines of code:

```
<h3><?php echo $v_name;?></h3>
  <div class="vm_infopage_image">
    <a href="<?php $db->p("vendor_url") ?>" target="blank">
      <img border="0" src="<?php echo IMAGEURL ?>vendor/<?php echo
$v_logo; ?>">
    </a>
  </div>
  <div class="vm_infopage_content">
    <div class="sectiontableheader">
      <strong><?php echo $VM_LANG->_('PHPSHOP_STORE_FORM_CONTACT_
LBL') ?></strong>
    </div>
  <div class="vm_infopage_address">
    <?php echo ps_vendor::formatted_store_address( true ); ?>
  </div>
  <div class="vm_infopage_other">
    <br /><?php echo $VM_LANG->_('PHPSHOP_STORE_FORM_CONTACT_LBL')
?>: <?php echo $v_title ." " . $v_first_name . " " . $v_last_
name ?>
    <br /><?php echo $VM_LANG->_('PHPSHOP_STORE_FORM_PHONE')
?>: <?php $db->p("contact_phone_1");?>
    <br /><?php echo $VM_LANG-
_('PHPSHOP_STORE_FORM_FAX') ?>: <?php echo $v_fax ?>
    <br /><?php echo $VM_LANG->_('PHPSHOP_STORE_FORM_EMAIL')
?>: <?php echo $v_email; ?><br />
    <br /><a href="<?php $db->p("vendor_url") ?>" target="_
blank"><?php $db->p("vendor_url") ?></a><br />
  </div>
  <div class="vm_infopage_desc">
```

```
            <?php $db->p("vendor_store_desc") ?>
        </div>
    </div>
```

4. Save the file and upload it to your server.

5. Point your browser to the vendor page. (`index.php?page=shop.infopage&vendor_id=1&option=com_virtuemart`). You should see the vendor page has changed completely.

Washupito's Tiendita

Contact Information
Washupito's Tiendita
100 Washupito Avenue, N.W.

Lake Forest, 92630

Contact Information: Mr. Demo Owner
Phone: 555-555-1212
Fax: 555-555-1212
Email: joseph@expertcms.net

http://vm.expertcms.net
We have the best tools for do-it-yourselfers. Check us out!

We were established in 1969 in a time when getting good tools was expensive, but the quality was good. Now that only a select few of those authentic tools survive, we have dedicated this store to bringing the experience alive for collectors and master mechanics everywhere.

You can easily find products selecting the category you would like to browse above.

Notes

Basically, what we did was replace the `<table>` and `<td>` tags with `<div>`. All `<tr>` tags were removed. We also added CSS class to allow the control of styles through CSS.

Ask seller page

The vendor page is pretty much similar to the manufacturer page. The processing is done in the file `shop.ask.php` and the template is `shop.ask.tpl.php`.

Exercise 5.7: Adding a radio button to the ask seller page

The default ask seller page allows the input of a name, e-mail address, and message only. In this exercise, we will add a radio button to the form. The value chosen in the radio button is passed back by adding it to the message. This provides more variety for the form within the same backend support.

Steps

1. Open your favorite text editor. Navigate to the VirtueMart administrator root.

2. Open the file `themes/default/templates/pages/shop.ask.tpl.php`.

3. Insert the following line before line 56 (before the line that starts with `document.emailForm.action`):

    ```
    document.emailForm.text.value="Enquiry Type: "+document.
    emailForm.enquiry_type.value+"<br />"+document.emailForm.text.
    value;
    ```

4. Insert the following lines of code before line 33 (that is, before the `contact_text` label):

    ```
    <label for="enquiry_type ">Enquiry Type</label><br />
    <br /><input type="radio" id="enquiry_type_1" name="enquiry_
    type" class="inputbox" value="General" checked="checked">
    <br /><input type="radio" id="enquiry_type_2" name="enquiry_
    type" class="inputbox" value="Sample Request">
    ```

5. Save the file and upload it to your server.

6. Point your browser to the ask seller page. (`index.php?page=shop.ask&product_id=1&option=com_virtuemart`). You should see the additional radio buttons on the ask seller page.

Return to product

Enter your Name

E-mail Address

Enquiry Type
  ○ General   Sample Request

Enter your Message

Send

Notes

1. This exercise uses a JavaScript to add the value of the **Enquiry Type** to the message before posting the data back to the server. This is not a perfect solution, but provides varieties of the form within the limit of the backend support. Otherwise, you will need to modify the `shop.ask.php` file to provide extra fields.

2. We use a radio button just for demonstration purposes. Other kinds of HTML form elements such as textbox, drop-down, or checkbox can be used as well. By using a more complex form of JavaScript, you can even hide or show a certain part of the form according to which the radio button is checked.

3. We hardcoded the radio button labels in English. If needed, it can be easily changed to support multi-language.

Home page template

The VirtueMart home page, or landing page, is the first page that shopper will come to when he/she visits the shop. So, a discussion on the look of VirtueMart is incomplete without a thorough discussion of the home page template.

The first thing we need to note is the VirtueMart home page is different from the Joomla! home page although you can make them the same. The Joomla! home page is the page displayed when a shopper just types the Joomla! root URL. By default, it will display the frontpage component (or actually the content component that points to the frontpage). This default can be changed in the Joomla! backend menu manager. If you set a menu item that points to a VirtueMart component as the default, the VirtueMart home page and Joomla! home page will be the same.

The URL of the VirtueMart home page is `index.php?option=com_virtuemart`. You can see this is a URL with the `option` parameter set to VirtueMart, but without a value for the `page` parameter. In that case, `page` will be set to `shop.index` by default. This default can be changed in the backend VirtueMart configuration on the **Security** tab. You are allowed to set this to other pages such as `shop.browse`, for example. If `shop.browse` is the home page, VirtueMart will start with the product list page when no `page` parameter is given (`category_id` is not set as well, so the product list will show all products).

In most cases, you probably will not change the home page setting in the configuration and so `shop.index` is, more often than not, the home page of your shop. The corresponding template is `shopIndex.tpl.php`, located in the `common` subdirectory of the VirtueMart templates root. So when we say VirtueMart home page, we actually mean the `shop.index` page.

shopIndex template

If you look at the `shopIndex.tpl.php` template, you will see that the structure for this is very simple. There are a few elements that will be displayed:

- `$vendor_store_desc`: This is actually the description you entered in the VirtueMart backend for the store. You can modify this in the VirtueMart backend by clicking the **Store/Edit Store** link on the left menu.

- `$categories`: This will show the full list of categories of the shop. The actual layout of this is determined by the template `categoryChildlist.tpl.php`, which also belongs to the `common` template group.

- `$recent_products`: This will show the products that have been visited in the same session. The template for this is `recent.tpl.php`.

- `$featured_products`: This is the list of products that have been set as featured products in the backend. The template for this is `featuredProducts.tpl.php`.

- `$latest_products`: This is the list of products that were added lately. There is no template set for this.

- `$paypalLogo`: This is obviously used to show the PayPal logo, if PayPal is activated for the site.

The recent products, featured products, and latest products will be discussed at greater detail in *Chapter 7, VirtueMart Templates And Joomla! Modules*. Here we will take a closer look at the `categoryChildlist` template and the `shopIndex` template.

Category child list template

The `categoryChildlist` template is used by both the home page template and the product list template to show the category child list. It basically loops through the child categories of a given category specified by `category_id` to display its name, thumbnail, and the number of products. For the case of home page, since no `category_id` is given, so the top categories will be displayed instead.

The child categories will be displayed by rows, if there are many categories. The number of child categories in a row can be modified in the head of the template.

Exercise 5.8: Changing the number of child categories per row

By default, the number of categories per row is 4. In this exercise, we will change this number to 2 instead.

Steps

1. Open your favorite text editor. Navigate to the VirtueMart frontend root.

2. Open the file `themes/default/templates/common/categoryChildlist.tpl.php`.

3. Replace line 6 (the line `$categories_per_row = 4;`) with the following line of code:

    ```
    $categories_per_row = 2;
    ```

4. Save the file and upload it to your server.

5. Point your browser to the VirtueMart home page (`index.php?option=com_virtuemart`). You should see that there are only two categories in each row.

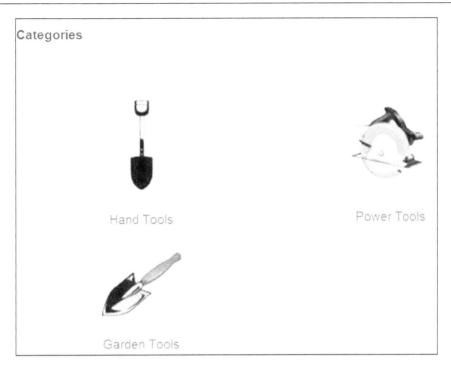

Notes

This is a very simple change. Unfortunately, VirtueMart does not have a setting for the number of categories per row. You can create one after we discuss how to create a custom theme in *Chapter 9, Theme Customizations*.

Exercise 5.9: Adding a manufacturer list to the landing page

The default `shopIndex` template only shows the list of categories. In this exercise, we are going to add a list of manufacturers as well.

Preparation

We will use manufacturer logos in the manufacturer list. So you need to have one ready for each manufacturer in your shop. We already created one in *Exercise 5.5*. If you have not tried that exercise, you will need to create one before performing this exercise.

Steps

1. Open your favorite text editor. Navigate to the VirtueMart frontend root.

2. Open the file `themes/default/templates/common/shopIndex.tpl.php`.

3. Insert the following lines of code before line 8 (that is, before the `$recent_products` section).

```php
<?php
  $db1 = new ps_DB;
  $q1 = "SELECT *
    FROM #__{vm}_manufacturer
    ORDER BY mf_name
  ";
  $db1->query($q1);
  echo '<div><b>Manufacturers</b></div>';
  while ($db1->next_record()) {
    echo '
    <div class="vm_manufacturer" style="float:left;text-
align:center;border:1px solid black;margin:5px;padding:2px;">
      <img src="'. IMAGEURL .'manufacturer_logo_'.$db1-
>f('manufacturer_id').'.png" />
    <br />
     ' . $db1->f('mf_name') . '<br />
    </div>
    ';
  }
  echo '<br class="clr" />';
?>
```

4. Save the file and upload it to your server.

5. Point your browser to the VirtueMart home page (`index.php?pageoption=com_virtuemart`). You should see the manufacturer list after the category list.

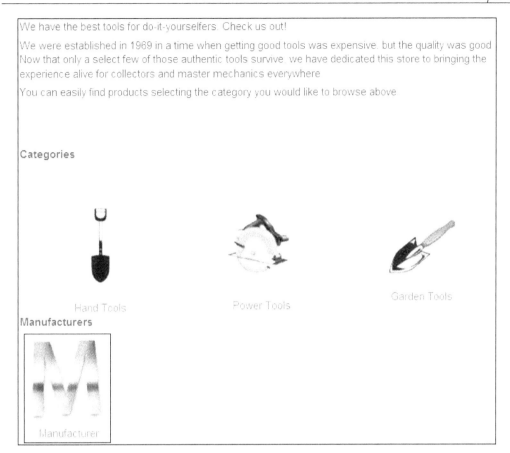

Notes

1. Normally, we should not access the database directly in a template file. However, since we are not passing any information about the manufacturers from the `shop.index.php` file and we do not want to change the core VirtueMart files, the only way we can do this is by fetching data directly from the database.

2. The coding will show all the manufacturers in the database. However, because we have only one manufacturer defined in the default VirtueMart install, that is the only one we can show. You can add more manufacturers to your site if you want to make sure this works.

Summary

In this chapter, we have looked at the structure of VirtueMart from the angle of web-page design. We glanced through the VirtueMart stylesheets and JavaScripts. We then saw how we can create a SEF-compatible URL and how multi-language elements are structured in VirtueMart. We also looked at a few more templates that affect the look of VirtueMart and learned how to customize them to add features that are originally not in the default theme. In the next chapter, we will continue our study with the templates from shop basket to the checkout pages.

6
From Shop Basket to Final Checkout

In this chapter, we will walk through the latter half of the shopping life cycle, from the time that a product is added to the shop basket to the time that the customer finishes with the order. We will first explain how the shop basket data is stored in the server and look at the various elements on the shop cart page. A major part of these discussions will focus around the `basket` template group. Next, we will cross the border to the `checkout` template group and follow every page in the checkout process. For each of the checkout steps, there are associated templates. We will look at each of the templates and see how they can be customized to fit our needs. While working through the exercises, we will introduce further techniques that can be employed to customize VirtueMart without hacking into the core files.

Briefly, in this chapter, we cover:

- Shop basket data and shop basket display
- Shop cart page
- Checkout steps
- Login/registration and shipping information
- Shipping methods and payment methods
- Final confirmation page
- Thank you page

Shop basket data and shop basket display

In the past three chapters, we have toured around most of the templates of the VirtueMart catalog system. The major goal of these templates is to show off your products and help shoppers to find the products that fit their needs. When they have found what they need, the next logical step is certainly to place the product into their shop basket. From time-to-time, the shopper may need to refer to this basket. So we need to have ways to show this basket to the shopper. This is exactly what we are going to look at in this section.

Session and shop basket

As you may know, web technology is based on a stateless communication scheme. This means that when a user navigates to another page, all previous information will be lost unless it is specifically stored by the server or browser using cookies. PHP has a special global variable called `$_SESSION` and a whole bunch of session functions to help record these data. This provision is used by VirtueMart to handle user permission and, in particular, the shop basket as the shopper navigates from page-to-page through the shop.

`$_SESSION` is actually an array created when a shopper first comes to the shop. Each piece of session data is recorded in it as an array element. For example, `$_SESSION['auth']` will record the user permission of the shopper and `$_SESSION['cart']` will record the products that are placed in the shop basket. As soon as the shopper starts to place a product into the basket, the `$_SESSION['cart']` element will be created. Since the shop basket can become complex as more and more products are added, the `$_SESSION['cart']` is created as an array by itself, so that we can add and remove structured data from it easily. Very often, VirtueMart will define another variable `$cart=$_SESSION['cart']` to make it easier to refer to the content. While `$_SESSION['cart']` and `$cart` are actually two different variables and should be distinguished carefully, they are basically the same thing, conceptually. For the sake of simplicity, we will refer to `$_SESSION['cart']` as `$cart` in the following discussion. This array has two sets of elements:

- `idx`: This is a named element that records the number of products that have been placed in the shop basket.

- Products: This is a series of integer-indexed elements starting from 0 onwards. So `$cart['0']` refers to the first product added to the basket, `$cart['1']` the second product, and so on.

Each of the product elements is an array in itself. The elements are:

- `product_id`: The identifier of the product. Note that different child products of the same product family will have their own `product_id` and will be recorded as a separate element in the shop basket. This will serve as the identifier of the product added to the basket most of the time. If the product has an advanced attribute or a custom attribute, the product with a different attribute will be recorded as a different element.

- `description`: The `description` element is used only for products with advanced or custom attributes. This is needed since products with different attributes will need to be handled differently during the checkout. (They may have different prices and certainly attribute information must be there to make sure the correct product will be shipped.)

- `quantity`: This records the quantity of products ordered.

- `category_id`: This is the category identifier of the product. Needed only for navigation purposes.

- `parent_id`: This is used for child products which record the `product_id` of the parent product. Needed only for navigation purposes. For non-child products, `parent_id=product_id`.

This may seem a little complex even to an experienced PHP coder. Maybe some examples will make it clearer. Let's suppose you have placed three products in the shop basket: two big Hammers (`product_id=6`) made of wood and metal and a Metal Ladder (`product_id=14`) which is a child product of Ladder (`product_id=2`).

Then the `$cart` array will contain three elements:

- `$cart['idx']=2` (because there are only two product items)
- `$cart[0]` contains details of the Hammer (PHP array index starts from 0)
- `$cart[1]` contains details of the Metal Ladder

Also, `$cart[0]` is itself an array with the following elements:

- `$cart['product_id']=6`
- `$cart['description']='size:big;material:wood_and_metal'`
- `$cart['quantity']=2` (two Hammers with the same attribute)
- `$cart['parent_id']=''` (no parent product)

Similarly, `$cart[1]` contains the following elements:

- `$cart['product_id']=14` (product ID of the Metal Ladder)
- `$cart['description']=''` (no attribute)

- `$cart['quantity']=1`
- `$cart['parent_id']=2` (product ID of the Ladder)

While this may look different from what you see when you come to the Shop Cart page, this is actually how the shop basket data is kept. What we see on the browser is a result of the processing and layout of this data. The processing and layout will vary with the page you are looking at; this certainly depends on which template is used for the display.

Basket templates

There are a number of situations when the shopper would like to check their shop baskets (and certainly, it is you who decides whether to provide function for checking). Basically, a shopper will need to look at the shop basket from time-to-time during the shopping process. VirtueMart provides a page `shop.cart` for this purpose. This is the page that we usually refer to as the shop cart or Shop Cart page. The Shop Cart page will be the focus of the next section.

Cart

Name	SKU	Price	Quantity / Update		Subtotal
Hand Shovel	G01-01	$5.48	1		$5.48
Color (Red) Size (Small)					
Hand Shovel	G01-03	$16.45	3		$49.35
Color (Blue) Size (Large)					
Circular Saw Size: XL (+ $1.10) Power: middle	P02	$243.54	1		$243.54
				Subtotal:	$298.37
				Total:	**$298.37**
				Tax Total:	$26.51

Check out with **PayPal**
The safer, easier way to pay

If you have a coupon code, please enter it below:

[Submit]

« Continue Shopping   » Checkout

The existence of the Shop Cart page is simply for checking what products are inside the basket. However, a shopper will need to refer to the basket during the whole checkout process. It will not be considered friendly if they have to switch back and forth between the checkout page and the shop cart page. VirtueMart includes the basket on every checkout page (except the thank you page) as shoppers proceed along, and so the basket template is included as an essential element on almost every checkout page. As we proceed through the checkout process, new information such as the shipping cost and revised tax will need to be added. However, to simplify the design, VirtueMart tries to make all those pages share the same template as far as possible.

However, there are still situations where different templates are needed. VirtueMart assumed that there may be very different basket requirements for B2B (business-to-business) and B2C (business-to-consumer) shoppers and so provides a template for each. Actually, VirtueMart's definition of B2B and B2C shoppers is very rough and is not prominent at all. So maybe you never noticed this before. According to VirtueMart, the only difference between a B2B and a B2C shopper is whether to show them the price including the tax or not. B2B shoppers will see the net price while B2C shoppers will see the tax included in the price. Whether to show the price with tax included will probably depend on the region of your targeted shoppers. In some regions, it is the law to show the price without tax. In such cases, all your shoppers belong to the B2B categories according to VirtueMart terminology, although in actual fact, all your shoppers are considered end consumers.

The setting for B2B and B2C shoppers is controlled by the shopper group. If you want to change this, you will need to go to an individual shopper group to make the change. In the following screenshot, you can see the checkbox in the **Shopper Group Form** for this purpose. To access the Shopper Group function, log into VirtueMart and click **Shopper** and then **Shopper Group** in the left Menu.

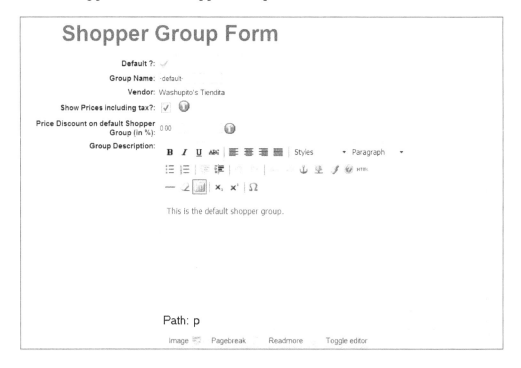

Another scenario that needs a different basket template is whether you want to allow changes to the shop basket during the checkout process. VirtueMart assumes that you allow shoppers to make modifications of the shop basket until the final confirmation. That's why it provides different basket templates for the final confirmation page. In these so called read-only basket templates, there are no quantity textboxes, no update buttons, and no delete buttons. All of the other pages share the same basket templates, which allow changes to the shop basket.

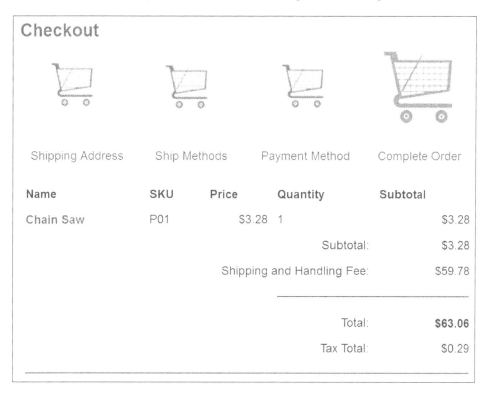

Name	SKU	Price	Quantity	Subtotal
Chain Saw	P01	$3.28	1	$3.28
			Subtotal:	$3.28
			Shipping and Handling Fee:	$59.78
			Total:	**$63.06**
			Tax Total:	$0.29

There are four basket templates in the `default` theme that cater to each of the above scenarios. All of these basket templates are placed in the `basket` template group.

Name ↓	Size	Last Modified	
⬆ Up to higher level directory			
includes		7/28/2010	12:58:00 AM
basket_b2b.html.php	4 KB	5/20/2010	12:00:00 AM
basket_b2c.html.php	4 KB	5/20/2010	12:00:00 AM
index.html		5/20/2010	12:00:00 AM
ro_basket_b2b.html.php	4 KB	5/20/2010	12:00:00 AM
ro_basket_b2c.html.php	4 KB	5/20/2010	12:00:00 AM

As you can see, the template names are self-explanatory. Templates that start with `ro_` are those for read-only shop baskets and are used only in the final confirmation page.

In addition to showing the basket on the main component area, VirtueMart also allows us to show the basket in a Joomla! module. VirtueMart itself is shipped with a number of modules that is using this function. There are also third-party modules that make use of this. The relation between templates and Joomla! modules will be the subject of *Chapter 7, VirtueMart Templates and Joomla! Modules*.

Shop basket functions

While the shop basket layout is controlled by the shop basket templates, data has to be pre-processed before passing it to the template. This processing is done by the pages `basket.php` and `ro_basket.php`, respectively. Other than showing what is inside the basket, the `basket.php` file also provides the following three functions:

- Update products: The file provides a textbox for changing the quantity and a button to update the quantity in the shop basket. This is passed to the template through the array element `'update_form'` of each product row.

- Delete product: The file provides a button to remove the product from the shop basket. This is passed to the template through the array element `'delete_form'`.

- Coupon discount: The file also provides a textbox for inputting the coupon code for performing coupon discount. Actually, the coupon form has a template `couponField.tpl.php` of its own which is separate from the basket templates. The `couponField.tpl.php` template belongs to the `common` template group instead of the `basket` template group.

These additional functions are not provided in the ro_basket.php file for obvious reasons. (Actually, the update product and delete product forms are created and passed into the template. However, there are some flaws in the coding and so they cannot be used.)

The basket.php file provides one update form for each product item. This means that changes can only be made to one product at a time when using this update form. If you need to have an update button for all products at the same time, you have to customize the basket.php for doing this. However, since basket.php is a part of the VirtueMart core, you can also consider putting all those processing logics in the basket templates instead. If you have basket templates from a third party that provide for additional basket functions, you probably will see lots of this additional coding placed in the template instead of hacking the VirtueMart core. In the following exercises, we will be using a similar approach.

Exercise 6.1: Adding product thumbnails to the basket

In the default theme, the basket templates do not show the thumbnail for the product. Adding a thumbnail image is straightforward if the information is passed down from the basket.php. Unfortunately, there is not enough information from the available fields in the basket templates to be used to deduce this information. Thus, we have to devise our own method to get the thumbnail. In this exercise, we are going to put some database logic into the template file to retrieve the appropriate information. This is not best practice, but can help to avoid hacking into the VirtueMart core.

Steps

1. Open your favorite text editor. Navigate to the VirtueMart frontend root.
2. Open the file themes/default/templates/basket/basket_b2c.html.php.
3. Insert the following line before line 32 (before the echo $product['product_price'] line).

   ```
   <td><?php echo $product['product_thumb'] ?></td>;
   ```

4. Insert the following line before line 24 (before the echo $VM_LANG->_ ('PHPSHOP_CART_QUANTITY') line):

   ```
   <th><?php echo 'Thumbnail'; ?></th>
   ```

5. Insert the following lines of code before line 19 (just before the ?> closing tag):

   ```
   // adding thumb image
   $db1 = new ps_DB;
   ```

```
$thumb_width=50;
$thumb_height=50;
$frontend_url= str_replace('shop_image/','',IMAGEURL);
for ($i=0;$i<count($product_rows);$i++) {
  $q1 = "SELECT product_full_image
    FROM #__{vm}_product
    WHERE product_sku='".$product_rows[$i]['product_sku']."'
  ";
  $db1->setQuery($q1);
  $product_image=$db1->loadResult();    $product_rows[$i]
['product_thumb']='<img src="'.$frontend_url.'show_image_in_
imgtag.php?filename='.$product_image
    .'&newxsize='.$thumb_width.'&newysize='.$thumb_height.'" />';
}
```

6. Save the file and upload it to your server.

7. Go to your VirtueMart site. Add some products to the shop cart and go to the Shop Cart page. You should see the product thumbnail for each product you have added.

Name	SKU	Thumbnail	Price	Quantity / Update	Subtotal
Chain Saw	P01		$164.61	1	$164.61
			Subtotal:		$164.61
			Total:		**$164.61**
			Tax Total:		$14.62

Notes

1. There are three steps (steps 3 to 5 in the preceding section) that you have to carry out before you can add a column to the shop basket table: prepare the data, add a column header cell, and add a column content cell. In order to make sure the line number is unambiguous, these steps are taken in reverse in the changes above.

2. Step 5 is the most important step to prepare the data. We define two variables to set the thumbnail size. These are set to 50 for this exercise, but you can change them to any value you think appropriate.

3. We derive the VirtueMart frontend URL from `IMAGEURL` by removing the `shop_image/` path from the URL. This is to make sure our code works in a SEF system. We cannot use the constant `URL`, as explained in the last chapter, because `URL` is for HTTP access only. As you may know, the shop basket is shown both in HTTP (shop cart page) and HTTPS (checkout pages) pages in many VirtueMart sites.

4. We use the `product_sku` value to get the value of `product_full_image` from the database. We should have used `product_id` instead. Unfortunately, `product_id` is not an available field in the template. `product_sku` should be fine so long if your `product_sku` is unique. If not, you will need to find another workaround. (For example, get the `product_id` directly from `$_SESSION['cart']`.)

5. We loop through all the elements in the `$product_rows` array, which has elements indexed by integer starting from 0. This means `$product_rows[0]` represents the first product, `$product_rows[1]` represents the second product, and so on. Each of these elements is itself an array indexed by property name. So, `$product_rows[0]['product_sku']` represents the `product_sku` of the first product.

6. We create a new index called `'product_thumb'` for each `$product_rows` element to make them available in the shop basket table. `product_rows[0]['product_thumb']` will therefore represent the thumb image location of the first product.

7. Step 4 adds the header cell to the shop basket table. We hardcoded the header value as `"Thumbnail"`. Feel free to change it to any other value or create a language element for it, as demonstrated in *Chapter 5, Changing the Look of VirtueMart*.

8. Step 3 is the actual step that adds the content cell to the shop basket table. This is pretty straightforward if you look at the neighboring lines in the coding.

9. This exercise only modified the template for B2C shopper groups. Creating one for the B2B shopper groups will be very similar.

Shop Cart page

We have looked at the shop basket in quite some detail previously. It's now time to take a closer look at the Shop Cart page. We should note that the Shop Cart page is a different object from the shop basket we have been discussing so far. Shop basket is just one common element shared by the shop cart and checkout pages. Shop Cart page is the page that VirtueMart used to show the content of the shop basket. When you click the link **Show Cart** or the **Cart** button on the add-to-cart pop-up, you will be brought to the Shop Cart page.

We purposely use a different terminology for distinguishing between shop cart and shop basket. As has been explained previously, the shop basket is included on the Shop Cart page and also on every checkout page. So it is important that you do not mix them up. The data processing of the Shop Cart page is controlled by the file `shop.cart.php`. The layout of the page is done in the template `shop.cart.tpl.php`. Just from the name of the template, you can guess that this template belongs to the `pages` template group. On the other hand, the shop basket data processing is done in the `basket.php` or `ro_basket.php` files and the templates belong to the `basket` template group.

Nevertheless, the major content of the Shop Cart page is the shop basket. Other than that, the Shop Cart page just provides two additional buttons at the bottom of the page to enable the shopper to go back to shopping or heading forward to the checkout. Customization of the Shop Cart page is pretty much the same as customization of the shop basket, despite the subtle difference.

Exercise 6.2: Using Ajax to update Shop Cart page

While Ajax is used in the product list and product details page to update the shop basket, this is not done on the Shop Cart page. In this exercise, we will add this function to the Shop Cart page. The customization is actually done in the basket template, but we use a special technique to restrict the change only to the Shop Cart page. This is essential as updating the shop basket during checkout will trigger changes in the shipping method, shipping cost, and many other things. Using Ajax to update the shop basket on the checkout page will need more complex consideration.

Preparation

This exercise is built upon the basket template we modified in *Exercise 6.1*. If you start from the original template file, the exact line numbers may differ.

Steps

1. Open your favorite text editor. Navigate to the VirtueMart frontend root.

2. Open the file `themes/default/templates/basket/basket_b2c.html.php`.

3. Insert the following lines after line 43 (after the `foreach ($product_rows` line):

```php
<?php
// use ajax to update cart if on shop cart page
if ($_REQUEST['page']=='shop.cart') {
    $product['update_form']=str_replace('<form ',
            '<form onsubmit="handleUpdateCart( this );return
false;"',
            $product['update_form']);
}
?>
```

4. Open the file `themes/default/theme.js`.

5. Insert the following lines after line 132 (that is, the bottom of the file):

```javascript
function updateCart() {
        var callbackCart = function(responseText) {
                $("vmMainPage").innerHTML=responseText;
        }
        var option = { method: 'post', onComplete: callbackCart,
data: { only_page:1,page: "shop.cart", option: "com_virtuemart" }
}
        new Ajax( live_site + '/index2.php', option).request();
}
function handleUpdateCart( frm ) {
        formCartAdd = $( frm );
        var callback = function(responseText) {
                updateCart();
                updateMiniCarts();
        }
        var opt = {
            method: 'post',
            data: $(frm),
            onComplete: callback,
            evalScripts: true
        }
        new Ajax(formCartAdd.action, opt).request();
}
```

6. Save the file and upload it to your server.

7. Go to your VirtueMart site. Add some products to the shop basket and go to the Shop Cart page. Try changing the **Quantity** textbox and click the **Update** button. The Shop Cart page should be updated on the fly without page refresh. If you have any shop cart modules on the same page, they should also be updated as well.

Notes

1. We have to change two files in this exercise.

2. The first change is done in the template file. We need to replace the `update_form` so as to insert the function call to `handleUpdateCart` before submitting the form. We check the `page` parameter to make sure that we are on the `shop.cart` page before performing any modification. This check restricts our changes only to the Shop Cart page. If you need the Ajax update function for checkout pages as well, you can remove this `page` parameter check. However, you will need to consider possible changes in the shipping method and shipping cost, and handle those changes as well. Otherwise, the data on the checkout page will not be consistent.

3. The second change, which is also the major one, is to add two functions to the `theme.js` JavaScript file.

4. We cannot explain all the details of the JavaScript here because this involves using the MooTools framework. However, this coding is basically a copy and paste of the coding on the same file and modifying them for our current situation.

5. The function `handleUpdateCart()` defines a callback function which is invoked when the Ajax call is done. It then posts the update form to the server to update the shop basket using Ajax. The callback function consists of two function calls. The first one, `updateCart()`, is to update the main page without a page refresh. The second one, `updateMiniCarts()`, is used to update all the shop cart modules existing on the page. Note that when using an Ajax call to update part of a page, we use `index2.php` instead of `index.php`. The `index2.php` differs from `index.php` in that it will only return the component part of the page.

Exercise 6.3: Restricting coupon usage to certain shopper groups

When **Enable Coupon Usage** is enabled in VirtueMart Global Configuration, any shopper can see the coupon field textbox below the basket table. This means that everyone is allowed coupon discount, if they can provide a valid coupon code. In this exercise, we will change the `couponField.tpl.php` file so that only shoppers from certain shopper groups can see the coupon field textbox.

Preparation

The standard VirtueMart install will create three shopper groups in the database. In addition to the **-default-** shopper group, you should see the other two shopper groups, **Gold Level** (`shopper_group_id`=6) and **Wholesale** (`shopper_group_id`=7), in the **Shopper Group List**. If you do not have any shopper groups other than **-default-**, you will need to create one by following steps 1 and 2 below. Otherwise, you can skip directly to step 3. If you are not sure, you can check by following step 1.

1. Log in to the VirtueMart backend. Click **Shopper** and then **Shopper Groups** in the left menu to open the **Shopper Group List**. If you have any shopper groups other than **-default-**, you can skip to step 3 directly. Otherwise, create a new shopper group by following the instructions in step 2.

2. Click **New** on the toolbar to open the **Shopper Group Form**. Enter **Gold Level** (or any other name you think appropriate) in the **Group Name** textbox and leave the default checkbox unchecked. Feel free to set any other fields as appropriate. They are irrelevant for this exercise. Remember to click the **Save** button on the toolbar after you are done with all the fields.

3. When you are back to the **Shopper Group List**, you should see your new shopper group has been created. Click the new shopper group (or any shopper group that you would allow to access the coupon field) to go to the **Shopper Group Form** and look for the `shopper_group_id` in the browser navigation bar. If you don't see `shopper_group_id` in the bar because the URL is too long, you can point your mouse to the bar and look for the value in the tooltip pop-up. Or you can click on the navigation bar to select the whole URL. Copy and paste the URL in to your editor and search for the `shopper_group_id`. The `shopper_group_id` is needed for this exercise.

4. You now need to create a user that belongs to the **Gold Level** shopper group. Click **Admin** and then **Users** on the left menu to open the **User List**. Click **New** in the toolbar to open the **Add/Update User Information** page. You can fill in everything just like you would for a new shopper. The only thing you need to make sure is the **Shopper Group** drop-down on the **Shopper Information** tab. Make sure that the value is **Gold Level** or the shopper group you will want to use.

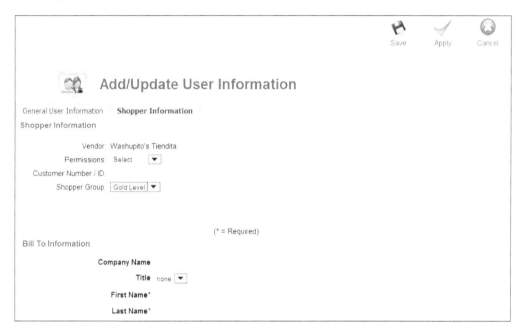

Steps

1. Open your favorite text editor. Navigate to the VirtueMart frontend root.

2. Open the file `themes/default/templates/common/couponField.tpl.php`.

3. Insert the following lines after line 55 (that is, the bottom of the file):

```php
<?php
        }
?>
```

4. Insert the following lines before line 21 (before the closing tag `?>`):

```php
$allow_shopper_groups = array (6,7,8,9,10);
$auth=$_SESSION['auth'];
$shopper_group=$auth['shopper_group_id'];
if (in_array($shopper_group,$allow_shopper_groups)) {
```

5. Save the file and upload it to your server.

6. Go to your VirtueMart site. Add some products to the shop basket and go to the Shop Cart page. You should not see the coupon field textbox. Log in to the VirtueMart frontend with the user you created in step 4 of the *Preparation*. You should now see the coupon field textbox.

Notes

1. In this exercise, an `if` condition is added to display the coupon field textbox. We make use of the `$_SESSION['auth']` element to check the `shopper_group_id`. If the `shopper_group_id` is within the `$allow_shopper_groups`, the coupon field textbox will display.

2. `$allow_shopper_groups` is an array variable. Here you should insert the `shopper_group_id` you found in *Preparation* step 3 here. You can also enter more than one shopper group, as we have done. Just make sure you separate the shopper groups with commas (,).

3. A user that is not logged in belongs to the **-default-** shopper group, which has a `shopper_group_id`=5, so he/she will not see the coupon field textbox.

4. This hack is not a bulletproof way to restrict coupon discount to certain shopper groups. Actually, this tweak just hides the textbox in the browser page for those shoppers who do not belong to the groups we allow. However, the server logic has not changed, so the coupon code is still accepted no matter which shopper group the shopper belongs to, if one is submitted to the server. As you perhaps know, people can create HTTP requests without using the browser and they can put in any parameter they like. In such cases, they can bypass our logic and will enjoy the coupon discount.

Checkout steps

Checkout is another major VirtueMart module other than the shop module. Though the major data processing is done in the `checkout.index.php` file, it comprises quite a number of steps. Each of the steps will have one or more template associated with it. All of these templates are grouped together into the `checkout` template group. There are five possible steps in a checkout including the following:

- Login/registration
- Get shipping address
- Get shipping method
- Get payment method
- Final confirmation

Since each web store may have a different checkout format, not all of these steps are needed in each VirtueMart site. VirtueMart allows you to customize the checkout format but not without restrictions. First of all you need to understand VirtueMart is a Joomla! component. So creating a login in VirtueMart is the same as creating a login in Joomla!. Using VirtueMart 1.0, only shoppers that have a registration in Joomla! can go to checkout. However, this is changed as from Version 1.1 onwards when VirtueMart introduced a no-registration option.

Actually, there are four registration options in VirtueMart 1.1. You can certainly have a **Normal Account Creation** option. There are also **Silent Account Creation**, **Optional Account Creation**, and the **No Account Creation** options. **Silent Account Creation** means a Joomla! login is created without the shopper knowing it, using the e-mail address and a randomly generated password. **No Account Creation** actually means no Joomla! login will be created, but still a shopper will be created in VirtueMart. **Optional Account Creation** optionleaves the registration choice to the shopper, so that he/she can choose to register or not.

No matter which option you select, the login/registration step remains a mandatory step in the checkout. Certainly, you can rename the title of the page, but logically the step is still there. Unfortunately, this login/registration step is not included specifically in the documentation and in the checkout bar. Sometimes, this will lead to confusion. Anyway, the login/registration step does have templates of its own and you can customize them to fit your needs. We also recognize that login/registration is different from the other steps and must be placed as the first step of the checkout.

There are two other mandatory steps in the checkout other than login/registration. They are the Get Payment Method step and the Final Confirmation step, respectively. This leaves only two steps that are optional in the ViruteMart checkout. For products that don't need shipping you can skip the Get Shipping Address and Get Shipping Method steps. You can configure VirtueMart whether to skip these steps in the backend VirtueMart **Configurataion**, on the **Checkout** tab.

VirtueMart also allows you to change the order of the checkout steps. You can, for example, set the get payment method before the get shipping method. Actually, this looks like the only possible swap of order of the checkout steps. It is definitely unreasonable not to put the final confirmation as the last step. It is also unconceivable to have the get shipping method before the get shipping address. VirtueMart also allows you to set two steps on the same page. You can, for example, put get shipping address and get shipping method on the same page. You can also put all the steps on one single page to simulate the single page checkout.

This brings up the checkout stage concept in addition to the checkout step. All steps that are placed on one page are said to be on the same stage. If you put all four steps on one single page, there will be only one checkout stage with four checkout steps. Sometimes, VirtueMart refers to this as one checkout step with four substeps. Despite the difference in nomenclature, the concept remains the same.

To give a shopper a clearer idea of which stage/step the checkout is on, VirtueMart provides a checkout bar showing the whole checkout life cycle with the current steps highlighted. This checkout bar has a template of its own so that you can customize it to fit your needs. If you look at the `checkout_bar.tpl.php` file, you will see that the bar is displayed as an HTML table with each table cell containing one stage (step). Of course, you need a different CSS style for the current stage (step) to make it stand out. For all of the earlier steps that the shopper has passed, the template will output a link to allow a shopper to go back. All future steps, however, are simply text labels so that the only way to go forward is by filling the form provided and clicking the next button.

Exercise 6.4: Customizing the checkout bar

The default theme checkout bar uses a different background to create a different checkout bar for different steps during the checkout. You do not need to follow this kind of design. In the exercise, we will customize the bar to use a tab system instead.

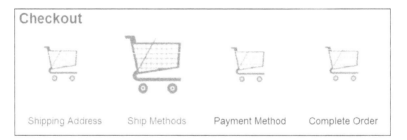

Steps

1. Open your favorite text editor. Navigate to the VirtueMart frontend root.

2. Open the file `themes/default/templates/checkout/checkout_bar.tpl.php`.

3. Replace line 31 (the line that starts with `echo '<table`) with the following line of code:

    ```
    echo '<table class="checkout-bar" border="0" cellspacing="0"
    cellpadding="0" align="center">
    ```

4. Replace line 22 (the line that starts with `$highlighted_style`) with the following line of code:

```
$highlighted_style = 'class="checkout-bar-highlight"';
```

5. Insert the following lines after line 19 (after the closing tag `?>`):

```
<style type="text/css">
  .checkout-bar td {
    border:1px solid #ccc;
    border-bottom:2px solid #333;
    vertical-align:middle;
    height:25px;
    text-align:center;
  }
  td.checkout-bar-highlight {
    font-weight:bold;
    border:2px solid #333 !important;
    border-bottom:none !important;
  }
</style>
```

6. Save the file and upload it to your server.

7. Go to your VirtueMart site. Add some products to the shop cart and head to the checkout. You should see a different checkout bar.

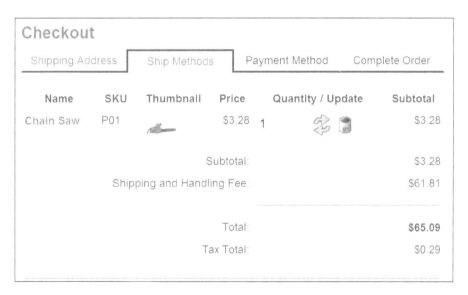

Notes

1. We have made three changes to the template file. Firstly, we replaced the table style attribute with a CSS class to provide more flexibility in controlling its style. This is especially important if you have a different team working on the CSS and you don't want them to touch your code. The CSS team will just change the style in the `theme.css` instead.

2. Secondly, we change the `$highlighted_style` variable to a CSS class instead of hardcoding the CSS style. Again, this is for more flexibility.

3. Final, we added a whole bunch of CSS styles to the template. This essentially changed the look of the bar to a tab form.

4. Obviously, the CSS style we added is very simple and may not fit your design standard. You can further fine-tune the tab to make it look better.

5. The tab system will look best when each step consists of just one single substep. Otherwise, the label of the tab may look too complicated.

Login/registration and shipping information

From this section onward, we start to look at each of the checkout steps and their associated templates one-by-one. The initial step is of course the login/registration step. No matter which registration option you have taken for your shop, the registration form is needed for allowing new shoppers to insert their customer information. This customer information is sometimes referred to as registration information, billing information, or even the billing address. But they are the same thing as viewed by VirtueMart.

VirtueMart has a default setting for the registration information in the standard install. The default setting includes all common fields needed so that your shop can be up and running right out of the box. If you want to change the fields or settings, you can go to the VirtueMart backend, click **Admin**, and then **Manage User Fields** to make changes.

Since registration information and shipping information are managed by the same User Fields Manager, it makes sense to put them together in the same section. As you will see when working through *Exercise 6.5* that follows, when you add a new user field, there are many possible options. The user field can be a checkbox, drop-down, textbox, date, and so on. You can even add a new `fieldset` delimiter to create a different group of user fields.

On the other hand, you can also configure the field for either the registration or shipping information or both. Also, there is a setting to show the field in account maintenance where the shopper can make changes as appropriate.

We will not go into the detail of every possibility but leave it for you to experiment with them yourselves. The good thing is, if you don't like a certain setting, you can always go back to the backend to make changes. We will demonstrate how this can be done in the exercise *Preparation* below, as an example for you.

The User Field Manager is definitely very useful. However, the many possible configuration options are provided at a big trade-off. The display of the user fields is pretty much hardcoded in the `ps_userfield.php` class file. As a result, we do not have many customization possibilities as we would probably refrain from hacking into the core. This applies also to the arrangement of the labels and the actual input field. It will be difficult, for example, if you want to have a single label that you want to put on the right-hand side instead of on the default left-hand side. However, if you want to set a common CSS style to all the labels and input fields, you can target the CSS class `.formLabel` and `.formField`, respectively.

The logic of data processing of all the checkout steps is done in the file `checkout.index.php`. The layout of the login/registration page is controlled by the `login_registration.tpl.php`. This is a very simple template which output the codes to control an accordion effect to show the login form and registration form. For a detailed layout, the template includes two page files, namely, `checkout.login_form.php` and `checkout_register_form.php` to provide the actual form. (Please note the difference in filename here.) These two files are part of the core and will probably get updated in future versions.

However, `checkout.login_form.php` uses the template `login_form.tpl.php` in the `common` template group to create the login form. So in case you need a custom login form, you can change it. On the other hand, `checkout_register_form.php` has no template of its own. It just simply calls the function `ps_userfield::getUserFields()` to list out the fields. As explained above, this means that you have to change the core file `ps_userfield.php` to customize the layout directly. Nevertheless, we can make changes indirectly using a special trick, as demonstrated in *Exercise 6.5*.

Exercise 6.5: Adding a user field that toggles with a checkbox

VirtueMart does not allow us to customize the layout of the user fields directly without hacking into the core. In this exercise, we will do the customization in an indirect way. We will add a new user field of the type checkbox. We will use this new field to toggle the display of the **Company** field in the registration form.

Preparation

We need to add a checkbox field to our user field. This can be easily done in the VirtueMart backend by following these steps:

1. Log in to your VirtueMart backend. Click **Admin** and then **Manage User Fields** to open the **Manage User Fields** page. Click **New** on the top toolbar to open the **Add/Edit User Fields** form.

2. Change the **Field type** to **Check Box (Single)**. Set the **Field name** to vm_private and **Field title** to **Private**. Make sure the **Show in registration form** drop-down is **Yes** and leave all other settings as default.

3. Save the form by clicking **Save** on the toolbar to go back to the **Manage User Fields** page.

Manage User Fields

Search

#		Field name	Field title	Field type	Required	Published	Show in registration form	Show in shipping form	Show in account maintenance	Reorder		Remove
1		vm_private	Private	checkbox	○	✓	✓	○	✓	▾	9	
2		delimiter_userinfo	Customer Information	delimiter	○	✓	✓	○	✓	▴ ▾	2	
3		email	Email	emailaddress	✓	✓	✓	○	✓	▴ ▾	3	
4		username	Username	text	✓	✓	✓	○	✓	▴ ▾	4	
5		password	Password	password	✓	✓	✓	○	✓	▴ ▾	5	
6		password2	Confirm Password	password	✓	✓	✓	○	✓	▴ ▾	6	
7		delimiter_billto	Bill To Information	delimiter	○	✓	✓	○	✓	▴ ▾	7	
8		address_type_name	Address Nickname	text	✓	✓	○	✓	○	▴ ▾	8	

4. In the last but one column, you will see a set of numbers. This is the sort order of the fields and will determine the order that the fields will be displayed in the frontend. By default, a newly created item like vm_private will be set as the first item. Change the number of vm_private from 1 to 9 to make it go under address_type_name. Click the Disk icon in the column header to save the sort order. (The Disk icon is on the column header and not on the toolbar.)

Steps

1. Open your favorite text editor. Navigate to the VirtueMart frontend root.

2. Open the file themes/default/templates/checkout/login_registration.tpl.php.

3. Add the following JavaScript to the end of the file (after line 61):

```
<script type="text/JavaScript" language="JavaScript">
function ToggleCompany(el) {
  if (el.checked) {
    $("company_div").style.display="none";
    $("company_input").style.display="none";
    $("company_br").style.display="none";
  } else {
    $("company_div").style.display="block";
    $("company_input").style.display="block";
    $("company_br").style.display="block";
```

```
      }
   }
</script>
```

4. Add the following CSS style before line 62 (before the section of code added in step 3).

```
<style type="text/css">
  #company_div label {padding-left:10px}
</style>
```

5. Replace line 38 (the `include PAGEPATH` line) with the following lines of code:

```
<?php
ob_start();
include(PAGEPATH. 'checkout_register_form.php');
$html = ob_get_contents();
ob_end_clean();
$html = str_replace('name="vm_private" id="vm_private_field"',
  'name="vm_private" id="vm_private_field" onclick="ToggleCompany(
this)"',$html);
$html = str_replace('<br style="clear:both;" /><div id="company_
div"',
  '<br id="company_br" style="clear:both;" /><div id="company_
div"',$html);
echo $html;
?>
```

6. Save the file and upload it to your server.

7. Go to your VirtueMart site. Make sure you are logged off. Otherwise you will not see the registration form. Add some products to the shop cart and head to checkout. You should see the login/registration. Click **New? Please Provide Your Billing Information** to see the Registration Form. You should see the additional **Private** checkbox under the **Bill To Information** section. Also, there is a slight indentation for the **Company Name** line.

8. Check the **Private** checkbox and you will see that the **Company Name** line will become hidden.

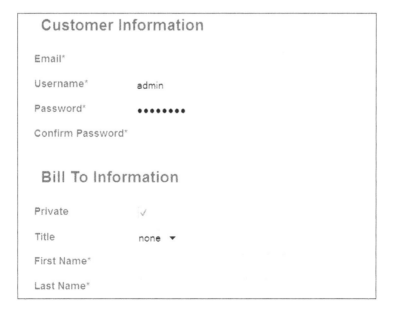

Notes

1. We made three changes to the file so as to accomplish our goal. The steps are in reverse just to make sure the line number will not mess up when new code is added.

2. Basically, the display of the registration form is controlled by the `ps_userfield` class, which is pretty complex because of the many possibilities of user fields and because of the mixing of HTML and PHP code. To avoid messing with this complex core file, we used the text replacement technique we met several times before, but this time with a different trick.

3. As we know, a PHP application is developed to send HTML code to the browser. There are a number of ways that we can control this sending process. Instead of directly sending the text generated to the browser, we can request PHP to use an output buffer as a temporary storage for the text and do further processing before actually sending the final HTML to the browser. The function `ob_start()` is used to start this output buffer, `ob_get_contents()` is used to fetch the content in the browser, and `ob_end_clean()` is to stop the output buffering. In step 5 above, we activated the output buffer to make a temporary store of the output of the `ps_userfield` class (called by the processing file `checkout_register_form.php`). The HTML coding is stored in the temporary variable `$html`.

4. We then used the `str_replace()` function to add the `onclick` event handler `ToggleCompany` and also gave an `id` to the `<br>` tag so that we can manipulate it as well. VirtueMart gave an `id` to each of the registration form fields. That's why we can use `id="vm_private_field"` to make sure we replaced the correct tag. (In case you are not sure what the `id` is, you can cheat by right-clicking the web page on your browser and use **View Page Source** to peek at the actual HTML code.)

5. In step 3, we add the JavaScript code to provide the `ToggleCompany()` function. This code is straightforward. We just change the display style of the three elements (`company_div`, `company_input`, `company_br`) to toggle the display when the checkbox is enabled. Note that `company_br` is the new `id` we added to the `<br>` tag in step 5. This is needed so that the extra space between lines is also toggled when the **Company Name** line is hidden.

6. In step 4, we added a CSS style to indent the **Company Name** line. This is an optional step. We added this coding just to demonstrate how we can change the style of an individual field. Since VirtueMart gives an `id` for each field label and field input, we can make use of these to tweak individual elements.

In *Exercise 6.5*, the trick is applied only to the registration form. If you want a similar trick in the shipping address form and/or account maintenance form, a separate customization will be needed for each page individually. The shipping address form template is `account.ship_to.tpl.php` and the account maintenance form template is `account.billing.tpl.php`. Both of these templates belong to the `pages` template group and the data processing is done in `account.ship_to.php` and `account.billing.php`, respectively. These two templates are similar to the `login_registration` template. Actually, they are simpler as we don't need to handle the login form as well. We will not go into detail here.

After passing through the registration step, the next in the step list is the get shipping address step. The template for this page is called `get_shipping_address.tpl.php` located in the checkout template group. Obviously, we don't want the shopper to re-enter everything if his/her shipping address is the same as the billing address. So in this template, VirtueMart shows a list of shipping addresses already on file instead of showing the shipping address form directly. The template calls another child template `list_shipto_addresses.tpl.php` for doing this. For new customers, the only shipping address on file is the default billing address. The get shipping address template also provides a link to the shipping address form in case a shopper wants to add or edit an address.

Exercise 6.6: Modifying the shipping address list

The `default` theme shipping address list is pretty lengthy when you have a few possible shipping addresses. We will customize this to make it look shorter in this exercise.

Preparation

In this exercise, we want to experiment changing the address list display. So we will need a user who has more than one set of shipping addresses. If you already have one, you can skip this preparation. Otherwise, you need to create a test user that has more than one shipping address. Adding an address is available both in the frontend and the backend. You can do it in either place. As this is pretty straightforward, we will not spend time with this here.

Steps

1. Open your favorite text editor. Navigate to the VirtueMart frontend root.

2. Open the file `themes/default/templates/checkout/list_shopto_addresses.tpl.php`.

3. Add the following JavaScript to the end of the file (after line 79):

```
<script type="text/JavaScript" language="JavaScript">
  function ToggleAddresses(el) {
    var labels = $$(".label_address_active");
    for (var i=0; i<labels.length;i++) {
      labels[i].className="label_address";
    }

$("label_"+el.value).className="label_address_active";
  }
</script>
```

4. Add the following CSS style before line 80 (that is, before the section of code added in step 3):

```
<style type="text/css">
      #vmAddressTable td {vertical-align:top}
      .label_address {display:none}
      .label_address_active {display:block}
</style>
```

5. Replace lines 20–79 with the following lines of code (this pretty much replaces everything except the code added in the steps 3 and 4):

```
<table id="vmAddressTable" border="0" width="100%" cellpadding="2"
cellspacing="0">
  <tr class="sectiontableentry1">
    <td>
<?php
$checked = '';
$display='class="label_address"';
if( $bt_user_info_id == $value || empty($value)) {
  $checked = 'checked="checked" ';
  $display = 'class="label_address_active"';
}
echo '<input onclick="ToggleAddresses(this)" type="radio"
name="'.$name.'" id="'.$bt_user_info_id.'" value="'.$bt_user_info_
id.'" '.$checked.'/>'."\n";
echo 'default';
$html = '<label '.$display.' id="label_'.$bt_user_info_id.'"
for="'.$bt_user_info_id.'">'
```

```
          .$VM_LANG->_('PHPSHOP_ACC_BILL_DEF').'</label>
';
while($db->next_record()) {
  $checked = '';
  $display='class="label_address"';
  if ( $value == $db->f("user_info_id")) {
    $checked = 'checked="checked" ';
    $display = 'class="label_address_active"';
  }
  echo '<br /><input onclick="ToggleAddresses(this)" type="radio"
name="'
      .$name.'" id="' . $db->f("user_info_id") . '" value="'
      . $db->f("user_info_id") . '" '.$checked.' />'."\n";
  echo '<strong>' . $db->f("address_type_name") . "</strong> ";
  ob_start();
  echo '<label '.$display.' id="label_'.$db->f("user_info_id").'"
for="'.$db->f("user_info_id") . '">';

  echo $db->f("title") . " ". $db->f("first_name") . " ". $db-
>f("middle_name") . " ". $db->f("last_name") . "\n";
  echo '<br />'."\n";
  if ($db->f("company")) {
    echo $db->f("company") . "<br />\n";
  }
  echo $db->f("address_1") . "\n";
  if ($db->f("address_2")) {
    echo '<br />'. $db->f("address_2"). "\n";

  echo '<br />'."\n";
  echo $db->f("city");
  echo ', ';
  // for state, can be used: state_name, state_2_code, state_3_
code
  echo $db->f("state_2_code") . " ";
  echo $db->f("zip") . "<br />\n";
  // for country, can be used: country_name, country_2_code,
country_3_code
  // (not displayed in default template)
  echo $VM_LANG->_('PHPSHOP_CHECKOUT_CONF_PHONE').': '. $db-
>f("phone_1") . "\n";
  echo '<br />'."\n";
  echo $VM_LANG->_('PHPSHOP_CHECKOUT_CONF_FAX').': '.$db->f("fax")
. "\n";
  echo '<br />'."\n";
```

```
    $url = SECUREURL . "index.php?page=account.shipto&user_info_id="
. $db->f('user_info_id')."&next_page=checkout.index";
    echo '<a href="'.$sess->url($url).'">'.$VM_LANG->_('PHPSHOP_
UDATE_ADDRESS').'</a>'."\n";
    echo '</label>';
    $html.=ob_get_contents();
    ob_end_clean();
}
?>
    </td>
      <td>
        <? echo $html; ?>
      </td>
    </tr>
</table>
```

6. Save the file and upload it to your server.

7. Go to your VirtueMart site. Add some products to the shop cart and head to checkout until you come to the shipping address page. You should see a different display of the address list.

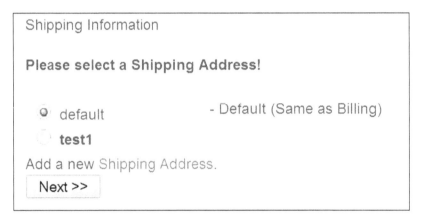

8. Click the **test1** radio button and you will see the address display changes to fit the selection.

Notes

1. Again, we made three changes to the file so as to accomplish our goal. The steps are in reverse, just to make sure line number will not mess up when new code is added.

2. In step 5, what we did is put the **Address Nickname** radio buttons on the left and the address display (defined as a label tag) on the right. We used the PHP output buffer mechanism to help us to build the HTML for the display on the right. In this way, we don't need to rewrite the original coding but just need to move it around to fit our new display requirement. We also added an `onclick` event handler `ToggleAddresses()` to the radio buttons. In this way, we will be able to toggle the address display when the radio button changes.

3. CSS class is added to the labels so as to control their display style. For a selected radio button, the corresponding label is assigned to a class `label_address_active`. Otherwise, the class is `label_address`.

4. The CSS styles added in step 4 are supposed to make the address labels invisible, except what is selected. The style for `td` is just cosmetic.

5. The JavaScript added in step 3 is to toggle the display of the address labels. The `$$` function is a special function in MooTools. It will return an array of elements with the given selection criteria. The selection criteria string accepts all CSS-acceptable selectors. So `$$(".label_address_active")` returns an array of elements belonging to the CSS `class="label_address_active"`. We need to loop through all `label_address_active` labels to turn them invisible (actually we have only one label that belongs to this class but since `$$` returns an array, we still need to use a loop). Finally, we need to set the label of the selected address to be visible by setting its class to `label_address_active`.

Shipping and payment methods

After passing through the get shipping address step, we will probably come to either the get shipping method or get payment method steps. These two steps share many similarities and so we group them together in the same section.

Both steps have a template of their own called `get_shipping_address.tpl.php` and `get_payment_method.tpl.php`. Both templates are similar in the way that after displaying the checkout bar, they called a function in the `ps_checkout` class to list out the available methods. The `ps_checkout` functions in turn uses the `list_shipping_methods.tpl.php` and `list_payment_methods.tpl.php` to do the actual work. All the templates we mentioned are found within the checkout template group.

To add to the list of similarities, both shipping and payment methods have their own API for a third party to extend VirtueMart. API is the acronym for Application Programming Interface and is the specification describing how you can write programs to interact with the existing system. By adhering to the shipping method and payment method API, you can write your own shipping and payment handler.

Despite all these similarities, there is one major difference between shipping and payment method handling. The shipping method API gives the shipping method developer the freedom of using his/her own HTML code. So there is no standard regarding the format and data provided in a shipping method. This means there is no way you can control the display of the shipping methods without hacking the individual shipping method code.

However, the payment method API prescribes the ways that payments can be handled and places them into different types. The payment method types are:

- Use payment processor: This means the payment processing is done through an external payment gateway. VirtueMart will get credit card information from a shopper and communicate this through the payment method code with the payment gateway to receive payment online.

- Credit card: This will display a credit card form for a shopper to fill in. Transaction will be done offline manually.

- Use HTML form (PayPal type): In this method, the shopper will be redirected to the respective website to carry out the payment.

- Bank debit: The shopper will be charged to the bank account they supply on registration.

- Address only: This means no additional payment information is needed. Payment will be done offline manually.

These payment types are further put into two groups: cc (credit card) and non-cc group. For payment processor type and credit card type, VirtueMart will display a form for a shopper to fill in the credit card detail. For the rest of the payment types, no further information is needed from the shopper and so VirtueMart only displays the methods as a radio button list for a shopper to choose from.

Exercise 6.7: Showing PayPal-type methods as preferred payment methods

The default theme `list_payment_methods` template shows the methods as a table with one row and two columns. It will display the cc payment group on the left and all other methods on the right.

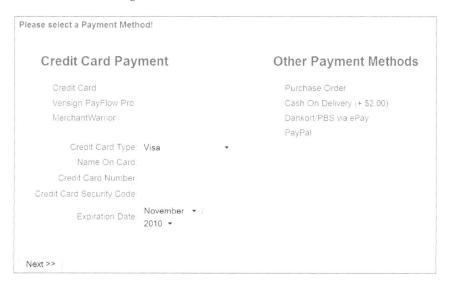

As you can see, all those methods are grouped together and the shopper will not be able to see which one is the preferred method. As from Version 1.1.5, a new button for checkout through PayPal Express was added at the top. This button will show only when PayPal Express is selected as a payment method. If PayPal Express is your preferred payment method, this fits your needs. If not, you will need a customization to highlight your preferred method.

In this exercise, we will move PayPal-related methods out from the right column. Instead, we will move it to the top to make it more prominent.

Preparation

To make the PayPal-related methods more prominent, we need to disable the PayPal Expression method. This can be done in the VirtueMart backend. Log in to the VirtueMart backend. Click **Store** and then **List Payment Methods** on the left menu.

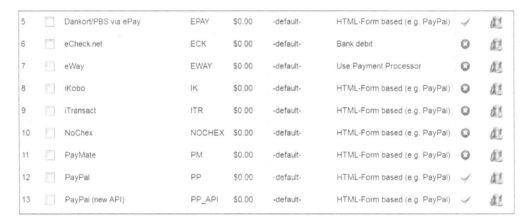

Click the **Check** icon against the **PayPal (new API)** line to unpublish the payment method.

Steps

1. Open your favorite text editor. Navigate to the VirtueMart frontend root.

2. Open the file `themes/default/templates/checkout/list_payment_methods.tpl.php`.

3. Replace line 121 (the `list_paypalrelated` statement) with the following line (simply remove the statement but leave `?>` there to make sure the `<?php` tag has a matching closing tag):

```
?>
```

4. Insert the following lines of code after line 19 (that is, at the top of the code):

```
echo '<fieldset>
        <legend>Paypal Related</legend>
        <div id="paypalrelated_payments">
';
$ps_payment_method->list_paypalrelated($payment_method_id,
false);
echo '</div>
</fieldset>';
```

5. Save the file and upload it to your server.

6. Go to your VirtueMart site. Add some products to the shop cart and head to the checkout until you reach the payment method page. You should see a different payment method listing.

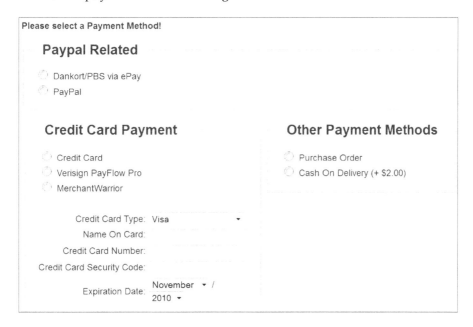

Notes

1. We have made two changes to the template file. Basically, we just move the `$ps_payment_method->list_paypalrelated($payment_method_id, false);` from the second column of the table out to the very beginning of the template. The removal is done in step 3 and the addition is done in step 4. The rest of the coding is just cosmetic to make the box look nicer.

2. You can use similar coding to move other types of payment methods to the top, making it look like a preferred method. You can also add explanations, graphics, and HTML elements as appropriate.

In the previous exercise, we can only move the whole bunch of PayPal-related methods to the top. This is not a big restriction as you probably will only use one PayPal-related method at a time. In case you have to use two or more methods in the same type and have a preferred one, you probably need to use a manual method to display the payment methods. This simply means you list out the payment methods all by yourselves without using the function provided by the class `$ps_payment_method`. Actually, this manual method is not very complicated and has much flexibility. The only catch is you need to use the correct `payment_method_id` to identify each method. In case of doubt, use the automatic method and use **View Page Source** on your browser to look at the ultimate HTML code. You can then rearrange the payment method list manually with all the `payment_method_id` intact.

We do not provide an exercise on customizing the shipping method page. There is little we can do with the shipping methods without hacking into individual shipping method coding. If you need to change the CSS style of some elements inside the shipping method, you can add a wrapper to the whole list of methods and target CSS at the element inside this wrapper element. This is a standard technique for employing CSS to elements that are beyond our control and so we don't need to give the detail here.

Final confirmation page

Final confirmation is the last step of the checkout before committing the order. This page is used to provide information and accept confirmation from the shopper. The template that controls the layout is `get_final_confirmation.tpl.php`.

The template can be divided into four sections: header, information needs to be verified, additional information needed for confirmation, and the final confirmation button.

The header includes the checkout bar, the read-only shop basket table, as well as the header for final confirmation. You probably don't need much customization on this section as the checkout bar and shop basket are controlled by two other templates. You may, if you wish, add some static text here to explain what this page is all about.

The information that needs to be verified is a big table with three table rows, one for each of shipping address, shipping method, payment method. This section is up to you to customize the layout of various pieces of information. Just make sure everything you want the shopper to confirm is there.

The additional information section includes the `customer_note` textarea, the agree-to-service checkbox. If you have configured to show the legal info message, it will also be displayed here. You can customize the `customer_note`, for example, by turning it into a textbox, a drop-down or any other form element. You can also add other elements to this part. But since any new input fields will not be processed in the backend, you will need to devise your own trick to make use of the new input.

The final confirmation button is just a submit button to confirm the order. There is JavaScript here to make sure the shopper has checked the agree-to-service checkbox before form submission. If you have anything you want to check before submission, you can customize the JavaScript code here.

Exercise 6.8: Adding a calendar to final confirmation

VirtueMart order data table does not include too many fields. Sometimes it may be necessary to include additional fields to store the information you need from customers, for example, a preferred delivery date. Adding the calendar may not be a big challenge as you have many good calendar controls available freely on the Internet. In fact, Joomla! itself has a calendar control that you can add to your template with a single line of code. The complexity of adding the calendar is how to send it back to the server and have it recorded in the order data table. You will need to modify the structure of the order data table, and subsequently several core files may need to be changed as well. This certainly involves some coding effort and will cause upgrade headaches in the future.

In the order data table, there is a field called `customer_note`. This is a text field and so can be used to store a lot of information. In this exercise, we are going to use this field to store a calendar date. Using `customer_note` has many advantages. The most important of all is you don't need anything additional to hack into the core files and database. What we need is a simple JavaScript handler, as we are going to demonstrate in this exercise.

Steps

1. Open your favorite text editor. Navigate to the VirtueMart frontend root.

2. Open the file `themes/default/templates/checkout/get_final_confirmation.tpl.php`.

3. Replace lines 134–146 (the lines that start with `if( PSHOP_AGREE_TO_TOS_ONORDER )` with the following lines of code:

```
if(  PSHOP_AGREE_TO_TOS_ONORDER == '1' ) {
  echo vmCommonHTML::scriptTag('', "function submit_order( form )
```

```
      if (!form.shipping_date.value) {
        alert (\"Please select a date.\");
        return false
      } else {
        form.customer_note.value=\"Shipping Date: \"+form.shipping_
date.value;
      }
      if (!form.agreed.checked) {
          alert( \"". $VM_LANG->_('PHPSHOP_AGREE_TO_TOS',false) ."\"
);
          return false;
      }
      else {
          return true;
      }
}" );
} else {
  echo vmCommonHTML::scriptTag('', "function submit_order( form )
{
    if (!form.shipping_date.value) {
      alert (\"Please select a date.\");
      return false
    } else {
      form.customer_note.value=\"Shipping Date: \"+form.shipping_
date.value;
    }
}" );
}
```

4. Insert the following line before line 92 (before the `div` that contains the customer note):

   ```
   <?php echo JHTML::calendar('','shipping_date','shipping_date'); ?>
   ```

5. Save the file and upload it to your server.

6. Go to your VirtueMart site. Add some products to the shop cart and head to the checkout until the complete order page. You should see the calendar above the customer note textarea.

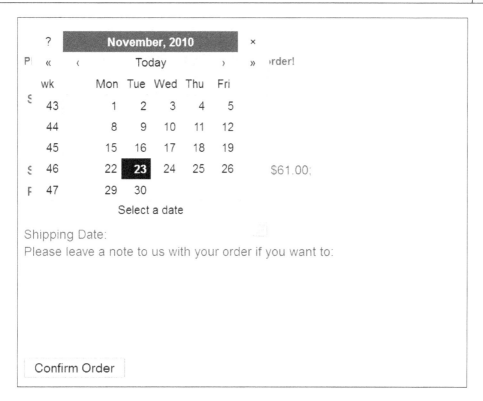

Notes

1. In step 4, we used a built-in function of Joomla! to create the calendar control. This is very handy as it only involves a single line of code. The function `JHTML::calendar()` accepts five parameters:

   - ° `$value`: This is the default value of the calendar date and also the value attribute of the input textbox that will be created.

   - ° `$name`: The name attribute of the input textbox.

   - ° `$id`: The ID attribute of the input textbox.

   - ° `$format`: The date format for the calendar. The default value is `'%Y-%m-%d'`, meaning the date will be in yyyy-mm-dd format.

   - ° `$attr`: Other attributes of the input textbox. You can add an event handler through this, if needed.

2. Step 3 simply added an extra step before the confirmation form is submitted to the server. We will check whether the shipping date is empty. If it is empty, the form will not be submitted. If not, the value will be stored in the `customer_note` textarea. Note that `shipping_date` is not a database field and will not be processed when posted back to the server. However, `customer_note` is a field in the order data table and so will be stored to the database.

Thank you page

After the order is confirmed, VirtueMart will follow two different routes depending on the payment method selected. If the payment method uses a payment processor (that is, payment will be done through a payment gateway directly through VirtueMart), it will post the order to the payment gateway until payment is confirmed or the shopper cancels the order. With payment confirmed, VirtueMart will create the order, store it in the database, send out the order e-mail, and redirect the shopper to the `checkout.thankyou` page.

If the payment method is not of payment processor type, VirtueMart will create the order, store it in the database, and send out the order e-mail without payment confirmation. The `order_status` will be set to pending though. After the order e-mail is sent, the shopper will also be redirected to the `checkout.thankyou` page.

The `checkout.thankyou.php` page actually does nothing other than getting data from the database and passing the data to the template. Some of the processing logic is left to the template file and so the `checkout.thankyou.tpl.php` template is not just a template in its strictest sense. As the filename suggests, the template is named according to the processing page `checkout.thankyou`. So this must be a template that belongs to the `pages` template group.

The template will check the payment method type and act accordingly. For PayPal-related payment methods, the template will include the payment code of the payment method and pass execution to it. This `payment_extrainfo` code will show a link informing a shopper to pay through the payment gateway or if the payment method so decided, the shopper will be redirected right away to the payment gateway website to finish the payment. For non-PayPal type payments, the template will just print out the thank you message and a link to the `account.order_details` page.

Before leaving this section, it is worth noting that the `checkout.thankyou` page is normally the final stage of a checkout. So you will need to create an order before you can reach this page. However, creating an order takes several steps. If you just want to test your `checkout.thankyou` template, there is a shortcut. We recall that the URL for a VirtueMart is of the form `index.php?option=com_virtuemart&page={module.page}`. In a similar vein, the `checkout.thankyou` page can be accessed with the URL `index.php?option=com_virtuemart&page=checkout.thankyou`. This URL will bring up the thank you page if you just need to test the layout. If you need data to test your logic, you should add the `order_id` parameter as well so the URl becomes `index.php?option=com_virtuemart&page=checkout.thankyou&order_id={order_id}`. You should replace `{order_id}` with the order number you want to test with.

Exercise 6.9: Printing order details on the thank you page

The default theme `checkout.thankyou` template only shows a thank you message and a link to the `account.order_details` page. Actually, the order data has been passed to the template but is not used directly in the thank you template. In this exercise, we are going to print out some order details from the data passed in by modifying the template.

Steps

1. Open your favorite text editor. Navigate to the VirtueMart frontend root.

2. Open the file `themes/default/templates/pages/checkout.thankyou.tpl.php`.

3. Insert the following lines of code after line 31 (just after the `PHPSHOP_THANKYOU_SUCCESS` message):

    ```php
    <?php
      global $CURRENCY_DISPLAY;
      echo '<br /><br />';
      echo 'Order Number: '.$db->f('order_id');
      echo '<br />Order Total: '. $CURRENCY_DISPLAY->getFullValue(
    $db->f('order_total'));
      echo '<br />Customer Note: '.$db->f('customer_note');
    ?>
    ```

4. Save the file and upload it to your server.

5. Go to your VirtueMart site. Add some products to the shop cart and head to the checkout until you reach the thank you page. You should see the additional order details.

Thank you for your order.

Your order has been successfully placed!

Order Number: 5
Order Total: $16.45
Customer Note: Shipping Date: 2010-11-30

A confirmation email has been sent to: **test@expertcms.net**

Follow this link to view the Order Details.

Notes

1. The processing page `checkout.thankyou.php` sends a variable `$db` into the template. `$db` is actually a database class and contains the order information grabbed from the database. For details of this variable, please refer to *Appendix, VirtueMart Template Reference.*

2. The function `$db->f()` was used to get the value of the database field. The name of the database field was passed in as a parameter.

3. We also made use of the global variable `$CURRENCY_DISPLAY` to print out the `order_total`. The function `$CURRENCY_DISPLAY->getFullValue()` will convert a passed in number into the corresponding currency and appropriate decimal places.

4. `order_id` and `order_total` are not the only fields available. There are several other fields as well. You can refer to *Appendix, VirtueMart Template Reference,* to see what other fields are available. If needed, you can even retrieve other order data from the database using the `order_id` as a key.

Summary

In this chapter, we have looked at all major templates from the shop basket to final checkout. We learnt how the shop basket data is stored in the server and how it relates to the shop basket display. We also saw why different basket templates are needed to fit various scenarios. After that, we walked through the checkout steps from Login/Registration, Get Shipping Address, Get Shipping Method, Get Payment Method, and Final Confirmation one-by-one, working on some customization exercises along the way. Finally, we also learnt the structure of the thank you page and how to add order data to the template. This wraps up our discussion of the templates, as related to the whole shopping life cycle. In the next chapter, we will turn our attention to the relationship between VirtueMart templates and Joomla! modules.

7
VirtueMart Templates and Joomla! Modules

In this chapter, we will look at the customization of the various Joomla! modules that come with VirtueMart. We will also touch on the templates for some peripheral elements on a flypage: recent products, related products, and so on.

Briefly, in this chapter, we cover:

- Joomla! modules that come with VirtueMart
- The Minicart
- The Product Snapshot
- Addendum elements in Shop pages

Joomla! modules that come with VirtueMart

As we all know, Joomla! modules are those small widgets you can place on a Joomla! page. Their execution is independent of the component (which controls the main content) of the page and are independent of each other. They can be activated and deactivated on each individual page. Joomla! modules provide supplementary functions that are otherwise not available through the main component, or may supply functions of one component while the visitor is navigating on another component. That means you can have a Joomla! module that is providing a VirtueMart function while a visitor is browsing a `com_content` article.

One typical use of Joomla! modules is to provide a menu or supplementary menus. In this regard, `mod_mainmenu` is probably the most important Joomla! module. Another important Joomla! module is the `mod_search` module which provides a search function while the visitor is navigating through the pages.

VirtueMart is actually a bundle of applications for Joomla!. The main element in the bundle is the component `com_virtuemart` which provides all the pages that help you build your web store. VirtueMart also comes with many useful Joomla! modules to provide various functions to make navigating your shop easier or otherwise make your shop stand out. The number of modules that come with VirtueMart may vary from version to version. As for VirtueMart 1.1.5, the Joomla! modules included are:

- `mod_product_categories`
- `mod_productscroller`
- `mod_virtuemart_featureprod`
- `mod_virtuemart_latestprod`
- `mod_virtuemart_randomprod`
- `mod_virtuemart_topten`
- `mod_virtuemart_cart`
- `mod_virtuemart_currencies`
- `mod_virtuemart_login`
- `mod_virtuemart_manufacturers`
- `mod_virtuemart_search`
- `mod_virtuemart`

Among those modules, `mod_product_categories` is probably the most used Joomla! module for VirtueMart. This module will automatically generate a hierarchical menu listing all the product categories in the shop. This is of course a very useful function, especially when you have lots of product categories or categories that are constantly changing. Another very popular module is the `mod_virtuemart` module, which is in fact an all-in-one module combining the functions of `mod_product_categories`, `mod_virtuemart_login`, `mod_virtuemart_cart`, and `mod_virtuemart_search` into one. If you don't like the rigid layout of `mod_virtuemart`, you can mix and match the standalone modules to build your own module system.

While you may be familiar with the different Joomla! modules VirtueMart provided, you may not have noticed that half of these modules are intimately related to the VirtueMart theme and template system. So if you change your theme, the layout of these modules will also change accordingly. That's why we need to have a separate chapter dedicated to the discussion of the templates related to Joomla! modules.

Actually, there are only two templates that are used by these modules, namely, `minicart.tpl.php` and `productsnapshot.tpl.php`. Both of these templates are shared by different modules and so they are placed in the `common` template group. In the next two sections, we will go over the detail of these two templates.

The Minicart

In *Chapter 6, From Shop Basket to Final Checkout*, we explained how the shop basket is stored in the session. The basket templates are actually different ways of showing the content in the basket. Many site owners prefer to have the shop basket showing in all pages, or at least within the pages related to the online shop. That's where the Joomla! cart modules come in. The `mod_virtuemart_cart` module is VirtueMart's answer to this request. The same function is also available in the all-in-one `mod_virtuemart` module. Some third parties also provide a similar function using their own modules. Basically, the principle is the same. We can use the default Minicart template or customize it for our needs.

While the name Minicart may seem to indicate that the cart is small, the actual content of that cart depends on the actual template code. You can make it a giant cart if you like. But, of course that may interfere with the whole design of the page. A giant cart will probably over-shadow the main content of the component. That's why the VirtueMart development team planned to have just a summary of the cart to be shown. A link to the shop cart page is provided, in case the shopper wants to see details in the cart.

The `mod_virtuemart_cart` module is just a wrapper. The function of this Minicart is provided by a VirtueMart module page `shop.basket_short.php`. Yes, this is a VirtueMart module page. So you can see the Minicart in the main area by using the URL `index.php?option=com_virtuemart&page=shop.basket_short`. The following screenshot shows the look of the page when the browser points to this link. You will see the Minicart in the main area.

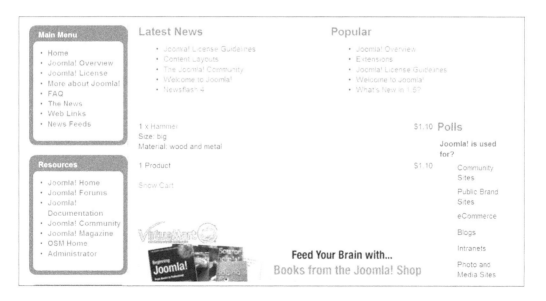

I don't think anyone would like to show such a minicart in the main content area since you can also show the full cart. However, just so you can understand, this is a VirtueMart module page which we can show using the standard VirtueMart URL by changing the `page` parameter.

The same code is used in the `mod_virtuemart` Joomla! module and so the Minicart in both the modules are exactly the same. This also means we can use the same code to include this Minicart into our custom Joomla! module. The code is surprisingly simple:

```
<div class="vmCartModule">
 <?php
 include (PAGEPATH.'shop.basket_short.php');
 ?>
 </div>
```

The `<div>` element is used just as a container to give this part of code a handle (you can give it an `id` as well, if you want to) so that we can refer to it in JavaScript. The class name `vmCartModule` is very important if you use Ajax to update the shop basket. The JavaScript will update the Minicart as well, if the shop basket Ajax update is successful. It assumes everything inside an element with class name `vmCartModule` contains the Minicart. (It is the class name that matters. The actual HTML element is not important. You can use `<div>`, `<span>`, `<td>`, or even `<p>`.)

The VirtueMart module page `shop.basket_short.php` will get necessary data from the `$cart` session variable as well as the database and pass the information to the `minicart.tpl.php` template file. So, when you change the template file, the Joomla! module display will change accordingly.

The Minicart template is not very complicated. You should be able to figure out what the code is doing by referring to the *Template Reference* in *Appendix, VirtueMart Template Reference*. The only thing we need to mention is the variable `$vmMinicart` which is not very intuitive. `$vmMinicart` is a flag telling the template to show only the summary of the cart contents. In this case, only the number of products and the cart total is displayed. Otherwise, the template will show the cart content as well.

Exercise 7.1: Adding a checkout link to the Minicart

In the `default` theme `minicart.tpl.php` template, there is only a link to go to the shop cart. Going to checkout will need two mouse-clicks. In this exercise, we are going to add a checkout link to the Minicart so that the shopper can go directly to checkout at any time.

Preparation

This exercise makes customizations to the `minicart.tpl.php` template. You need to publish the module `mod_virtuemart_cart` in order to see the effect. If you don't see the module in your frontend, please log in to your backend and go to **Module Manager** to check this. You can open the **Module Manager** by pointing to **Extensions** on the top menu and then clicking **Module Manager** in the drop-down. This will bring up the list of modules installed in your site.

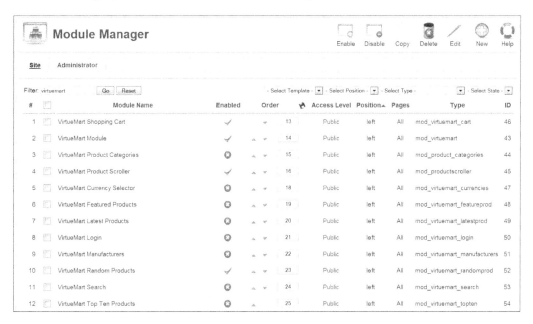

Make sure you see the "check" icon next to the **VirtueMart Shopping Cart** module. If not, you just need to click the "cross" icon to publish the module. (If you don't see the `mod_virtuemart_cart` in the backend, you probably did not have it installed. This module is available in the standard installation package. However, you need to install it manually. After you have downloaded the VirtueMart package from the site and unpacked the package, you should see a modules directory where the `mod_virtuemart_cart` is located.)

Once you have the `mod_virtuemart_cart` published, it should be displayed in the frontend somewhere. Even if you have no products in the shop basket, the module should still show the **Empty Cart** text. The following screenshot shows the Minicart published on the left of the page. If you don't see the module when it is published, you will need to check whether the module is published in a template position visible in the Joomla! template.

VirtueMart Shopping Cart	If you want to dis Joomla!, you are the terms of the (
1 x Chain Saw $3.28	License. If you ar license, you migh
1 Product $3.28	Apply These Tern the 'GNU Genera
Show Cart	The Joomla! licer GPL.
	Last Updated on W

Steps

1. Open your favorite text editor. Navigate to the VirtueMart frontend root.

2. Open the file `themes/default/templates/common/minicart.tpl.php`.

3. Insert the following lines of code before line 48 (after the `echo $show_cart` line):

    ```php
    <?php
      $checkout_link=str_replace(
        'page=shop.cart',
        'page=checkout.index',
        $show_cart);
      $checkout_link=str_replace(
        $VM_LANG->_('PHPSHOP_CART_SHOW'),
        $VM_LANG->_('PHPSHOP_CHECKOUT_TITLE'),
        $checkout_link);
      echo '  '.$checkout_link;
    ?>
    ```

4. Save the file and upload it to your server.

5. Go to your VirtueMart site. Add some products to the shop cart. You should see the additional **Checkout** link in the **VirtueMart Cart** module to the right of the **Show Cart** link.

Notes

1. The **Checkout** link is not an available field in the `minicart.tpl.php` template. So we need to build it ourselves. There are plenty of ways that this can be accomplished. In step 3 above, we rebuild the link from the **Show Cart** link. We understand that the shop cart page has a parameter `page=shop.cart`. We look for this text and replace it with `page=checkout.index`. We also look for the **Show Cart** text and replace it with **Checkout**.

2. The technique in step 3 may not work, if you have SEF enabled. In that case, you probably need to use something different but the concept should be the same.

Exercise 7.2: Showing the Minicart as a drop-down box

Sometimes, you don't want the Minicart to occupy too big a space because you are short on browser space, yet you want to make the Minicart available when shopper needs it. This exercise will minimize the space occupied by a Minicart to just a button which when clicked will show the whole Minicart.

Preparation

This exercise is based on the code customized in *Exercise 7.1*. If you start from the original code, line numbers may differ.

Steps

1. Open your favorite text editor. Navigate to the VirtueMart frontend root.

2. Open the file `themes/default/templates/common/minicart.tpl.php`.

3. Insert the following lines before line 60 (that is, after the line `</div><br/>`):

   ```
   </div>
   ```

4. Insert the following lines before line 15 (before looping through the `$minicart`):

   ```
   ?>
       <style type="text/css">
         .visibleCart {
           display:block;
           border:1px solid black;
           padding:2px;
           position:absolute;
           background:white;
           width:150px
         }
         .hiddenCart {
           display:none
         }
         #vm_cart_button {
           background:#333;
           border:1px solid black;
           color:white;
           padding:2px;
           cursor:auto;
           width:150px
         }
       </style>
       <script language="JavaScript" type="text/JavaScript">
         function ToggleCart() {
           var myCart = $("vm_cart_dropdown");
           if (myCart.className=="hiddenCart") myCart.
   className="visibleCart";
           else myCart.className="hiddenCart";
         }
       </script>
       <div id="vm_cart_button" onclick="ToggleCart()">Mini Cart</
   div>
       <div id="vm_cart_dropdown" class="hiddenCart">
   <?php
   ```

5. Save the file and upload it to your server.

6. Go to your VirtueMart site. Add some products to the shop cart. You should see Minicart has been shrunk to a button.

When you click the Mini Cart button, the full cart will show.

Notes

1. We need to add two `<div>` tags to the HTML. The `vm_cart_button` is added to act as the toggle button. The `vm_cart_dropdown` is the wrapper for the whole Minicart. It is given the class `hiddenCart` so as to make it hidden initially.

2. Step 3 is to close the `<div>` tag for the `vm_cart_dropdown`.

3. Step 4 is the major code that needs to be added. There are three sections of code: the CSS styles, the JavaScript, and the HTML elements.

4. An `onclick` event handler `ToggleCart()` was added to `vm_cart_button` so that when it is clicked the `ToggleCart()` function is applied.

5. The JavaScript function `ToggleCart()` should be straightforward. It just toggles the class of the `vm_cart_dropdown` `<div>`.

The product snapshot

Product snapshot is a special concept in VirtueMart. The product is certainly the most important object in a web store. There are various situations that we may need to show off the products. Sometimes we need details. Sometimes we just need a summary. A concise description of the products is required, especially in the Joomla! modules where the real estate is very limited. To provide an easily accessible concise description of products, the VirtueMart development team has designed a special function in the `ps_product` class. This function is named `product_snapshot()` which is used in most of the Joomla! modules that are used to highlight VirtueMart products. These include `mod_productscroller`, `mod_virtuemart_featureprod`, `mod_virtuemart_latestprod`, and `mod_virtuemart_randomprod`. All these modules share the same layout pattern. The difference is in the criteria to select the appropriate products or whether to show the products as a scrolling element. The only exception to the list is `mod_virtuemart_topten` which does not use the product snapshot because only a product name and link is needed.

The `ps_product::product_snapshot()` function accepts the product data as an input. It will then do some further processing before feeding the data to the template `productsnapshot.tpl.php` to do the actual layout. If you want to change the layout of the Joomla! modules that highlight VirtueMart products, this is the template that you need to work on.

There is no reason to restrict product snapshots only to Joomla! modules. In principle, it can also be used in a Joomla! content plugin. As you may recall, `com_content` is one of the most important components. It is used to create HTML content to be displayed in the main content area. Joomla! allows you to embed a special tag inside the content. The Joomla! content plugin is a small application that will parse through the content, replacing these special tags with the full content they should represent. VirtueMart development also provides a content plugin for including product content and somehow decided to use the product snapshot instead of the full content. Unfortunately, the content plugin only shares the name. It does not use the product snapshot as provided by the `ps_product` class. So, if you want to customize the `productsnapshot` plugin, you will need to hack into the `vmproductsnapshot` plugin code.

Exercise 7.3: Adding product fields to the product snapshot

The available product fields in the `productsnapshot.tpl.php` template are very limited. It can only access the `product_id`, `product_name`, product flypage URL, price, and `product_thumb_image`. In this exercise, we will demonstrate how to make other fields available.

Preparation

You will need to have the **VirtueMart Random Products** module (`mod_virtuemart_randomprod`) activated on your frontend to see the effect. If you do not have the module **VirtueMart Random Products** published, you need to do so now. Log in to your Joomla! backend. The steps to enable this module are basically the same as in *Exercise 7.1*. (If you don't see the `mod_virtuemart_randomprod` in the backend, you probably did not have it installed. You can find it in the standard VirtueMart package.)

After publishing the **VirtueMart Random Products** module, you should see it in your frontend. The exact layout of the module may vary with your VirtueMart settings and Joomla! template, but the basic information should be the same.

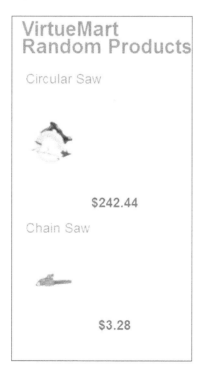

Steps

1. Open your favorite text editor. Navigate to the VirtueMart frontend root.

2. Open the file `themes/default/templates/common/productsnapshot.tpl.php`.

3. Insert the following lines at the end of the file after line 54:

```
<br style="clear:both" />
</div>
```

4. Replace line 5 with the following line of code. This essentially removes the style attribute from the `<div>` tag.

```
<div>
```

5. Replace line 12 with the following line of code. This essentially removes the style attribute from the `<div>` tag.

```
<div>
```

6. Insert the following lines before line 21 (that is, before the product price DIV):

```
<?php
    echo '<div>Weight: ';
    $product_weight=ps_product::get_field( $product_id,'product_
weight');
    $product_weight_uom=ps_product::get_field( $product_
id,'product_weight_uom');
    echo number_format($product_weight,1).' '.$product_weight_uom;
    echo '</div>';
?>
```

7. Insert the following lines before line 3 (that is, before the product name DIV):

```
<?php if (!defined('PRODUCTSNAPSHOT_CSS')) {
  define('PRODUCTSNAPSHOT_CSS',1);
?>
<style type="text/css">
 .productsnapshot_container {
  padding:5px;
  border:1px solid #ccc
}
.productsnapshot_container div {
  text-align:center !important;
}
</style>
<?php } ?>
<div class="productsnapshot_container">
```

8. Save the file and upload it to your server.

9. Go to your VirtueMart site. You should see the additional **Weight** information in the **VirtueMart Random Products** module.

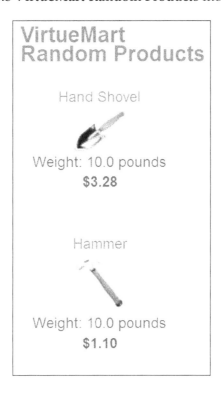

Notes

1. We made five changes to the file. The steps are listed in reverse so as to make the line numbers unambiguous.

2. The major code change is in step 6, where we get the product information by using the `ps_product::get_field()` function. This is a class function that can grab the necessary product field from the database. You need to pass in two parameters. The first one is the `$product_id` which is needed to identify the product. The second parameter is the name of the product field you need. We want to use both the `product_weight` and `product_weight_uom` (the unit). So we need to call the function twice. The rest of the code is sending a `<div>` tag for the information and also formatting the information to fit our needs.

3. Step 7 adds CSS code to style the product snapshot to make it look better. You can modify this to fit your own design and needs. We also added a `<div>` with CSS class `productsnapshot_container`. This is used so that we can target the appropriate HTML elements using CSS. Since the `productsnapshot` template will be invoked several times in a page, we define a constant `PRODUCTSNAPSHOT_CSS` to avoid the CSS being added more than once.

4. Steps 4 and 5 essentially removed all the hardcoded styles for the `<div>` tag. This makes our code more flexible and also removed some weird hardcoded styles that do not fit all situations.

5. Step 3 was used to close the `productsnapshot_container <div>`.

Exercise 7.4: Making the snapshot template configurable

The snapshot template in the `ps_product` class is hardcoded to `common/productsnapshot.tpl.php`. This is not convenient as you sometimes may want a different template based on the modules. In this exercise, we are going to build a configurable snapshot template for the `mod_virtuemart_randomprod` module.

Preparation

You will need to have the **VirtueMart Random Products** module (`mod_virtuemart_randomprod`) activated on your frontend to see the effect. If you did not work on *Exercise 7.3* and do not have **VirtueMart Random Products** published, please follow the *Preparation* section of *Exercise 7.3* to publish the module.

This exercise will also customize the `mod_virtuemart_randomprod` module. So please backup the `modules/mod_virtuemart_randomprod` directory first before you proceed.

You may also want to take a look at the configuration page of the module. Log in to the Joomla! backend. Point to **Extensions** and then click **Module Manager** to open the **Module** list. Click **VirtueMart Random Product** in the list to go to the module edit form.

There are a number of configurable items for this module, shown on the right of the screenshot. We are going to add the **Snapshot Template** configuration to the list.

Steps

1. Open your favorite text editor. Navigate to the `modules` directory of your Joomla! root.

2. Open the file `mod_virtuemart_randomprod/ mod_virtuemart_randomprod.xml`.

3. Insert the following lines before line 20 (just after the `<params>` line):

```
<param name="template" type="filelist"
default="productsnapshot.tpl"
     label="Snapshot Template" description="Template to use to
create the snapshot"
   directory="components/com_virtuemart/themes/default/templates/
common"
       filter="productsnapshot" exclude="" stripext="1" />
```

4. Save the file and upload it to your server.

5. Open the file `mod_virtuemart_randomprod/ mod_virtuemart_randomprod.php`.

6. Insert the following line after line 41 (before the `require_once` statement):

```
$_REQUEST['productsnapshot_template']=$params->get( 'template',
'productsnapshot.tpl' );
```

7. Save the file and upload it to your server.

8. Navigate to the VirtueMart frontend root. Open the file `themes/default/templates/common/productsnapshot.tpl.php`.

9. Insert the following lines to the top of the file after line 3:

```php
<?php
  $myTemplate = $_REQUEST['productsnapshot_template'];
  if ($myTemplate!='productsnapshot.tpl' && file_exists(dirname(__
FILE__).'/'.$myTemplate.'.php')) {
    include (dirname(__FILE__).'/'.$myTemplate.'.php');
    return;
  }
?>
```

10. Save the file and upload it to your server.

11. Create a new file and insert the following lines of code:

```php
<?php if( !defined( '_VALID_MOS' ) && !defined( '_JEXEC' ) ) die(
'Direct Access to '.basename(__FILE__).' is not allowed.' ); ?>
<?php if (!defined('PRODUCTSNAPSHOT_CSS')) {
  define('PRODUCTSNAPSHOT_CSS',1);
?>
<style type="text/css">
 .productsnapshot_container {
  padding:5px;
  border:1px solid #ccc
}
.productsnapshot_container div {
  text-align:center !important;
}
</style>
<?php } ?>
<div class="productsnapshot_container">
<!-- The product name DIV. -->
 <?php if( $show_product_name ) : ?>
<div>
<a title="<?php echo $product_name ?>" href="<?php echo $product_
link ?>"><?php echo $product_name; ?></a>
<br />
</div>
<?php endif;?>
<!-- The product image DIV. -->
<div>
<a title="<?php echo $product_name ?>" href="<?php echo $product_
link ?>">
  <?php
    // Print the product image or the "no image available" image
    echo ps_product::image_tag( $product_thumb_image,
"alt=\"".$product_name."\"");
```

```
        ?>
    </a>
    </div>
    </div>
```

12. Save the file as `productsnapshot_1.tpl.php` and upload it to the same
    directory as `productsnapshot.tpl.php` on your server.

13. Log in to the Joomla! backend. Point to **Extensions** and then click
    Module Manager to open the module list. Click **VirtueMart Random
    Product** in the list to go to the module edit form. You should now see
    an additional **Snapshot Template** drop-down box on the right. Select
    `productsnapshot_1.tpl` and then click **Save** in the top toolbar to save
    the configuration.

14. Go to your VirtueMart site. You should see a different **VirtueMart Random
    Products** layout.

Notes

1. This is perhaps the most complex customization we have done so far as this involves four files.

2. In step 3, we added a parameter to the `mod_virtuemart_randomprod.xml` file. `filelist` is a special parameter in Joomla! which will show a drop-down filled with the files in a specified directory. The attributes for this parameter are:

    - `name`: This is the name of the parameter. We set it as `"template"`.

    - `type`: This is the type of the parameter. Must be `"filelist"` as we need to create a file list drop-down.

    - `default`: The default value for the parameter. In our case =`"productsnapshot.tpl"`.

    - `label`: The label parameter. We use **Snapshot Template** here. You can use anything you like.

    - `description`: Explanation of the use of the parameter. You can use anything you like.

    - `directory`: This is the directory where the file selection can be found. We have to set it to `components/com_virtuemart/themes/default/templates/common` unless you plan to put the snapshot template, in some other directory.

    - `filter`: The regular expression for filtering the list. We use `productsnapshot` to exclude other template files in the common template group. You can leave this blank but you will see all the templates even if those templates do not apply to product snapshot.

    - `exclude`: The regular expression for excluding files from the list. We don't use this. You can use it if you have specific files to be excluded.

    - `stripext`: Whether to strip the extension (`.php` in our case). Use `"1"` to strip, and `""` or `"0"` otherwise.

    You can refer to the Joomla! documentation at `http://docs.joomla.org/Filelist_parameter_type` for further explanation of this parameter type.

3. In step 6, we modified the `mod_virtuemart_randomprod.php` file to make use of the template parameter passed in. It is a challenge to pass this parameter to the template since we have to go through the `ps_product::show_snapshot()` function which does not provide for such a parameter. As we don't want to hack into the core VirtueMart files, we have to take another route. The `$_REQUEST` global variable can be retrieved anywhere in the PHP code. So we use it to pass our parameter with the name `productsnapshot_template`.

4. In step 9, we modify the default `productsnapshot.tpl.php` file to check if the `productsnapshot_template` has a value and if this template file really exists. If it does, we will include the template directly and then finish the template parsing. Otherwise, the template will continue to parse the template normally. Note that the passed in parameter only contains the filename without path and extension information. We will need to fill in the path (through `dirname(__FILE__)`, a PHP standard function that will return the path information of the current file), and extension (`.php`) information by ourselves.

5. In step 11, we create a different template called `productsnapshot_1.tpl.php`. This is basically the same template file as `productsnapshot.tpl.php` with all information removed except the product name and product thumbnail. You can customize this file in any other ways you like. The filename is also arbitrary. But it has to start with `productsnapshot` to pass through the module `filelist` parameter filter.

6. In step 13, we go to the backend to configure the module template parameter to make use of the new template we created. Of course, you need to change it to something that matches the filename you gave to the template as explained in step 5.

Addendum elements in shop pages

When we discussed the product list templates and product details templates in *Chapter 3*, *Product List Templates* and *Chapter 4*, *Products Details Templates*, we came across a number of what we call addendum elements such as recent products, related products, and featured products. These elements are not part of the product itself but will serve either as enticers or useful links for shoppers. They are also product highlights and apparently good candidates for using the product snapshot. To provide more flexibility, however, VirtueMart does not apply the product snapshot template directly. Instead, each of these elements has a template of its own. The templates are put in the `common` template group as they will be shared by various different pages.

The following screenshot shows the **Featured Products** list in the product list page:

Depending on your preference or design, you can still use the product snapshot template if you want to. Otherwise, you have full freedom to tailor the template to your site. The template `relatedProducts.tpl.php` is a good example. This is supposed to be a template for displaying the related products. When you look at this template, you will see the code is very simple:

```php
<?php if ( !defined( '_VALID_MOS' ) && !defined( '_JEXEC' ) ) die(
'Direct Access to '.basename( __FILE__ ).' is not allowed.' ); ?>

<hr/>

<h3><?php echo $VM_LANG->_('PHPSHOP_RELATED_PRODUCTS_HEADING') ?></h3>

<table width="100%" align="center">
  <tr>
    <?php
    while( $products->next_record() ) { ?>
        <td valign="top">
            <?php echo $ps_product->product_snapshot( $products-
>f('product_sku') ) ?>
        </td>
    <?php
```

```
      }
    ?>
      </tr>
  </table>
```

Other than the header and the containing table, the code just invokes the function `$ps_product->product_snapshot()` to list out the product highlights. In case you need to reuse the snapshot product template in any other templates, you can use the same technique. However, you need to take care because the parameter passed in is the `product_sku` instead of the normal `product_id`. This is apparently a design overlook of the development team.

VirtueMart used a different strategy for the recent products and featured products. The recent products are supposed to be simple links to the products that the shopper has looked at. So this is not a surprise to see that the template `recent.tpl.php` used a simpler way to list out the products. On the other hand, it is a little bit strange to see the `featuredProduct.tpl.php` template does not use the snapshot products template as what has been done for the Joomla! module `mod_virtuemart_featureprod`. So you will find that the featured product appears differently in the Joomla! module than in the product detail page. Anyway, so now you know the strategy of VirtueMart and you know how to invoke the product snapshot template in a template (just use similar code as related products above). It is just a snap to port the related products template for use in featured products.

On the other hand, if you do not like the `featuredProduct.tpl.php` template and the `productsnapshot.tpl.php` template does not fit your needs, you can customize the template as we are going to do in *Exercise 7.5*.

Exercise 7.5: Using a product scroller in the product list page

The product list templates of the `default` theme do show a window of featured products. The featured product list is static. In this exercise, we will make it scroll from right to left.

Steps

1. Open your favorite text editor. Navigate to the VirtueMart frontend root.
2. Open the file `themes/default/templates/common/featuredProduct.tpl.php`.

3. Insert the following lines of code at the end of the file:

```php
<?php
echo '
</tr>
</table>
</marquee>';
?>
```

4. Replace lines 15 to 39 with the following lines (that is, the section of code within the `foreach $featuredProducts` loop):

```php
  <td style="width:150px;text-align:top;padding:0px;vertical-align:top" >
        <a title="<?php echo $featured["product_name"]
?>" href="<?php $sess->purl(URL."index.php?option=com_
virtuemart&amp;page=shop.product_details&amp;flypage=".$featured["
flypage"]."&amp;product_id=".$featured["product_id"]) ?>">
       <h4><?php echo $featured["product_name"] ?></h4></a>
       <?php echo $featured['product_price'] ?><br />
           <?php
      if ( $featured["product_thumb"] ) { ?>
              <a title="<?php echo $featured["product_
name"] ?>" href="<?php $sess->purl(URL."index.php?option=com_
virtuemart&amp;page=shop.product_details&amp;flypage=".$featured["
flypage"]."&amp;product_id=".$featured["product_id"]) ?>">
        <?php echo ps_product::image_tag( $featured["product_
thumb"], "class=\"browseProductImage\" border=\"0\"
alt=\"".$featured["product_name"]."\"");
        ?></a><br /><br/>
            <?php
      }?>
   </td>
<?php
}
```

5. Insert the following lines of code before line 13 (before the `foreach $featuredProducts` loop):

```php
echo '<marquee
style="border:1px solid #ccc;margin:2px;padding:5px;"
behavior="scroll"
direction="left"
height="150"
width="300"
scrollamount="5"
```

```
scrolldelay="180"
truespeed="true"
onmouseover="this.stop()"
onmouseout="this.start()">
<table><tr>
';
```

6. Delete lines 3 to 8.

7. Save the file and upload it to your server.

8. Go to your VirtueMart site and navigate to the **Hand Tools** category. You should see the featured product list scrolling from right to left.

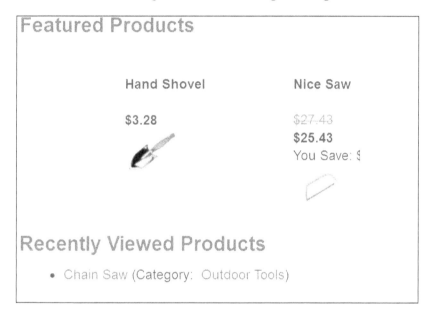

Notes

1. We made four changes in this exercise. The steps are listed in reverse so as to make the line numbers unambiguous.

2. The major code change is in step 5, which makes use of the `marquee` elements to achieve the scrolling effect.

3. Step 3 closed the `marquee` and table row.

4. In step 4, we changed the original `<div>` elements to a table cell `<td>`. We also removed the product price and add-to-cart form for simplicity's sake. If you need the price and add-to-cart form, you can retain them as well.

5. In step 6, we delete the lines of code which are irrelevant since the scroller should be on a single row to avoid complication.

This exercise demonstrated how you can make use of technology you learnt elsewhere in the template. The `<marquee>` tag is used in the product scroller. While this maybe a somewhat outdated technology, we use it here just because it is easy to copy and paste the code and reuse it in our example. Basically, the code is almost an exact copy of the product scroller and encloses the featured product list inside this `<marquee>` tag. The product scroller effect can be added to any template (for example, the shop cart page) you wish. We did not put in the configuration values as defined in the product scroller module just for the sake of simplicity. If you think you have a need to add the configuration, you can always add them back in.

Summary

In this chapter, we have looked at the relationship between Joomla! modules and VirtueMart templates. We learnt how to customize the `minicart` template and the `productsnapshot` template. We also saw how the addendum elements in the product list and product details pages relate to the template. In the next chapter, our focus will shift again to the theme structure and we will see how different components of a theme work together.

8
VirtueMart Theme Anatomy

In this chapter, we will look at the detailed structure of a VirtueMart theme. We will first look at the VirtueMart theme class and how the whole theme system works. Then we will focus on each of the components: the images, the JavaScript, the CSS file, the theme file, and the theme configuration. Finally, we will try to see how we can add new configurations to the theme configurator.

Briefly, in this chapter, we cover:

- VirtueMart theme system
- The `default` theme images
- The `default` theme class
- Theme configuration

VirtueMart theme system

The VirtueMart theme is a collection of files that work together to present VirtueMart shop pages to shoppers. While the `default` theme is the only theme that comes with VirtueMart, you are free to develop a theme of your own or purchase one from a third party. We will tell you how to create a theme in the next chapter. But before that, we need to understand the basic building blocks of a VirtueMart theme.

vmTemplate class

VirtueMart makes use of a class called `vmTemplate` to provide the function of a theme. (Yes, this class is named as Template. Yet, it is used to provide basic theme function. Apparently, the development team did not make a clear distinction between theme and template or maybe because they had a hard time finding an appropriate wording to call it.) The class file is named `template.class.php` and is located in the `classes` subdirectory of the VirtueMart `administrator` directory.

The `vmTemplate` class has a number of functions. But for a template user, just a handful of them may be useful:

- `get_cfg`: This function is used to get the value of a configuration setting defined in the theme. This accepts two parameters, namely, `$var` and `$default`. `$var` is the name of the config that needs to get and `$default` is the default value. If `$name` exists in the config, its value will be returned. Otherwise, the function value will be `$default`.

- `set_cfg`: This function is used to set the value of a configuration setting. In most cases, we don't need to bother with this function. In the rare case you want to change a configuration value dynamically, you can use this function to change the configuration value.

- `fetch`: This function is used to parse a given template and return the resulting HTML. It accepts only one parameter, `$file`, which is the path of the template file relative to the theme templates path.

- `set`: Before calling the `fetch()` function, you may need to pass the appropriate variables (the so called available fields) into the template. You use the `set` function to do this. It accepts two parameters, `$name` and `$value`. The variable will then be accessible in the template.

vmTheme class

The `vmTemplate` class is a parent class that is not actually used directly. All VirtueMart themes must define a `vmTheme` class which will inherit from the `vmTemplate` class. (Inheritance is a programming concept that we cannot explain here in detail. For the purpose of this book, you only need to understand that `vmTheme` inheriting from `vmTemplate` means that all the functions and variables defined in `vmTemplate` will also be available in `vmTheme`. That is to say the `get_cfg()`, `set_cfg()`, `set()`, and `fetch()` functions can also be found in the `vmTheme` class.) The `vmTheme` class has to be declared in a special PHP file named `theme.php` located in the root of the theme directory. You have probably seen this file before in the `default` theme root directory.

Name ↓	Size	Last Modified	
images		11/9/2010	12:43:00 PM
templates		7/27/2010	11:58:00 PM
admin.css	4 KB	5/20/2010	12:00:00 AM
admin.styles.css	18 KB	5/20/2010	12:00:00 AM
theme.config.php	1 KB	11/20/2010	1:21:00 AM
theme.css	9 KB	11/9/2010	12:50:00 PM
theme.js	5 KB	11/19/2010	5:39:00 PM
theme.php	6 KB	12/11/2010	1:15:00 AM
theme.prototype.js	4 KB	5/20/2010	12:00:00 AM
theme.xml	6 KB	5/20/2010	12:00:00 AM

⇧ Up to higher level directory

Recall in *Chapter 2, The VirtueMart Default Theme,* we saw that the VirtueMart configuration has a setting on the **Site** tab that allows you to set the theme. Whenever VirtueMart starts up, it will check the theme, load the theme.php file, and then create a vmTheme object. It will subsequently use the set() function of this vmTheme object to inject data into the templates and use its fetch() function to get the template result.

You can also define some additional functions in the theme.php to fulfil your theme needs. If you need another JavaScript framework, for example, you will need to load it here.

Theme configuration

Each theme will have its own specific functions and features. Some of these features can be configured. The VirtueMart theme system has a provision to allow theme developers to create their own configuration page. Among the set of files in the default theme directory, there are two files theme.config.php and theme.xml that are responsible for configuring the theme.

Actually, the theme configuration page is a function set up by VirtueMart itself. As we saw back in *Chapter 2*, *The VirtueMart Default Theme*, there is a **Configuration** link under the theme selection drop-down box.

When you click on this link, VirtueMart will call up the page `admin.theme_config_form.php` to show the configuration page. While the engine for showing the page is the same, the items that are configurable will be different for different themes. This is where the `theme.xml` file comes into place. All the configurable items and their possible options are stored in this `theme.xml` file. On the other hand, the settings selected by a user are stored in the file `theme.config.php`.

The theme configuration is a very interesting and useful feature when you want to create your own theme. We will study this in more detail in a later section.

Major building blocks

While `theme.php`, `theme.xml`, and `theme.config.php` are the engines of the theme system, there are other essential user building blocks that assist in providing the features of a theme system. Images are obviously one of the major players in customizing the VirtueMart shop. By providing a different set of images, your VirtueMart shop can have a totally different look.

Of course, we cannot forget the templates which have been our major discussion focus in the previous five chapters. Their roles in the theme system are very prominent. We also came across the JavaScript files and the stylesheet files. All of them must fit together to create a complete theme.

To summarize this, the theme system contains the following six building blocks:

- Theme class: This is the major controller of the theme system. The theme class must be defined in the file `theme.php`, but you can supplement this with other files, if necessary.

- Theme configuration: This helps to provide configurable items for a theme. The configurable items are defined in the `theme.xml` file. The selected settings are saved in the file `theme.config.php`.

- Images: The graphic files that are used in various parts of the VirtueMart and, in particular, used by the templates. All the images are stored in the `images` subdirectory.

- Templates: The major presenter that builds the HTML code for sending to the browser. All the templates are stored in the `templates` subdirectory. They are further divided into seven template groups and are the most commonly customized files in the theme.

- JavaScripts: They provide the special functions and behaviors of the web page displayed on the browser. There are only two JavaScript files in the default theme: `theme.js` and `theme.prototype.js`. The latter file seems legacy code and is no longer used in the `default` theme.

- Stylesheets: They provide the styles for individual HTML elements. There are three CSS files: `theme.css`, `admin.css`, and `admin.styles.css`. Only `theme.css` is used in frontend pages. The admin CSS files are only for controlling the styles of the backend administration pages.

Since we have taken quite a thorough look at the templates, the JavaScripts and the stylesheets in previous chapters, we will focus our discussion only on the remaining three building blocks for the rest of this chapter.

The default theme images

Graphic is a major part of every website design. VirtueMart has a set of professionally designed images that come with the `default` theme. If you are not very demanding, you can live with these `default` theme graphics. The major drawback of keeping these images is that your site will look very similar to other sites built with the `default` theme. Replacing these images will definitely give your site a fresh new look. People won't recognize so easily that you are using a "canned" solution.

Customizing the images is simple for anyone who has been working in the fields of graphic design or website design, so there is not much that we can say about them. But it will be worthwhile to have a brief look at the images and how they are used. The following screenshot shows the content of the images subdirectory of the default theme:

Name ↓	Size	Last Modified	
Up to higher level directory			
administration		7/27/2010	11:58:00 PM
availability		7/27/2010	11:58:00 PM
checkout		7/27/2010	11:58:00 PM
stars		7/27/2010	11:58:00 PM
add-to-cart.gif	2 KB	5/20/2010	12:00:00 AM
add-to-cart_blue.gif	2 KB	5/20/2010	12:00:00 AM
add-to-cart_blue1.gif	2 KB	11/9/2010	12:38:00 PM
add-to-cart_blue_r.gif	2 KB	11/9/2010	12:43:00 PM

As you can see, there are more than 40 images within the root itself. Also, the images directory itself has four subdirectories: administration, availability, checkout, and stars. Let's check out the content of each of those directories before we come back to the root images.

The administration images

You can tell that this directory contains all of the graphics that are used in the backend administration.

Name ↓	Size	Last Modified	
Up to higher level directory			
dashboard		7/27/2010	11:58:00 PM
header		7/27/2010	11:58:00 PM
menu		7/27/2010	11:58:00 PM
toolbar		7/27/2010	11:58:00 PM
cal.gif	1 KB	5/20/2010	12:00:00 AM
header_bg.png	1 KB	5/20/2010	12:00:00 AM
header_logo.png	17 KB	5/20/2010	12:00:00 AM
history.png	1 KB	5/20/2010	12:00:00 AM

There are four further subdirectories within this directory. The `dashboard` subdirectory contains the graphics that are used in the home page or the **Control Panel** page of the VirtueMart backend, where you see a number of buttons that help you to access the commonly used VirtueMart functions easily.

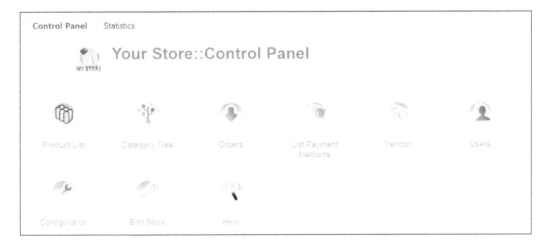

The `header` images are the icons that are shown beside the page heading of each of the individual administration pages. The **MY STORE** icon shown next to the **Control Panel** header above is just one of them. All of the icons are 48 x 48 and so look bigger than normal icons. The `menu` images are the icons that are shown on the left menu. These images are 16 x 16 and so are smaller.

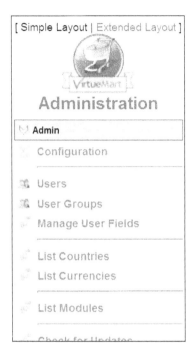

The `toolbar` images are the icons that are shown on the top toolbar. The size of these icons are 32 x 32.

In the `administration` parent directory, you will find miscellaneous images that are used elsewhere in the VirtueMart backend, such as the VirtueMart logo.

You may think that there is little need to customize the `administration` images as these images are used only in the backend. That is only partly correct. The `administration` images are tied to the theme. So if you want to create a new theme, as we are going to do in the next chapter, you will need to take care of these images.

The availability images

The `availability` images are the graphics that are used to show availability in the frontend when you have configured your shop to show the availability of products.

1-2 months	1-4 Weeks	2-3 Days	3-5 Days	7 Days	14 Days
1-2m.gif	1-4w.gif	2-3d.gif	3-5d.gif	7d.gif	14d.gif
24 h	48 h		Not Available	On Order	
24h.gif	48h.gif	index.html	not_available.gif	on-order.gif	Thumbs.db

VirtueMart is not intelligent enough to decide which graphic to show according to the product. This is something you have to set individually for each product in the backend Product Form. When you add a new graphic to the `availability` directory, it will show up in the drop-down box under the **Product Status** tab of the backend Product Form, as shown in the following screenshot:

The checkout images

The `checkout` directory contains the images that are used in the checkout bar, as we discussed in *Chapter 6, From Shop Basket to Final Checkout*.

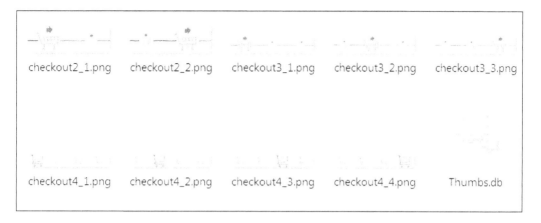

Since the filenames are tied to the number of steps and the current step number, you have to make sure the filename is exact. Otherwise, the image will not show. You can certainly customize the checkout bar template, as we have done in *Chapter 6, From Shop Basket to Final Checkout*.

The stars images

The stars directory contains the star images used in product ratings.

A shopper can rate a product on a scale of 0 to 5. Each scale has its own graphic. (Note: The product review form only shows up when a shopper is logged in.)

Again, because the filename depends on the rating scale, you have to make sure the filename is exact for each rating.

Miscellaneous images

In addition to the preceding four groups, there are more than 40 images used in different VirtueMart pages.

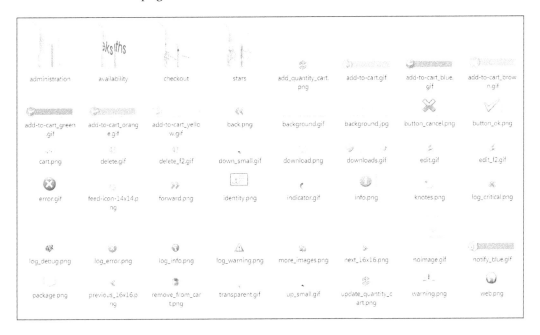

We will not discuss them in detail here as they are self-explanatory.

The default theme class

As we have pointed out previously, theme.php must be there in order for a theme to work. There are no prescribed functions that must exist in the vmTheme class though. You can just simply inherit (or extend, in terms of PHP) from the vmTemplate class without adding any extra code, if that fits your needs.

In the default theme, the theme.php file contains a few lines of initialization code before actually defining the vmTheme class. There are four additional functions defined in the class. The following screenshot shows the major elements in this PHP file:

```php
global $mainframe;

// include the stylesheet for this template

if( vmIsJoomla('1.0') && mosGetParam($_REQUEST,'option') != VM_COMPONENT_NAME) {
    // This can only be a call from a module or mambot
    // In Joomla 1.0 it is not possible to add a JS or CSS into the HEAD from a module or
content mambot,
    // using addcustomheadtag, that's why we just print the tags here
    echo vmCommonHTML::scriptTag(VM_THEMEURL.'theme.js');
    echo vmCommonHTML::linkTag(VM_THEMEURL.'theme.css');
} else {
    $vm_mainframe->addStyleSheet( VM_THEMEURL.'theme.css' );
    $vm_mainframe->addScript( VM_THEMEURL.'theme.js' );
}
class vmTheme extends vmTemplate {

    function vmTheme() {
    function vmBuildFullImageLink( $product ) {
    /**
     * Builds a list of all additional images
     *
     * @param int $product_id
     * @param array $images
     * @return string
     */
    function vmlistAdditionalImages( $product_id, $images, $title='', $limit=1000 ) {
    /**
     * Builds the "more images" link
     *
     * @param array $images
     */
    function vmMoreImagesLink( $images ) {
    // Your code here please...

}
```

Initialization code

The initialization code is placed before the vmTheme class definition. This will enable the code to run as soon as the file is included. The intention of the code is clear. It just instructs the PHP to add theme.js and theme.css to the output HTML. We want to add this to the HTML as soon as possible. The best location for this is, of course, the <head> section. However, as the comment among the code explains, for Joomla! 1.0, there is no way to add this code to the header. That's why VirtueMart decides to put this outside the class definition of vmTheme, to make the inclusion of the JS and CSS sooner. For Joomla! 1.5, this code can be placed safely inside the vmTheme class.

vmTheme constructor

The first function of the vmTheme class is a function of an identical name vmTheme. This is a PHP way of defining the *constructor* function of a class. This function will be executed whenever a new object vmTheme is created.

```
function vmTheme() {
  parent::vmTemplate();
  vmCommonHTML::loadMooTools();
}
```

As the coding reveals, the function calls the constructor of its parent vmTemplate first to make sure all necessary initialization is done. The only thing it adds to the list is to load the MooTools library. MooTools is the JavaScript framework chosen by VirtueMart. (Joomla! will load MooTools as well. However, due to historical reasons, VirtueMart has to use its own MooTools library. This will, in some cases, cause conflicts between the two libraries. But that is something beyond our scope.). MooTools is needed for the functioning of the default theme. However, if you decide to develop your own theme JavaScript, you can safely remove the loading of MooTools.

On the other hand, if you need to load your own JavaScript framework or additional JavaScript code files to be shared among the templates, you can do it here.

Additional vmTheme functions

There are three more additional vmTheme functions:

- vmBuildFullImageLink: This function is used to build the **Full Image** link that will pop up when the product thumbnail is clicked. It adds the lightbox or greybox effect to the thumbnail as set in the theme configuration.

- vmlistAdditionalImages: This function is used to list additional images of a product in the product details page. The additional images will show only if you have more than one image in the product. We have been playing around with this one in *Chapter 4, Product Details Templates*. Please refer to that chapter for details.

- vmMoreImagesLink: This function is used to place a **More Image** link in the product details page. This differs from the vmlistAdditionalImages() function in that only a link is shown and the additional images will open in a pop-up when the link is clicked.

These three functions are for image display and are meant for the product details page. However, there is no restriction to limit these functions to flypage templates only, provided you have the appropriate parameters fed into the function. The `$images` parameter, for example, is only available in the flypage templates. So, you have to craft your own code to get the image list before you can use this function in templates other than the flypage templates.

To call any of these functions (or any other functions you added to your theme file), you can use the form `$this->function_name()`. `$this` is a special PHP variable for a class object to refer to itself. The variable `function_name` will be the name of the function that you want to call. We will demonstrate how to do this in the following exercise.

Exercise 8.1: Adding a theme function to insert Joomla! article

Perhaps you have thought of inserting a Joomla! article into one of your product pages. This is especially useful if the message will apply to all products, but it will change at a certain time interval. Obviously, you want to make this as simple to your client or any non-technical people that manage your store. Using a Joomla! article to prepare the message will be more accessible to a layperson user.

Preparation

In this exercise, we are going to use a function to insert a Joomla! article into the product details page. So we need a Joomla! article. I have created an uncategorized article for that purpose.

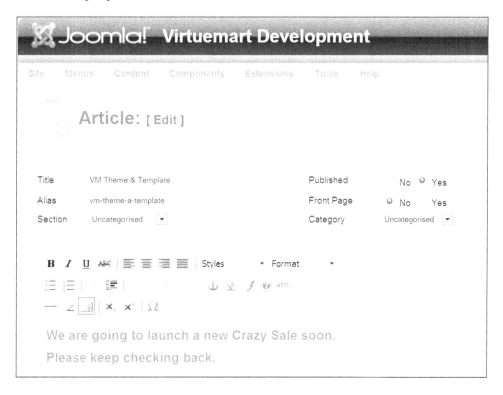

Actually, any article already existing in your site can be used. We only need to know the article ID. To do that, you can log in to your backend, if you are not already there. Go to the **Article Manager** to view the article list. Point your mouse towards the article you want to use in this exercise. You should see the link in the status bar at the bottom of your browser.

Note the number after `cid[]=`. This is the article ID; in this case, the number is **46**.

This exercise will build upon the `flypage.tpl.php` template we have worked in *Exercise 4.5*. If you skipped that exercise, the line number and layout may differ.

Steps

1. Open your favorite text editor. Navigate to the VirtueMart frontend root.

2. Open the file `themes/default/theme.php`.

3. Insert the following lines before line 148 (just before the closing brace }):

```
function insertJoomlaArticle( $id ) {
    $db = new ps_DB;
    $q = "SELECT CONCAT(`introtext`,' ',`fulltext`) FROM #__
content WHERE id='$id'";
    $db->setQuery($q);
    $text = $db->loadResult();
    return $text;
}
```

4. Save the file and upload it to your server.

5. Open the file `themes/default/templates/product_details/flypage.
tpl.php`.

6. Insert the following lines before line 22 (before the `<table>` tag). The number `46` is the article `id` you found in the preceding *Preparation* section. This number may be different for you. Feel free to change it.

```
<?php
    echo $this->insertJoomlaArticle(46);
?>
```

7. Save the file and upload it to your server.

8. Go to your VirtueMart site and browse to any product details page. You should be able to see the Joomla! article there.

Notes

1. We made two changes, one to the `theme.php` file and the other to the `flypage.tpl` template.

2. In Step 3, we created the `insertJoomlaArticle()` function. This function accepts one parameter which is the article ID of the message that we want to show. Through the query `$q`, the ID is passed into the database to get the appropriate article.

3. In this example, we retrieved both the `introtext` and the `fulltext` of the article and added them together. You can use just the `introtext` or the `fulltext`. The coding is pretty much similar.

4. In Step 6, we added the function call to the `flypage.tpl.php` template. Here we hardcoded the article ID to 46. This can be dynamically created when the article `id` varies with the product. But obviously, you need to craft a relation between the product and the article. (For example, you can use the `category_id` to match it with the article `id`.) Note how we call the function `insertJoomlaArticle` with the variable `$this` in the coding.

5. We invoked the function from a flypage template, just as an example. You can use the function from whichever template you want. This means you can insert an article in the browse page in accordance with the category.

The default theme configuration

In the VirtueMart configuration **Site** tab, there is a **Configuration** link below the theme selection box. When you click the **Configuration** link, the **Theme Settings** page will come up.

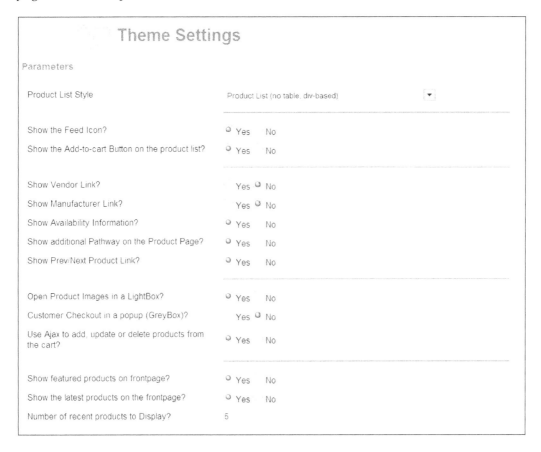

We have seen this page before in *Chapter 2*, *The VirtueMart Default Theme*, when we talked about the theme settings. When you save the settings, the data will be stored in the file theme.config.php, the content of which is shown in the following screenshot:

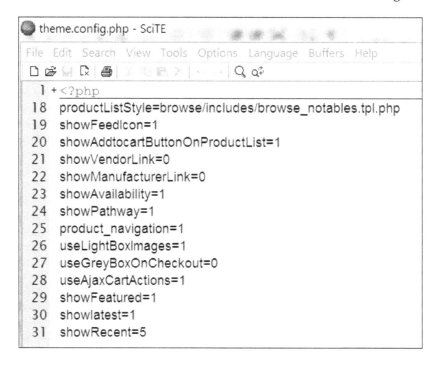

This is basically a text file (other than a section of standard comment for any VirtueMart file) with each setting on one line. The name of the setting and its values are separated by the symbol =. There is nothing special about this file. You can change the text file manually and the new settings will take effect after you save and upload it back to the server.

How does VirtueMart know what settings are available for the theme and is it a drop-down or textbox? All the secrets lie in the file theme.xml. As the file extension suggests, this is an XML file, so its structure has to conform to the requirements of XML data.

Simplified XML file rules

Before we look at the detail of the `theme.xml` file, let's have a brief look at the XML requirements. XML is the acronym for eXtensible Markup Language. This is designed to provide a standard way to represent data, and so there is a very restrictive set of rules for writing a well-formed XML file. In essence, an XML file is a structured document with a hierarchy of elements and attributes. (There are other elements as well. However, as this subsection name suggests, we are trying to simplify it and make it easier to understand.) In this format, an XML file is not much different from an HTML file. Actually, we can write HTML in a form that conforms to XML requirement. Such a document is coined as an XHTML document. The rules for XML documents are as follows (please note, we have overly simplified it):

- The document consists of elements and attributes. Both elements and attributes have names. Element names and attribute names must consist of alphabetical and numerical characters and the hyphen symbol.

- All element names are enclosed in angle brackets `<>`. So an HTML element will be written in the document as `<html>`, `</html>`, or `<html />`. `<html>` is called the start tag, `</html>` is called the end tag. For an empty element, you can use `<html />` which is a short form of `<html></html>`.

- Elements are hierarchical, meaning that one or more elements can be enclosed within another element. However, both the start tag and end tag of the child elements must be fully enclosed within its parent elements. So you cannot have `<html><head></html></head>`.

- The outermost element is called the root or document element of the document. There must be one and only one root element in an XML document.

- Elements can have attributes. Attributes are written within the angle brackets of the start tag after the tag name. The attribute value is enclosed within double quotation marks. So `<div style="font-size:12pt">` is a `div` element with an attribute `style`. The value of the `style` attribute is `font-size:12pt`.

- Within an XML document, you cannot have any text that contains `<`, `>`, or `&`. If you need to use them, you have to write them as `&lt;`, `&gt;`, and `&amp;` instead.

So, you see, XML is not very complicated. So long as you follow these regulations, you can produce a well-formed XML document. However, if you break any of these rules, the document will not be recognized. Even a small error will make the whole document unreadable (by computer, not human being, of course).

theme.xml

Let's take a look at the `theme.xml` file of the default theme. The following screenshot shows the basic structure of this file:

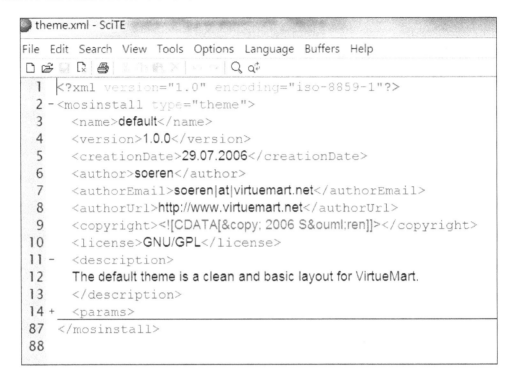

We have folded the major element `params` in this screenshot so as to make the document fit within the page. We will go back to the `params` element in a moment. As you can see, the root element in this XML file is `mosinstall`. All the child elements of `mosinstall`, except the `params` element, are self-explanatory. So, let's move on to talk about the `params` element.

```
  <params>
    <param name="productListStyle" type="list" default=
"browse/includes/browse_layouttable.tpl.php" label="Product List Style" description="Select the
style of the product listings (=browse page)">
        <option value="browse/includes/browse_layouttable.tpl.php">Product Listing with a table (default)</option>
        <option value="browse/includes/browse_listtable.tpl.php">Flat Product List (fixed to 1 product per row,
using a table)</option>
        <option value="browse/includes/browse_notables.tpl.php">Product List (no table, div-based)</option>
    </param>

    <param name="@spacer" type="spacer" default="" label="" description="" />

    <!-- Begin Product Listing Configuration -->
    <param name="showFeedIcon" type="radio" default="1" label="Show the Feed Icon?" description=
"Show/Hide the Feed Icon Link so customers can subscribe for the Product News Syndication.">
      <option value="1">Yes</option>
      <option value="0">No</option>
    </param>
    <param name="showAddtocartButtonOnProductList" type="radio" default="1" label="Show the
Add-to-cart Button on the product list?" description="Show/Hide the add-to-cart button on the
main product listings. Customers will then be able to purchase the product from the details page
only.">
        <option value="1">Yes</option>
        <option value="0">No</option>
    </param>

    <param name="@spacer" type="spacer" default="" label="" description="" />

    <!-- Begin Product Details Configuration -->
```

When unfolding the params element, you will see that there are a number of param
elements within this parent element. Each param element represents a configuration
setting of the theme. For example, the first param element has a name attribute
productListStyle. This corresponds to the first configuration setting in the **Theme
Settings** page. It is not difficult to see the meaning of the several attributes of this
param element:

- name: This is the name of the configuration setting.
- type: This is the setting type. It can be a list (drop-down), radio (radio
  button), text (textbox), or spacer (separator).
- default: This is the default value when none is selected.
- label: This is the text to be displayed when describing the setting.
- description: This is the full description for the setting. This description
  will show as a tool tip when the mouse is pointing to that setting.

Some of the param elements do not have any child elements, some do. All of the child
elements of the param element in this document are option elements. Obviously,
they represent different possible values for a radio button list or a drop-down list.

By conforming to the rules of XML and the semantics of the different elements,
you will be able to modify or add to the settings.

Exercise 8.2: Adding a new configuration setting to the default theme

In *Chapter 5, Changing the Look of VirtueMart*, while discussing Product Details templates, we customized the theme.js JavaScript file to give a longer time for showing the pop up when the shopcart is updated using Ajax. In this exercise, we will add a setting to the theme configuration to allow users to change the value of pop-up duration.

Preparation

This exercise is based on the code customized in *Exercise 5.2*. If you skipped that exercise previously, you will have to complete it before continuing with this one. In case you find it difficult to understand this coding, you may also need to refer to that exercise to make sure you understand what the pop up is and what pop-up duration means.

The modification of theme.php is based on the custom file in *Exercise 8.1*. While the line numbers do not differ, the final file may not be the same if starting with the original theme.php file.

Steps

1. Open your favorite text editor. Navigate to the VirtueMart frontend root.

2. Open the file themes/default/theme.xml.

3. Insert the following lines of code before line 73 (after the closing the </param> tag of the useAjaxCartActions param):

```
    <param name="popUpDuration" type="radio" default="3"
label="Duration of the ajax popup" description="When shopcart is
updated, there will be a popup asking shopper whether to continue
shopping or go to shopcart. You can change the popup duration with
this value.">
        <option value="1">1</option>
        <option value="2">2</option>
        <option value="3">3</option>
        <option value="4">4</option>
        <option value="5">5</option>
        <option value="6">6</option>
        <option value="7">7</option>
        <option value="8">8</option>
        <option value="9">9</option>
        <option value="10">10</option>
    </param>
```

4. Save the file and upload it to your server.

5. Open the file `themes/default/theme.php`.

6. Insert the following lines before line 40 (before the closing brace } of the `vmTheme()` function):

```
echo '<script type="text/JavaScript" language="JavaScript">
  popUpDuration='.($this->get_cfg('popUpDuration',3)*1000).';
</script>';
```

7. Save the file and upload it to your server.

8. Log in to your VirtueMart backend. Click **Admin** and then **Configuration** on the left menu. Go to the **Site** tab and click on the **Configuration** link below the theme selection drop-down box. You should see a new configuration **Duration of the ajax popup** below the **Use Ajax to update** setting. Change the pop up duration to **5**.

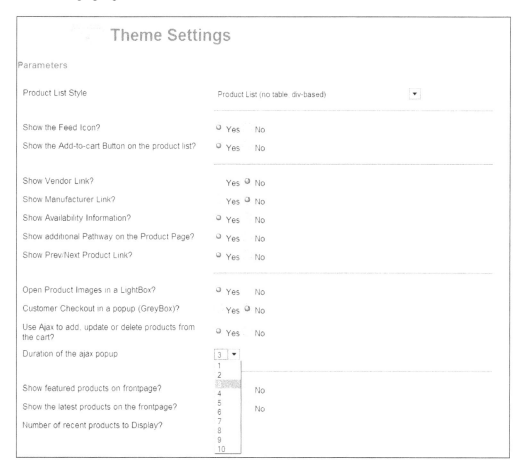

9. Go to the frontend. Navigate to any product that has an **add-to-cart** button. When clicking the button, you should see a different pop-up duration.

Notes

1. We made two changes, one to each of the files `theme.xml` and `theme.php` respectively.

2. In Step 3, we added a param `popUpDuration` of `type` list to the XML. This adds a new setting to the **Theme Settings** page. Since the list `type` param will show the options as a drop-down box, a new drop-down box appears in the **Theme Settings** page. We added options from 1 to 10. You are free to add more or less options. The script will still work.

3. In Step 6, we modified `theme.php` to make use of the new setting to output a JavaScript assignment statement. The function `$this->get_cfg()` is used to get the value of the `popUpDuration` setting. We need to multiply this by 1000 as the JavaScript delay is measured in milliseconds (thousandth of a second). For a setting of 3, the pop-up duration will become 3000 milliseconds or 3 seconds.

Adding a theme setting to the **Theme Settings** page is not complicated, but simply adding the setting has no effect. You need to consider how to use that configuration setting, and at least one more file has to be modified to make use of the setting. In *Exercise 8.2*, we modified the `theme.php` as well to add the JavaScript to the page.

Summary

In this chapter, we have looked at the various building blocks of a theme: theme class, theme configuration, theme images, templates, JavaScripts, and stylesheets. We focused on the first three elements as the other three have been discussed before. We browsed through all the `default` theme images and then had a closer look at the theme class and theme configuration. We learnt how to customize the theme class to provide a function to insert Joomla! articles to the product details page. We also learnt how to add a configuration into the theme in order to change the Ajax pop-up duration when a product is added to the shopcart. In the next chapter, we will go on further to investigate how to create a new theme.

9
Theme Customizations

In this chapter, we will look at the details of customizing or creating a VirtueMart theme. We will first look at the differences between customizing and creating a theme. Then we will discuss the pros and cons of creating a new theme rather than customizing the `default` theme. We will then proceed to the various issues that we need to consider before creating a new theme. After that, we will demonstrate how to integrate JavaScript utilities and the Joomla! plugin with a VirtueMart theme. Finally, we will take a brief look at how to use custom VirtueMart classes to provide your own logics into VirtueMart.

Briefly, in this chapter, we will cover:

- Theme customization and new theme
- Planning a new VirtueMart theme
- Integrating with JavaScript utilities
- Inegrating with the Joomla! plugin
- Modifying the core VirtueMart classes

Theme customization and new theme

In the previous chapter, we saw the basic building blocks of a VirtueMart theme and customized the `default` theme. We are now ready for a more thorough customization of the VirtueMart theme or even to build a theme of our own.

Creating a new VirtueMart theme

Customizing a VirtueMart theme is actually not much different from creating a new theme. When you modify any one building block of a VirtueMart theme such as a single template, your theme is already different from the original theme and so can be considered as a new theme. However, since the theme has the same name as the original theme, it is not considered a new theme for VirtueMart's sake. You create a new theme only when you give a different name to the modified theme and put it in a different subdirectory under the themes directory.

Exercise 9.1: Cloning the default theme

In this exercise, we will make a copy of the default theme and give it a new name. This is the simplest way to create a new theme.

Steps

1. Open your favorite FTP client program (or the file manager in your operating system, if your website is created on your local machine). Navigate to the VirtueMart themes directory, that is, components/com_virtuemart/themes. Create a new subdirectory called packtpub (or any other name you like).

2. Make a copy of the theme.php file from the default theme and save it to the new subdirectory packtpub (If you don't recall what the theme.php file is, please refer to the previous chapter).

3. Log in to your VirtueMart backend. On the left menu, click **Admin** and then **Configuration**. Click on the **Site** tab and the theme drop-down box on the right. You will see our new theme **packtpub** is already there to select.

4. However, if we select **packtpub** as our new theme and then save the configuration, you will see this new screen:

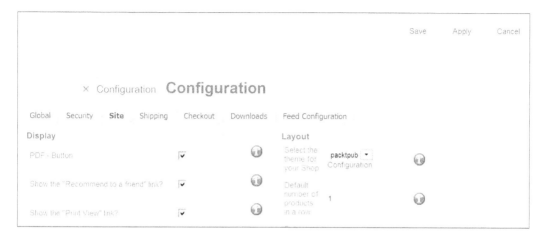

Now all the image buttons/icons disappear. This is because our theme is basically empty. In particular, we do not have any `admin` images and so all the `admin` images on the page are gone.

5. Make a copy of all the files and directories under the `default` theme to our new `packtpub` theme. Go back to the VirtueMart backend, and you will see that everything is back to normal. (Note that sometimes the browser will cache the previous CSS file and you may need to click refresh to make sure the updated CSS file is loaded.)

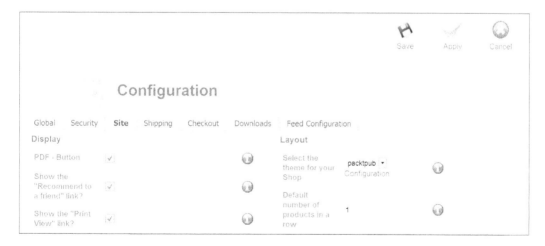

Notes

1. In this exercise, we created a new theme by cloning the `default` theme to another directory. This is the simplest way of creating a new theme.

2. After cloning the theme, you can further customize the theme and add functions and features that are not originally available.

Benefits of creating a new theme

Now you have a brand new VirtueMart theme named `packtpub`. But this theme is exactly the same as that of our custom `default` theme (assuming that you have followed all our customizations). Functionally, our custom theme behaves exactly as our custom `default` theme. So, do we gain anything by creating a new theme?

There are two major benefits of creating a new theme rather than customizing the default theme:

1. A new theme provides an alternative theme rather than overwriting the original `default` theme. The new theme will appear as an option in the VirtueMart theme selection drop-down. You can easily set the theme to the new theme by changing the theme settings in the configuration. Similarly, you can revert to the `default` theme by simply resetting the VirtueMart theme settings. This is especially useful when you are working on a live site. When an unexpected problem emerges as you switch to the new theme, you can revert back to the `default` theme.

2. A new theme makes your site less prone to upgrade problems. Since all the modified files are in its own directory, any changes in the core `default` theme can be updated without any problems. Provided the core theme logic and available fields do not change, the new theme will work in the upgraded version even when the `default` theme has changes.

A corollary of these benefits: if you want to sell your customized theme, you better make it as a new theme. Otherwise, your client will need to overwrite their `default` theme to install your theme, a destructive action that may cause concern for your potential clients. By distributing your theme with a different theme name, your client can revert to the `default` theme when your theme does not work for one reason or another. This provides a safety net for your client and so will make your theme more user-friendly.

Planning a new VirtueMart theme

In *Chapter 8, VirtueMart Theme Anatomy*, we saw all the building blocks of a theme: theme class, theme configuration, images, templates, theme JavaScript, and theme stylesheets. To create a new theme, you can customize any one block or a combination of these blocks. There is no restriction on how you customize them. However, customizing the images and stylesheets can be done separately from the rest of the building blocks. Also, changes in images and stylesheets usually do not have big upgrade issues. So, you should feel free to do customizations of this kind without much worry. If your customizations are limited to only these two categories, you can do it in the `default` theme without creating a new theme.

When you decide to create a new theme, you will probably add a set of new functions/features to it. Some new functions/features are standalone, meaning that it works on a single VirtueMart page without any effect on all other pages. However sometimes your new features may affect more than one VirtueMart page. You probably will want them to appear more coherently.

Also, when adding a new feature, you will consider whether there are possible options for using the feature. You can, for example, set two options — yes and no — to allow your user to enable or disable the feature.

In either case, you will need to make a thorough plan before starting your customizations. Your customizations may affect more than one building block of the theme and they must fit into one another. So before you go ahead, you need to write down which block(s) the customization will involve and the steps that will get the project completed. Making a new theme is not very different from embarking on a VirtueMart customization project. So, you should find the advice in *Chapter 1, The VirtueMart Engine*, helpful. There are a couple of additional points you may want to note though.

Template fallback mechanism

To create a custom theme, you will need at least a `theme.php` file placed in the root directory of the theme. All the other files are not mandatory but will have an effect here and there. Some of the filenames are hardcoded in the core files. So you have to make sure the filenames are named accordingly. Otherwise, you are free to use different subdirectory names and filenames. For a smooth transition, you will probably have a clone of the `default` theme in the new theme directory and start from there.

One important feature you should be aware of is the template fallback mechanism. For most of the files, if VirtueMart does not find a file, it will most probably flag an error. But for the template files, if it does not find a template, it will search it in the default theme trying to locate one. So, if it does not find a template named `browse_1.tpl.php` in the `packtpub` theme directory, it will try to look for it in the `default` theme. This is what we call the template fallback mechanism.

The template fallback mechanism is useful when you are making changes to only a few templates. You just need to place the modified templates in the new theme instead of cloning everything. VirtueMart will use the `default` theme templates for those it does not find in the new theme. This will save you some time (though very minimal) and storage for copying those templates.

There are a few benefits of relying on the fallback mechanism instead of copying the whole set of templates to the new theme:

- You can just put templates that have been modified in the new theme. For those unmodified templates, rely on the fallback mechanism to retrieve the `default` theme template. In this way, it will be clear what files have been customized for the new theme. This is especially helpful when you have several custom themes when maintaining which files have been modified becomes a headache.

- When you need to upgrade to a VirtueMart version, sometimes the template files also change. If the original template has been copied to the new theme, you will need to copy the modified files to the new theme again to make sure they work with the new code. If you rely on the fallback mechanism, then the new template files will be picked up automatically. Again, the more custom themes you have, the more useful this will become.

- During the development phase, especially on a live site, you may need to test the template of your new theme from time to time. But the template may not be fully implemented yet and so you may need to remove it immediately after testing. This is not a huge job but can cause trouble when you need to switch it back and forth. You can set your theme to the new theme and give different names to the templates that are not ready to go live. Rename the template to the true name when testing and switch back you have finished testing. The fall back mechanism of VirtueMart will guarantee that the correct template will be used.

While the fallback mechanism has its merits, there are some pitfalls that we need to note:

- For VirtueMart configuration and also for product category edit page, the template selection drop-down will look for files in the theme directory only. That is, if the theme is `packtpub`, the flypage template drop-down will search in the `packtpub/product_details` subdirectory for possible options. If you rely on the fallback mechanism for the template, only those templates in the `packtpub` theme will be included. The templates in the `default` theme will not be available for selection.

- When changing the theme, make sure the `default` templates for the browse and flypage are available in the new theme. Often, users find that their product list and product details suddenly go blank. One of the reasons is that the new theme does not have the template that you have configured in the VirtueMart configuration or in the category edit form.

Making your theme backward compatible

Avoiding version upgrade headache is one of the reasons that we want to create our own theme. So to make it backward compatible as much as possible should be our goal. That being said, we should understand that there is no way to ensure our theme works in whatever version upgrade. There is always a possibility of upgrade changes that will break our code. Creating a new theme in itself already minimized that possibility. Here are a few hints to further reduce the impact of version changes:

- Try to minimize the number of code changes. Restrict changes to as few files as possible.

- Use the template fallback mechanism, if possible. If there are no changes to a file, there is no point to clone one into your theme. On the other hand, feel free to make a clone if you need the theme file there for configuration purposes.

- Avoid accessing the database directly. Try to use built-in VirtueMart functions. Use database code in theme/template file only as the last resort.

Exercise 9.2: Adding CSS configuration

Changing CSS usually has no connection with the theme configuration. However, it is still possible to control the CSS with configuration if you want to. In this exercise, we will add CSS configurability to the theme. We will demonstrate this using two simple stylesheets.

Our customization will be based on the `theme.xml` we did in *Exercise 8.2*. If you skipped that exercise, the line number will still be the same but the final file you get may be different. The same remark applies to the `theme.php` file.

Steps

1. Create a subdirectory `css` in the directory `themes/packtpub/` of your VirtueMart frontend root.

2. Create a new CSS file that contains the following stylesheet and save it with the name `white.css`. Upload the file to the `css` subdirectory created in Step 1.

   ```
   #vmMainPage {
     background:white;
   }
   ```

3. Create a new CSS file that contains the following stylesheet and save it with the name `yellow.css`. Upload this file to the `css` subdirectory created in Step 1.

   ```
   #vmMainPage {
     background:yellow;
   }
   ```

4. Open the file `themes/packtpub/theme.xml` of your VirtueMart frontend root.

5. Insert the following lines before line 21 (the first `@spacer` param):

   ```
   <param
     name="cssStyle" type="filelist"
     default="white.css"
   directory="/components/com_virtuemart/themes/packtpub/css"
     filter="\.css$"
     hide_none="1"
     hide_default="1"
     label="Color Scheme"
     description="Select the Color Scheme"
   />
   ```

6. Save the file and upload it to your server.

7. Open the file `themes/packtpub/theme.php` of your VirtueMart frontend root.

8. Insert the following lines before line 40 (after the `loadMooTools` call):

   ```
   global $vm_mainframe;
   ```

```
$colorStyle =$this->get_cfg('cssStyle','white.css');
$vm_mainframe->addStyleSheet( VM_THEMEURL.'css/'.$colorStyle
);
```

9. Insert the following lines at the end of file:

```
<?php
  class mosHTML extends vmCommonHTML {
  }
?>
```

10. Save the file and upload it to your server.

11. Log in to the backend. Click on **Admin/Configuration**. On the left side of the **Site** tab, click **Configuration** under the theme drop-down. This will bring up the **Theme Settings** page. You should see a new setting for **Color Scheme** under **Product List Style**. Change the **Color Scheme** to **yellow.css** and save the settings.

12. Go to your frontend and browse any VirtueMart page. You will now see the background has changed to yellow.

Notes

1. This exercise demonstrated how we can add CSS configuration to the theme. We first created a new subdirectory to hold the CSS files that we can configure. Obviously, you can use any name for this subdirectory as long as it matches what will be used in the configuration. (See the following third note.) This technique can also be applied to theme settings that control other features such as the image selection, and so on.

2. We created two CSS files `white.css` and `yellow.css` to simulate the possible change in the styles. You can add as many stylesheets to this file as you please. We use background color just to demonstrate the effect. There is no limit to which CSS style you can use. You can create many more CSS files. Just place them all under the `css` subdirectory we created in Step 1.

3. In Step 5, we added a new `<param>` element `cssStyle` to the file. This `<param>` is of `type` filelist because we want the config to pick up the files in the `css` subdirectory we created automatically. The `directory` attribute specifies the location of the CSS directory. The `filter` attribute is a regular expression. We use `\.css$` to make sure the drop-down box will only include filenames ending in `.css`. If the setting is for image selection, we can change this to `\.jpg$|\.png$|\.gif`. (Actually, you can also use `<param>` type `imagelist` for that purpose.)

4. Step 8 added the coding to insert the appropriate CSS file to the HTML. It used the `get_cfg()` function to grab the value of the `cssStyle` setting. `$vm_mainframe` is a global variable. We need it to access the `addStyleSheet()` function.

5. Step 9 looks strange. This code section is applied just to fix a VirtueMart bug. Somehow, when VirtueMart upgraded the coding, it forgot to rename all the old classes. `mosHTML` is an obsolete class and has been renamed to `vmCommonHTML` in the new version. Unfortunately, the old class `mosHTML` still remains in the `<param>` filelist processing code. We need to define the `mosHTML` class to be same as the `vmCommonHTML` class to fix this loophole. (Note: this problem has been fixed in version 1.1.8.)

Up to now, we have introduced a number of techniques that we can use to extend or customize the theme functions. All these new features are inherent in VirtueMart and do not need external help. We can also make use of external utilities to help provide more features. In the next two sections we are going to see how we can accomplish this.

Integration with JavaScript utilities

There are many useful open source JavaScript utilities on the Internet. Integrating these JavaScript utilities into your theme will definitely add value to it. You can add special effects to your images such as reflection effect and zoom capabilities, add accordion menu to checkout page, add TreeView control to show detail of certain product, and add a color picker to allow shopper to pick color, just to name a few examples. We will demonstrate how to do this using an exercise below.

The image reflection JavaScript

Image reflection is a common technique used to enhance graphics. You have probably encountered them in some of your design projects, or even know how to create one using graphic manipulation programs such as Photoshop. Adding the effect is not difficult but just takes quite a number of steps. To create the effect for just one of your product image is not a big deal. However, it will be lots of effort if you want to have the effect for all your product images. Even if you have created a Photoshop action which allows you to batch process all the product image files, you still need to create them and upload them to your web server, taking special care to make sure the product image and its reflection will match with each other.

It will be really nice if all this can be made automatically on the web server or even on the web browser itself. Not too long ago, Christophe Beyls has written a JavaScript that does exactly the same trick on a web browser. By simply integrating this script into VirtueMart theme, you can create the reflection effect to any of your product images by adding a CSS class to the `<img>` element. The `reflection.js` is released in MIT license and you can download and distribute it for free. You can even redistribute it together with a commercial product.

The `reflection.js` is available for download at the URL `http://www.digitalia.be/software/reflectionjs-for-mootools`. Since there are detailed instructions and documentation on how to use the script, we will not go into the details of the usage of the script here. Instead, we will concentrate on how to integrate the script with a VirtueMart theme.

To integrate the script with our theme, we certainly need to download it and place it within our theme files. There are two flavors of the `reflection.js` script, either the jQuery or MooTools JavaScript framework. In this exercise, we have chosen MooTools which already exists in VirtueMart. If you want to use the jQuery flavor, you will also need to insert the jQuery framework within your theme directory.

Another important issue is the version. The latest version 1.43 of `reflection.js` is developed with MooTools 1.2. However, the version of MooTools that comes with VirtueMart is MooTools 1.11. So we will need the older version 1.33 instead. (MooTools 1.2 is supported from VirtueMart 1.1.8 onwards, although you can stay with 1.11. If you are using MooTools 1.2, remember to use version 1.43 for the `reflection.js`.)

Initial considerations

Before we actually do the integration and theme customization, we need to think about what images will need the reflection effect. Most probably, we will want it to be available in both the product detail page as well as the product list page. You can also add the effect to the product snapshot image used in several VirtueMart modules. If you just need the effect for one single template, the reflection.js can be included there. To make the effect available for any VirtueMart shop page, we will include the reflection.js in the theme initialization script. We also need to customize any template that will use the reflection effect. In addition, if we want to allow the user to decide which page will use the reflection effect, we will also customize the theme.xml so that the effect becomes configurable in whatever pages we want to show the effect.

Here are the steps needed to integrate the reflection.js JavaScript with your theme:

- Add configuration settings to theme.xml to allow the user to configure whether to use the reflection effect on the flypage, browse page, and the product snapshot.Also, to let user to control the reflection image height

- Modify theme.php to load the reflection.js script

- Modify the flypage templates to use the reflection image effect

- Modify the browse templates to use the reflection image effect

- Modify the snapshot template to use the reflection image effect

Exercise 9.3: Adding reflection effect to product images

This exercise consists of several changes to the theme files. To make it easier to follow, we will break the exercise into several parts. You will need to complete all the parts (at least the first two parts and one of the rest) to have a fully functional hack.

Preparation

Before you continue with this exercise, you will need to download the reflection-mootools 1.1 package from the preceding URL, unzip the package, and then upload the file reflection.js to the root of the packtpub theme directory. (There are two reflection.js files in the package. The one we need is located inside the js directory.)

Exercise 9.3.1: Adding configuration settings

In this exercise, we will add a configuration setting to the theme by modifying the `theme.xml` file. Our `theme.xml` is based on the custom file from *Exercise 9.2*. If you skipped that exercise, the line numbers may differ.

Steps

1. Open your favorite text editor. Navigate to the VirtueMart frontend root.

2. Open the file `themes/packtpub/theme.xml`.

3. Insert the following lines before line 71 (before the `useLightBoxImages` param):

```
    <param name="FlypageReflection" type="radio" default="1"
label="Use Image Reflection in flypage?"
      description="Use Image Reflection in the product detail
page.">
      <option value="1">Yes</option>
      <option value="0">No</option>
    </param>

    <param name="BrowseReflection" type="radio" default="1"
label="Use Image Reflection in browse page?"
      description="Use Image Reflection in the product list
page.">
      <option value="1">Yes</option>
      <option value="0">No</option>
    </param>

    <param name="SnapshotReflection" type="radio" default="1"
label="Use Image Reflection in product snapshot?"
      description="Use Image Reflection in the product snapshot.
This will affect most joomla modules.">
      <option value="1">Yes</option>
      <option value="0">No</option>
    </param>

    <param name="reflectionHeight" type="list" default="0.5"
label="Reflection Image Height"
      description="Height of the reflection image from 10% to 100%
of the image height.">
      <option value="0.1">10%</option>
      <option value="0.2">20%</option>
      <option value="0.3">30%</option>
      <option value="0.4">40%</option>
      <option value="0.5">50%</option>
      <option value="0.6">60%</option>
      <option value="0.7">70%</option>
```

```
<option value="0.8">80%</option>
<option value="0.9">90%</option>
<option value="1.0">100%</option>
</param>

<param name="@spacer" type="spacer" default="" label=""
description="" />
```

4. Save the file and upload it to your server.

5. Log in to the backend. Click **Admin/Configuration**. On the left side of the **Site** tab, click **Configuration** under the theme drop-down. This will bring up the **Theme Settings** page. You should see the four new settings for the **Image Reflection**.

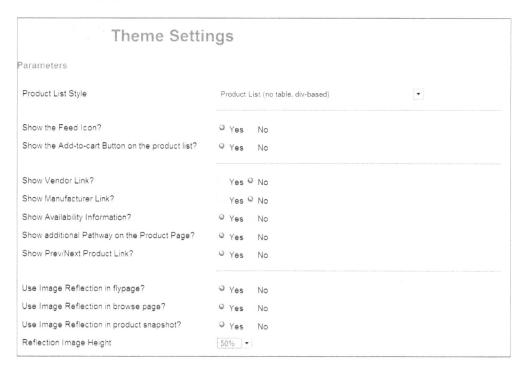

Notes

1. We added five `<param>` elements to the XML. The last one is just a separator that creates the line after the set of **Image Reflection** settings.

2. The first three settings are just yes/no settings to allow users to decide which page(s) will need the **Image Reflection** effect.

3. The last setting is to let user configure the reflection image height. In the `reflection.js` script, this value can be a fraction from 0 to 1 or a number greater than 1. Fractional values will be considered as a percentage in terms of the original image height (1=100% and so on). For values greater than 1, it will be interpreted as height in pixel. We use a drop-down box from 0.1 to 1.0 to make it easier for the user. By using this strategy, user will no longer be able to specify the height in pixel. If you want to allow users to use pixel, you can change this to a `text` type `<param>`.

4. There are many additional options for the reflection effects. For simplicity, we did not provide all the settings here. You can definitely use a similar method to create more `<param>` elements to let users control these additional settings.

Exercise 9.3.2: Inserting reflection.js JavaScript

This exercise will insert the `reflection.js` JavaScript to the `theme.php` file so that the script can be used when needed. We will build upon the `theme.php` file created in *Exercise 9.2*. If you skipped that exercise, the following steps may not work.

Steps

1. Open your favorite text editor. Navigate to the VirtueMart frontend root.

2. Open the file `themes/packtpub/theme.php`.

3. Insert the following lines before line 40, after the `global $vm_mainframe` line:

```
    if ($this->get_cfg('reflectionFlypage',1) ||
$this->get_cfg('reflectionBrowse',1) || $this->get_
cfg('reflectionSnapshot',1)) {
        $vm_mainframe->addScript( VM_THEMEURL.'reflection.js' );
    }
```

4. Save the file and upload it to your server.

Notes

1. We added code to load the `reflection.js` JavaScript only when one of the pages uses the Reflection Image effect. Otherwise, there is no point in loading the script.

2. `$vm_mainframe` is a global variable that we already added in *Exercise 9.2*. We need it to access the `addScript()` function.

3. The changes to `theme.php` have no visible effect in the frontend because the VirtueMart templates have not been modified yet. The template changes will be done in the next three exercises.

Exercise 9.3.3: Modifications to the product details template

This exercise will modify the flypage template to use the reflection effect. We will build upon the `flypage.tpl.php` file created in previous exercises up to *Exercise 8.1*. If you skipped those exercises, the line numbers will differ.

Steps

1. Open your favorite text editor. Navigate to the VirtueMart frontend root.

2. Open the file `themes/packtpub/templates/product_details/flypage.tpl.php`.

3. Insert the following lines before line 35 (that is, the line `echo $product_thumb; `):

```
    if ($this->get_cfg('flypageRelection',1)) {
        $product_thumb = str_replace('<img','<img class="
reflectFlypage "',$product_thumb);
        if (!defined('VM_REFLECTION_SCRIPT_FLYPAGE')) {
          echo '
<script language="JavaScript" type="text/JavaScript">
window.addEvent("domready", function() {
  $$($$("img").filter(function(img) { return img.
hasClass("reflectFlypage"); })).reflect(
    {
      height:'.$this->get_cfg('reflectionHeight',0.5).',
      opacity:0.5
    });
});
</script>
        ';
        define ('VM_REFLECTION_SCRIPT_FLYPAGE',1);
      }
    }
```

4. Save the file and upload it to your server.

5. Point your browser to the Circular Saw product (URL is `index.php?page=shop.product_details&flypage=flypage.tpl&product_id=8&category_id=2&option=com_virtuemart`), you should see the reflection of the product image.

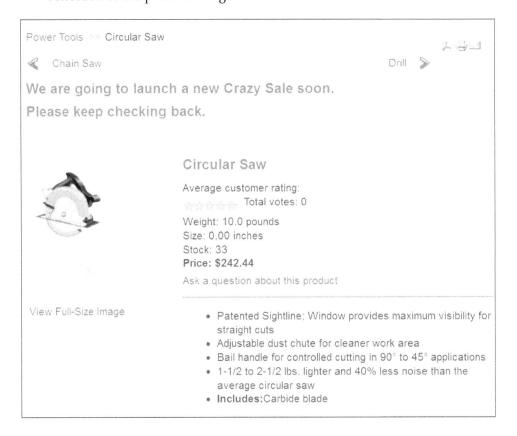

Notes

1. The code logic is in Step 3. The outermost `if` condition is obvious. We will add the code only when the config `flypageReflection` is 1.

2. We then added the CSS class `reflectFlypage` to the `<img>` tag. This is the standard way of adding the reflection effect to an image. For the detail of using this technique, please refer to the documentation on the website.

3. Since the reflection effect may be added to a Joomla! module (see *Exercise 9.2.5*) in addition to the VirtueMart component, we need to define a flag `VM_REFLECTION_SCRIPT_FLYPAGE` to make sure the JavaScript is loaded only once. We will check this flag before spitting out the JavaScript. If it is defined, we will skip the code.

4. The `window.addEvent` code is actually a clone from a file downloaded with the `reflection.js` script. While the code looks a little cryptic, what it does is simply pick up all the `<img>` tags in the HTML document, filter it with those that have a CSS class `reflectFlypage`, and then execute the `reflect()` function to all those `<img>` tags. We only pass two options to the `reflect()` function. The `height` option makes use of the config `reflectionHeight`. The `opacity`, on the other hand, is hardcoded to `0.5`. You can definitely set the `opacity` as another config (refer to *Exercise 9.3.1*) or add other options here. For the available options that you may use, please refer to the website www. digitalia.be.

5. Finally, we will define the flag `VM_REFLECTION_SCRIPT_FLYPAGE` after loading the JavaScript to make sure the script will not be loaded again.

6. In this exercise, we only modified one flypage template `flypage.tpl.php`. To make sure all other templates will use the reflection effect, each of those templates will need to be modified, but the modifications should be very similar.

Exercise 9.3.4: Modifications to the product list template

This exercise will modify the core browse template to use the reflection effect. We will build upon the `browse_1.php` file created in previous exercises up to *Exercise 3.6*. If you skipped those exercises, the line numbers will differ.

Steps

1. Open your favorite text editor. Navigate to the VirtueMart frontend root.

2. Open the file `themes/packtpub/templates/browse/browse_1.php`.

3. Replace lines 21–32 (the section of code for the `browseProductImageContainer <div>`) with the following lines of code:

```php
<?php
  $image_class = 'class="browseProductImage"';
  if ($this->get_cfg('reflectionBrowse',1)) {
    $image_class = str_replace('class="','class="reflectBrowse
',$image_class);
    if (!defined('VM_REFLECTION_SCRIPT_BROWSE')) {
      echo '
<script language="JavaScript" type="text/JavaScript">
window.addEvent("domready", function() {
  $$($$("img").filter(function(img) { return img.
hasClass("reflectBrowse"); })).reflect(
    {
      height:'.$this->get_cfg('reflectionHeight',0.5).',',
```

```
            opacity:0.5
        });
    });
    </script>
        ';
        define ('VM_REFLECTION_SCRIPT_BROWSE',1);
        }
    }
?>
        <div class="browseProductImageContainer">
            <script type="text/JavaScript">//<![CDATA[
            document.write('<a href="JavaScript:void window.
open(\'<?php echo $product_full_image ?>\', \'win2\', \'status=no,
toolbar=no,scrollbars=yes,titlebar=no,menubar=no,resizable=yes,wid
th=<?php echo $full_image_width ?>,height=<?php echo $full_image_
height ?>,directories=no,location=no\');">');
            document.write( '<?php echo ps_product::image_
tag( $product_thumb_image, $image_class . ' border="0"
title="'.$product_name.'" alt="'.$product_name .'"' ) ?></a>' );
            //]]>
            </script>
            <noscript>
                <a href="<?php echo $product_full_image ?>"
target="_blank" title="<?php echo $product_name ?>">
                <?php echo ps_product::image_tag( $product_thumb_
image, $image_class.' border="0" title="'.$product_name.'"
alt="'.$product_name .'"' ) ?>
                </a>
            </noscript>
        </div>
```

4. Save the file and upload it to your server.

5. Point your browser to the All Product List page (the URL is `index.php?page=shop.browse&category=&option=com_virtuemart&Itemid=1`), you should see the reflection of the product image.

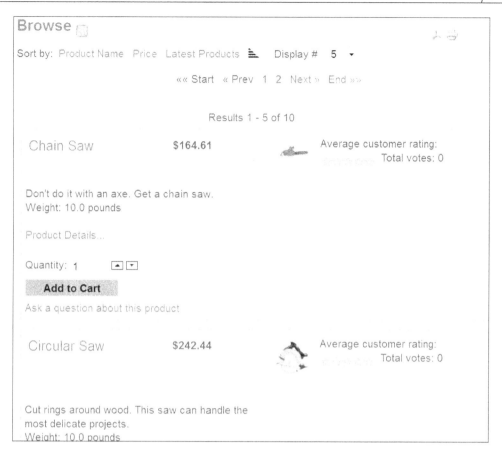

Notes

1. The coding in this exercise is not very different from that in *Exercise 9.3.3*. There are some coding differences due to the difference in the rendering of the image. Also, there is a different config `browseReflection` that controls the reflection effect on the product list page. We also need a different CSS class `reflectBrowse` and different constant `VM_REFLECTION_SCRIPT_BROWSE` to allow the browse page and flypage reflection effect to operate independently of each other.

2. Again, we only modified one template `browse_1.php`. You should change all the templates that may be used to ensure the reflection effect is also available in those templates.

Exercise 9.3.5: Modifications to the product snapshot template

This exercise will modify the product snapshot template to use the reflection effect. We will build upon the `productsnapshot.tpl.php` file created in *Exercise 7.4*. If you skipped that exercise, the line numbers will differ.

Steps

1. Open your favorite text editor. Navigate to the VirtueMart frontend root.

2. Open the file `themes/packtpub/templates/common/productsnapshot.tpl.php`.

3. Replace lines 35–38 (section of code for showing the thumb image, just after the line `<a title="<?php echo $product_name ?>" href="<?php echo $product_link ?>">`) with the following lines:

```
<?php
$image_attribute = 'alt="'.$product_name.'"';
if ($this->get_cfg('snapshotRelection',1)) {
  $image_attribute = 'class="reflectSnapshot" '.$image_
attribute;
    if (!defined('VM_REFLECTION_SCRIPT_SNAPSHOT ')) {
      echo '
<script language="JavaScript" type="text/JavaScript">
window.addEvent("domready", function() {
  $$($$("img").filter(function(img) { return img.
hasClass("reflectSnapshot "); })).reflect(
  {
    height:'.$this->get_cfg('reflectionHeight',0.5).',
    opacity:0.5
  });
});
</script>
      ';
      define ('VM_REFLECTION_SCRIPT_SNAPSHOT',1);
    }
  }

    // Print the product image or the "no image available" image
    echo ps_product::image_tag( $product_thumb_image, $image_
attribute);
  ?>
```

4. Save the file and upload it to your server.

5. Point your browser to any page that has the product scroller module (for example, `index.php?page=shop.product_details&flypage=flypage.tpl&product_id=8&category_id=2&option=com_virtuemart`), you should see the reflection of the product image in the product scroller module.

Notes

1. The coding in this exercise is not very different from that in *Exercise 9.3.3* and *9.3.4*. There is a different config `snapshotReflection` that controls the reflection effect on the product snapshot. We also need a different CSS class `reflectSnapshot` and different constant `VM_REFLECTION_SCRIPT_SNAPSHOT` to allow the snapshot reflection effect to operate independently from those for the browse page and flypage.

2. You can also use a module config to control the display of the reflection effect. This may be the way to go if you want a different reflection effect for different modules. In that case, you will need to add the config to the module and use the `$_REQUEST` variable to pass the config to the template. Please refer to *Exercise 7.4* for the steps to do this.

Integration with Joomla! plugins

Joomla! plugins are very useful gadgets that can take your VirtueMart theme to another level. We will discuss integration with the content plugin in this section.

Content plugins

We introduced Joomla! content plugins in *Chapter 7, VirtueMart Templates and Joomla! Modules*, when we discussed the product snapshot. VirtueMart snapshot plugin is not the only content plugin available. There are lots of content plugins available in the Joomla! extension directory (`http://extensions.joomla.org`). You can certainly integrate them into your theme if you want to.

As you will recall, content plugins are Joomla! extensions that will parse special tags in Joomla! content items and replace them with appropriate HTML code. For more detail about content plugins, you can refer to the Joomla! wiki site (`http://docs.joomla.org/Plugin`). Here are some of the HTML code that can be inserted into the content items:

- Image: Usually you just need to specify the image filename in a certain directory
- Photo gallery: Usually you need to specify a directory or define the list of files in the backend
- Slideshow: Similar to photo gallery
- Video: This includes WMV, AVI, QuickTime movies, flash movies, and even YouTube videos
- JavaScript: Insert special JavaScript functions to produce special effect
- Joomla! modules: Include Joomla! module by name, by ID, or by position
- Content items: Include content of other content items

This list is not exhaustive. Actually, anything you name can probably be included. The problem is whether that kind of plugin is available.

The Tab and Slide content plugin

The `Tab and Slide` content plugin is a plugin make available by JoomlaWorks (`http://www.joomlaworks.gr`). This plugin belongs to the JavaScript category and will insert JavaScript code that subdivides content items into tabs or accordion slides.

The Tab and Slide content plugin is distributed through a GNU/GPL license. You can download it from the JoomlaWorks website mentioned previously. Installation of the plugin is very simple. You just install it through the Joomla! **Extension/Install** menu in your Joomla! site backend.

Usage of Tab and Slide is also straightforward. The documentation comes with the free download, or you can always check out the JoomlaWorks website.

Exercise 9.4: Adding a tab system to the product details page

In this exercise, we are going to demonstrate how to integrate the content plugin into your theme. We will use the Tab and Slide plugin as an example. Much of the code can also be used for other plugins.

Preparation

We will need the Tab and Slide plugin from JoomlaWorks for this exercise. Please go to JoomlaWorks to download the plugin and install it to your Joomla! site before continuing.

Since we will be using content plugin, we need to have content plugin enabled in the VirtueMart configuration. You can log in to the VirtueMart backend to enable this. The setting is on the **Global** tab within the Frontend Features section. Make sure the **Enable content mambots/plugins in descriptions?** setting is enabled.

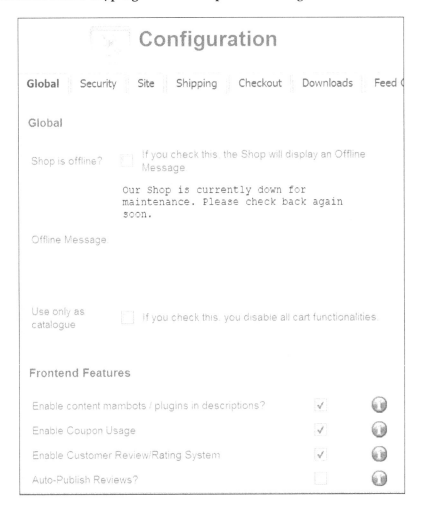

The setting is supposed to be for parsing Product Description only. However, we need to enable this before we can extend the parsing to all theme templates.

Exercise 9.4.1: Adding configuration to use content plugin

To make the content plugin parsing configurable, we need to add a setting in the theme configuration. This is the first step in this whole project. The `theme.xml` file will be based on the custom one we are working on from *Exercise 9.3.1*. If you skipped that exercise, the line number may differ.

Steps

1. Open your favorite text editor. Navigate to the VirtueMart frontend root.

2. Open the file `themes/packtpub/theme.xml`.

3. Insert the following lines before line 21 (just after the `productListStyle` param) with the following lines:

```
<param name="useContentPlugin" type="radio" default="1"
label="enabled Content Plugins?"
    description="Enable Content Plugin parsing of templates.">
    <option value="1">Yes</option>
    <option value="0">No</option>
</param>
```

4. Save the file and upload it to your server.

5. Log in to the backend. Click **Admin/Configuration**. On the left side of the **Site** tab, click **Configuration** under the theme drop-down. This will bring up the **Theme Settings** page. You should see the new setting for the **Enable Content Plugins?** after **Product List Style**.

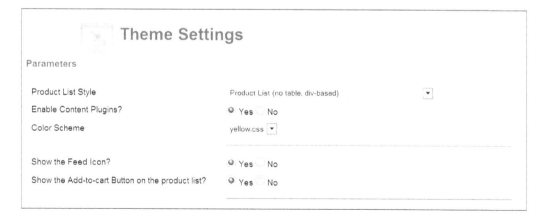

Notes

1. We added a new `<param>` for the **Enable Content Plugin** setting. By now, adding `<param>` should be straightforward.

2. If you need it, you can add configurations to allow user to turn on and off content plugin for individual template group or templates.

Exercise 9.4.2: Modifications to theme.php

We need to add code to the `theme.php` in order to work our magic. VirtueMart has a function to parse the content with Joomla! content plugins. We need to add the coding to the `fetch()` function which is responsible for parsing the template content. We based our `theme.php` from the previous exercises. So the line number will differ if you start from a different file.

Steps

1. Open your favorite text editor. Navigate to the VirtueMart frontend root.

2. Open the file `themes/default/theme.php`.

3. Insert the following lines before line 37 (before `function vmTheme`):

```
function fetch($file) {
  $content=parent::fetch($file);
  if ($this->get_cfg('reflectionFlypage',1)) {
    $contents=vmCommonHTML::ParseContentByPlugins($contents);
  }
  return $contents;                 // Return the contents
}
```

4. Save the file and upload it to your server.

Notes

1. We added a `fetch()` function to our `vmTheme` class. This overrides the original `vmTemplate` class `fetch()` function.

2. The `fetch()` function calls its parent `fetch()` function first to get the template content. It then checks the `useContentPlugin` config to see if content plugin parsing is needed. If yes, it will call the `ParseContentByPlugins()` function to parse the content. Special tags defined in the template file will then be replaced with appropriate HTML code.

3. The changes in the function should have no effect in the frontend as no template file has been modified yet.

Exercise 9.3.3: Modifications to the product details template

In this exercise, we will add the special tags to separate the product details content into different tabs. Please refer to the documentation that comes with the `Tab and Slide` download.

Steps

1. Open your favorite text editor. Navigate to the VirtueMart frontend root.

2. Open the file `themes/packtpub/templates/product_details/flypage.tpl.php`.

3. Replace the whole file with the following lines of code:

```php
<?php if( !defined( '_VALID_MOS' ) && !defined( '_JEXEC' ) ) die(
'Direct Access to '.basename(__FILE__).' is not allowed.' );
mm_showMyFileName(__FILE__);
 ?>
 <img src="components/com_virtuemart/shop_image/category_
banner_<?php echo $category_id ?>.jpg" /> <br />
<?php echo $buttons_header // The PDF, Email and Print buttons ?>

<?php
if( $this->get_cfg( 'showPathway' )) {
  echo "<div class=\"pathway\">$navigation_pathway</div>";
}
if( $this->get_cfg( 'product_navigation', 1 )) {
  if( !empty( $previous_product )) {
    echo '<a class="previous_page" href="'.$previous_product_
url.'">'.shopMakeHtmlSafe($previous_product['product_name']).'</
a>';
  }
  if( !empty( $next_product )) {
    echo '<a class="next_page" href="'.$next_product_url.'">'.
shopMakeHtmlSafe($next_product['product_name']).'</a>';
  }
}
?>
<br style="clear:both;" />
<?php
  echo $this->insertJoomlaArticle(46);
?>
<table border="0" style="width: 100%;">
  <tbody>
    <tr>
```

```php
<?php  if( $this->get_cfg('showManufacturerLink') ) { $rowspan =
3; } else { $rowspan = 2; } ?>
    <td width="33%" rowspan="<?php echo $rowspan; ?>"
valign="top"><br/>
<?php
  $thumb_width=100;
  $thumb_height=100;
  $thumb='<img src="components/com_virtuemart/show_image_in_
imgtag.php?filename='.$product_full_image
    .'&newxsize='.$thumb_width.'&newysize='.$thumb_height.'" />';
  $product_thumb = preg_replace('/<img [^>]+>/',$thumb,$product_
image);
  if ($this->get_cfg('flypageRelection',1)) {
    $product_thumb = str_replace('<img','<img
class="reflect"',$product_thumb);
    if (!defined('VM_REFLECTION_SCRIPT_FLYPAGE')) {
      echo '
<script language="JavaScript" type="text/JavaScript">
window.addEvent("domready", function() {
  $$($$("img").filter(function(img) { return img.
hasClass("reflect"); })).reflect(
  {
    height:'.$this->get_cfg('reflectionHeight',0.5).',
    opacity:0.5
  });
});
</script>
      ';
      define ('VM_REFLECTION_SCRIPT_FLYPAGE',1);
    }
  }
  echo $product_thumb;
?><br/><br/><?php echo $this->vmlistAdditionalImages( $product_id,
$images ) ?></td>
    <td rowspan="1" colspan="2">
    <h1><?php echo $product_name ?> <?php echo $edit_link ?></h1>
  <?php
    $product_rating = ps_reviews::allvotes( $product_id );
    echo $product_rating . '<br />';
     echo $product_price_lbl;
    echo $product_price;
  ?><br />
    <br /><?php echo $addtocart ?>
    </td>
  </tr>
```

```
<?php if( $this->get_cfg('showManufacturerLink')) { ?>
  <tr>
    <td rowspan="1" colspan="2"><?php echo $manufacturer_link
?><br /></td>
  </tr>
<?php } ?>
  <tr>
    <td colspan="2"><?php echo $ask_seller ?></td>
  </tr>
  <tr>
    <td colspan="3">
{tab=dimension}
    Weight: <?php echo number_format($product_weight,1) . ' ' .
$product_weight_uom ?><br />
  Size: <?php echo number_format($product_length,2) . ' ' .
$product_lwh_uom ?><br />
  Stock: <?php echo $product_in_stock ?><br />
      <?php echo $product_packaging ?><br />
{tab=description}
      <?php echo $product_description ?><br/>
{tab=reviews}
    <?php echo $product_reviews ?><br />
    <?php echo $product_reviewform ?><br />
{/tabs}
    </td>
  </tr>
  </tbody>
</table>
<?php
if( !empty( $recent_products )) { ?>
  <div class="vmRecent">
  <?php echo $recent_products; ?>
  </div>
<?php
}
if( !empty( $navigation_childlist )) { ?>
  <?php echo $VM_LANG->_('PHPSHOP_MORE_CATEGORIES') ?><br />
  <?php echo $navigation_childlist ?><br style="clear:both"/>
<?php
} ?>
```

4. Save the file and upload it to your server.

5. Point your browser to the Chain Saw product. (The URL is `index.php?page=shop.product_details&flypage=flypage.tpl&product_id=7&category_id=4&option=com_virtuemart`.) You should see the tab system under the product image.

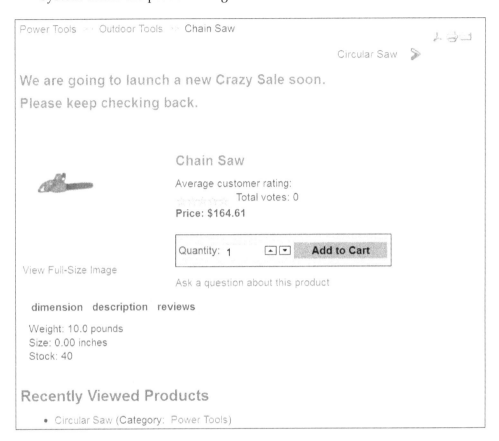

Power Tools ·· Outdoor Tools ·· Chain Saw

Circular Saw ➤

We are going to launch a new Crazy Sale soon.
Please keep checking back.

Chain Saw

Average customer rating:
Total votes: 0
Price: $164.61

Quantity: 1 ▲▼ **Add to Cart**

View Full-Size Image

Ask a question about this product

dimension description reviews

Weight: 10.0 pounds
Size: 0.00 inches
Stock: 40

Recently Viewed Products

• Circular Saw (Category: Power Tools)

Notes

1. The modifications to the flypage template seem quite extensive. The major problem is we need to rearrange the layout to make the tab system more logical.

2. We added three tabs **dimension**, **description**, and **reviews**. You certainly can add more tabs to fit your own product structure and need.

Modifying core VirtueMart classes

As you may be aware, all through the previous chapters, we never touch the core VirtueMart files. This is important in order to avoid headaches when we need to upgrade VirtueMart. If we modified the core files, they would be overwritten when upgrading and all our customizations will be lost. Obviously, this restriction limits our possibility of adding more useful functions to VirtueMart. Yet, we have to comply with this unless we would rather not do any upgrades or be willing to go to the trouble of updating our code whenever a new VirtueMart version comes out.

Starting from version 1.1.4, VirtueMart adds a new feature to allow us to write our own VirtueMart classes. This great enhancement is very similar to the templating system which allows us to supply our own template. As you may recall from *Chapter 1, The VirtueMart Engine*, VirtueMart classes are used to connect to the database and to provide underlying functions. Writing our own classes means we can override many important VirtueMart functions to incorporate our own logic. The theme class filesystem does not restrict our changes to only frontend and presentation items. The changes can also affect many backend functions and possibly interfere with the tax and price system. But of course, those changes will take much greater effort and must be very carefully planned.

Theme class file system

The best way to understand the working of this theme class file system is to look at a sample file. Not all core class files can be extended (Actually, I have no clue why VirtueMart does not allow extension of all class files. This will open more possibility for third-party developers.). Most files with filename starting with ps_ can be overridden. Otherwise, you have a 50 percent chance that the file allows custom theme class files. Let's look at the class file ps_cart.php (Remember all class files are placed in the classes subdirectory off the VirtueMart administrator directory.)

```
24 class vm_ps_cart {
688 // Check if there is an extended class in the Themes and if it is
    allowed to use them
689 // If the class is called outside VirtueMart, we have to make sure to
    load the settings
690 // Thomas Kahl - Feb. 2009
691 if (!defined('VM_ALLOW_EXTENDED_CLASSES') && file_exists(dirname(__FILE__
    ).'/../virtuemart.cfg.php')) {
692    include_once(dirname(__FILE__).'/../virtuemart.cfg.php');
693 }
694 // If settings are loaded, extended Classes are allowed and the class
    exists....
695 if (defined('VM_ALLOW_EXTENDED_CLASSES') && defined('VM_THEMEPATH') &&
    VM_ALLOW_EXTENDED_CLASSES && file_exists(VM_THEMEPATH.'user_class/'.
    basename(__FILE__))) {
696    // Load the theme user class as extended
697    include_once(VM_THEMEPATH.'user_class/'.basename(__FILE__));
698 } else {
699    // Otherwise we have to use the original classname to extend the
       core-class
700    class ps_cart extends vm_ps_cart{}
701 }
```

We have folded the main part of the class definition, leaving only the part to the bottom of the file where you see an additional section after the class definition. This additional Extensible Class section is added in VirtueMart 1.1.4 and is the part that makes the theme class file system work.

In line 695, you see the code that will load the theme class file, if your config allows it, and a file with the same filename (in this case, filename is ps_cart.php) exists in the user_class subdirectory of the theme directory. If the file does not exist, VirtueMart will define class ps_cart as synonymous to the class vm_ps_cart (line 700), which is actually the class defined in the file itself (see line 24). This means that you need to put a file ps_cart.php in the directory themes/packtpub/user_class in order for it to be used by VirtueMart. In that custom class file, we need to define the class ps_cart to provide all the cart functions that are expected.

All VirtueMart classes that can be overridden by a theme class file must have this Extensible Class section added after the main class definition. A prefix of vm_ is added to the original VirtueMart class (for example, vm_ps_cart) to keep the name different from the class (ps_cart) actually called by VirtueMart to do the real job. This may be a little overly complicated at first. Let's make it easier by looking at ps_cart as an actual example:

- VirtueMart uses the class ps_cart to manage the shop basket stored in the server. To add a product to the shop basket, for example, the function ps_cart->add() will be called.

- VirtueMart does not define the class ps_cart directly. Instead, it defines the class vm_ps_cart.

- If we want to use our own ps_cart class, we can create a class file with the same filename and put it in the user_class subdirectory of our theme directory. The class file must contain the definition for the class ps_cart.

- When VirtueMart loads the core class file, it will check whether a theme class file exists. If the theme class file does exist, it will be loaded. Otherwise, VirtueMart will define the class ps_cart by inheriting from vm_ps_cart to make sure the ps_cart is available for use by code elsewhere.

You may be intimidated by writing the whole class file yourself. But actually, we don't need to write everything. The simplest theme class file for ps_cart.php will look like this:

```php
<?php
class ps_cart extends vm_ps_cart {};
?>
```

This is a valid theme class file. What we did is defining ps_cart as a new class that extends vm_ps_cart. This means that ps_cart will inherit everything defined in the core VirtueMart ps_cart class. Of course, that also means we haven't added anything new to VirtueMart. While this seems a waste of time, this demonstrates how easy it is to build a new theme class base on the core VirtueMart class. Also, everything in VirtueMart still works as it should when we enable this new class.

OK. What if we want to add some new features? Simply define some functions to override one or more original function. Let's do this with a real-world exercise.

Exercise 9.5: Creating a template file for the recommend to friend page

If you check the VirtueMart template files defined in the `default` theme, you will see there is no template for the **recommend to friend** page. This is definitely a mistake in VirtueMart design. All the **recommend to friend** HTML is hardcoded in the class `ps_communication`. If you want to customize the e-mail form, you will need to hack into the core file `ps_communication.php` directly. Thanks to the new feature of the custom class file system; we can now do this using a custom class file. In this exercise, we are going to write a custom `ps_communication` to override the function `showRecommendForm()` to use a new VirtueMart template.

Preparation

Since we are going to use the theme class filesystem, we need to enable this in the VirtueMart config. Please log in to the VirtueMart backend. Click **Admin/ Configuration** on the left menu and then click the **Security** tab. You should see the **Allow the inclusion of extended classes from the theme-directory?** checkbox on the upper part of the **Security Settings**. Make sure this setting is enabled.

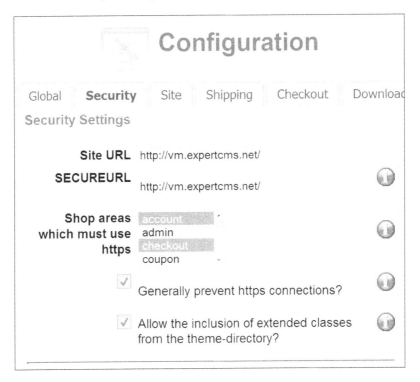

Steps

1. Open your favorite text editor with a blank new file.

2. Add the following lines of code to the file:

```php
<?php
if( !defined( '_VALID_MOS' ) && !defined( '_JEXEC' ) ) die(
'Direct Access to '.basename(__FILE__).' is not allowed.' );
?>
  <style type="text/css">
    #RecommendToFriend {margin:5px}
    #RecommendToFriend th {text-align:left}
  </style>
  <div id="RecommendToFriend">
  This is a customized Recommend To Friend form. You can write
instructions here, add graphic images etc.
    <form action="index2.php" method="post">
     <table border="0" cellspacing="2" cellpadding="1"
width="80%">
       <tr>
        <th><?php echo $VM_LANG->_('EMAIL_FRIEND_ADDR') ?></th>
        <td><input type="text" name="recipient_mail" size="50"
value="<?php echo $recipient_mail ?>" /></td>
       </tr>
       <tr>
        <th><?php echo $VM_LANG->_('EMAIL_YOUR_NAME') ?></th>
        <td><input type="text" name="sender_name" size="50"
value="<?php echo $sender_name ?>" /></td>
       </tr>
       <tr>
        <th><?php echo $VM_LANG->_('EMAIL_YOUR_MAIL') ?></th>
        <td><input type="text" name="sender_mail" size="50"
value="<?php echo $sender_mail ?>" /></td>
       </tr>
       <tr>
        <th colspan="2"><?php echo $VM_LANG->_('VM_RECOMMEND_FORM_
MESSAGE') ?></th>
       </tr>
       <tr>
        <td colspan="2">
          <textarea name="recommend_message" style="width:
100%;height: 200px;padding:5px"><?php echo $message; ?></textarea>
        </td>
       </tr>
     </table>
```

```
      <input type="hidden" name="option" value="com_virtuemart" />
      <input type="hidden" name="page" value="shop.recommend" />
      <input type="hidden" name="product_id" value="'.$product_id.'"
/>
      <input type="hidden" name="<?php echo $vmHash ?>" value="1" />
      <input type="hidden" name="Itemid" value="'.$sess-
>getShopItemid().'" />
      <input type="hidden" name="func" value="recommendProduct" />
      <input class="button" type="submit" name="submit" value="<?php
echo $VM_LANG->_('PHPSHOP_SUBMIT') ?>" />
      <input class="button" type="button" onclick="window.close();"
value="<?php echo $VM_LANG->_('CMN_CANCEL') ?>" />
    </form>
  </div>
```

3. Save the file under the name `shop.recommend.tpl.php` and upload it to the directory `themes/packtpub/templates/pages` of your VirtueMart frontend root.

4. Create another blank new file and add in the following lines of code:

```php
<?php
if( !defined( '_VALID_MOS' ) && !defined( '_JEXEC' ) ) die(
'Direct Access to '.basename(__FILE__).' is not allowed.' );


class ps_communication extends vm_ps_communication {

  function showRecommendForm( $product_id ) {
    global $VM_LANG, $vendor_store_name, $sess,$my;

    $sender_name = shopMakeHtmlSafe(vmGet( $_REQUEST, 'sender_
name', null));
    $sender_mail = shopMakeHtmlSafe(vmGet( $_REQUEST, 'sender_
mail', null));
    $recipient_mail = shopMakeHtmlSafe(vmGet( $_REQUEST,
'recipient_mail', null));
    $message = shopMakeHtmlSafe( vmGet( $_REQUEST, 'recommend_
message'));
    if (!empty($message)) {
      $message = stripslashes(str_replace( array('\r', '\n' ),
array("\r", "\n" ), $message ));
    } else {
      $message = sprintf($VM_LANG->_('VM_RECOMMEND_
MESSAGE',false),
        $vendor_store_name,
        $sess->url( URL.'index.php?page=shop.product_
details&product_id='.$product_id,
```

```
        true ));
      $message = shopMakeHtmlSafe(stripslashes( str_replace(
'index2.php', 'index.php', $message )));
    }
    $template = vmTemplate::getInstance();
    $template->set_vars( array(
      'sender_name'=>(!empty($sender_name)?$sender_name:$my-
>name),
      'sender_mail'=>(!empty($sender_mail)?$sender_mail:$my-
>email),
      'recipient_mail'=>(!empty($recipient_mail)?$recipient_
mail:''),
      'message'=>$message,
      'vmHash'=>vmCreateHash(),
      'Itemid'=>$sess->getShopItemid(),
      'product_id'=>$product_id
    ));
    echo $template->fetch('pages/shop.recommend.tpl.php');
  }
}
?>
```

5. Save the file under the name `ps_communication.php` and upload it to the directory `themes/packtpub/user_class` of your VirtueMart frontend root. You will need to create the `user_class` since it does not exist yet.

6. Point your browser to the **Chain Saw** product (URL is `index.php?page=shop.product_details&flypage=flypage.tpl&product_id=7&category_id=4&option=com_virtuemart`) or any other product. Click the e-mail icon on the top right of the page:

You should see a pop-up window with the **recommend to friend** page.

Notes

1. We created two files in this exercise. The first one is a template file and the second one is the theme class file for ps_communication.

2. In the template file, we added a section of CSS stylesheet, a paragraph of text, and changed some of the HTML tags. It is up to you to further customize the template to fit your needs. You can add instructions, e-mail addresses, graphics, and other elements that make the page more interesting. You can even add product thumb images. Note that most of the HTML here is a copy from the original HTML in the ps_communication function. (See Notes 4 below.)

3. We save this template file in the pages directory and name it shop. recommend.tpl.php just like the page it shows in the frontend. The name is actually arbitrary. You can name it in any other way. Just make sure it matches the code in Step 4.

4. In the theme class file `ps_communication`, we only overrode the function `showRecommendationForm()`. We removed the HTML from the original code and added the template invocation. We kept most of the original code just for the sake of simplicity. You can, for example, customize the default text in the `recommend_message` textarea or move the textboxes around.

5. The `ps_communication` file must be saved to the `user_class` subdirectory under the theme directory `packtpub`. This file does not exist before. So you need to create it.

In *Exercise 9.5*, we added a theme class file to the `packtpub` theme. Theme class file can also be added to the `default` theme. So don't think that you must create a theme to use the theme class files. We also created a brand new template for using with this new class. This is not mandatory. We just want to demonstrate how to create a new template as well. You can create subtemplates and make a sophisticated template system using the theme class files. Just feel free to explore this new VirtueMart feature.

Summary

In this chapter, we have looked at the various aspects of building a custom theme. We compared the pros and cons of building a custom theme with a customized `default` theme. We then discussed some of the issues that users need to be aware of when building a new theme. We also demonstrated how to build the `packtpub` theme by integrating it with Javscript utilities, Joomla! content plugin, and even extending VirtueMart using a theme class file. We made use of all these to provide for Image Reflection effect, and Tab and Slide effect, and created brand new VirtueMart template. All these techniques can be applied to other JavaScript utilities, content plugins, and class files. We are now done with all the basic techniques of working with VirtueMart themes and templates. In the next chapter, we will explore more customization possibilities.

10
Additional Customization Possibilities

In this chapter, we will look at some advanced customization possibilities for modifying the templates and themes. Most of the material is practical stuff and each section may not be related to the rest of the chapter. The only common thing among them may be that they are all interesting customization examples. We will talk about breaking complex templates into smaller manageable ones. We will talk about sharing templates between two template groups. We will work on using a images to display advanced attributes. We will use the product type template to include a file uploader. Finally, we will touch on some more exercises on using Custom VirtueMart class file to make various changes to the pricing system.

Briefly, in this chapter, we will cover:

- Managing big templates
- Sharing child templates
- More fun with advanced attributes
- The product type flypage template
- Hacking into core VirtueMart functionalities

Managing big templates

In the preceding chapters, we have seen many templates and completed a lot of exercises using them. So far there is one template group that we have not touched on. This is the `order_emails` template group. We left this template group to the very end because this group contains one of the most complex templates of all and is also the most difficult one to test. This is the `confirmation_email.tpl.php` template in the `order_emails` template group.

Big templates are difficult to manage as there are tons of HTML tags nested together. The best strategy to manage big templates is to break them into smaller supporting templates. The process of breaking down big chunks of code into smaller ones is so important in modern software development that a name has been coined: refactoring. **Refactoring** is the key to making our code easier to manage and quality assured. We will demonstrate how to refactor a big template in *Exercise 10.2*. Before that, we need to add a little trick to make it easier to test the `confirmation_email.tpl.php` template.

The challenge of testing the e-mail template is that you do not know the template effects until you see the e-mail. In VirtueMart, the order e-mail is sent only after an order has been completed. However, every time an e-mail is sent, the shop basket will become empty. You have to re-add a new product to the shop basket and go through all the steps of checking out to create another test. This is obviously very time-consuming. We need a way to enable us to test the template without going through these tedious steps every time.

Exercise 10.1: Interrupting order processing after order e-mail is sent

In this exercise, we will make use of the custom theme class system to work the magic of interrupting the normal VirtueMart order process. We will use a custom `ps_checkout` class to stop VirtueMart after the order e-mail is sent. This will enable us to test the `confirmation_email` template repeatedly without going through all the shopping steps.

Preparation

This exercise assumes you have done *Exercise 9.5: Creating a template file for the recommend to friend page*. If you skipped that exercise, you will have to create a `user_class` subdirectory in the `themes/packtpub/user_class` of your VirtueMart frontend root.

Steps

1. Create a blank new file and add in the following lines of code:

```php
<?php
if( !defined( '_VALID_MOS' ) && !defined( '_JEXEC' ) ) die(
'Direct Access to '.basename(__FILE__).' is not allowed.' );

class ps_checkout extends vm_ps_checkout {
  function email_receipt($order_id) {
    $result = parent::email_receipt($order_id);
```

```
    $template = vmTemplate::getInstance();
    if ($template->get_cfg('pauseAfterEmail',0)) {
       die( 'testing confirmation_email template. An email has been
sent out');
    } else {
       return $result;
    }
  }
 }
}
?>
```

2. Save the file with the name ps_checkout.php and upload it to the directory themes/packtpub/user_class of your VirtueMart frontend root.

3. Open the file themes/packtpub/themes.xml.

4. Insert the following lines before line 15, just before the productListStyle param:

```
    <param name="pauseAfterEmail" type="radio" default="0"
label="Pause VM after order email"
    description="Pause VM after order email to allow testing of
confirmation_email template.">
       <option value="1">Yes</option>
       <option value="0">No</option>
    </param>
```

5. Save the file and upload it to your server.

6. Log in to the backend. Click **Admin/Configuration**. On the left side of the **Site** tab, click **Configuration** under the theme drop-down box. This will bring up the **Theme Settings** page. You should see the new setting for **Pause VM after order email?** before **Product List Style**. Change this setting to **Yes**.

7. Go to the frontend to make an order through to final confirmation. Instead of the normal thank you page, you should see the following message:

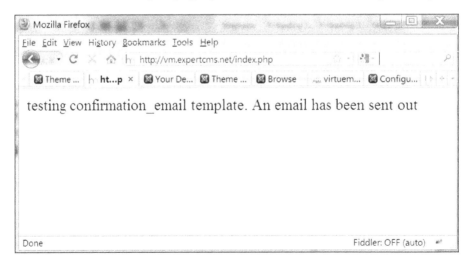

8. Even though VirtueMart is forcefully stopped by the script, the order is still intact. You can continue to refresh the page to put in the same order again and send another e-mail. Before clicking refresh to do testing, you can make further modifications to your `confirmation_email.tpl.php` template and the new modifications will be incorporated in the new order e-mail sent out.

Notes

1. In this exercise, we build a tool that will help us in the customization of `confirmataion_email.tpl.php`.

2. There are two ways that we can set up the control of this script to control when the pause of VirtueMart will be enabled. We used a configuration setting in this exercise. Another simpler way would be just renaming the class file `ps_checkout.php` when we are finished testing, say to `ps_checkout_.php`. When the filename is different, the theme class system will automatically switch back to use the core VirtueMart `ps_checkout` class. The configuration setting method certainly is more elegant but needs a bit more work.

Order e-mail template

In VirtueMart, you can send out order e-mail in HTML or plain text. Because of the complexity of the order, most shop owners will prefer an HTML format. Certainly, there will be a lot of projects that may involve customizing the order e-mail. The template for the order e-mail is `confirmation_email.tpl.php` and it is one of biggest templates among all the VirtueMart templates. (The other big one is `pages/account.order_details.tpl.php` which we will look at in the next section.)

Actually, the product details templates are more complex. But VirtueMart implemented the product details template by breaking many elements into child templates. You probably remember the `includes` subdirectory inside the main `product_details` template folder, which contains child templates to create the add-to-cart form, the child products, the advanced attribute, the custom attribute, and so on. Breaking the main template into several child templates makes the product details template much smaller in size.

While a bigger file may have its merits (you can see everything in one place), it is difficult to manage. It will be difficult to trace the code and make customizations. In the following exercise, we will break the `confirmation_email.tpl.php` template into smaller child templates before making some changes to the layout of the e-mail.

Exercise 10.2: Splitting the confirmation_ e-mail template into smaller templates

In this exercise, we will create a number of child templates for the order e-mail template `confirmation_email.tpl.php`. This will make the big template easier to manage. This is a long exercise since a lot of code is involved but it is not new. You just need to cut and paste the appropriate section of code from the `default` theme's `confirmation_email.tpl.php` template.

Preparation

I suggest you work through *Exercise 10.1* before attempting this one. During the modification of this complex template, you probably will encounter lots of glitches. Having the **Pause VM after order e-mail** system in place will reduce the time to troubleshoot problems in this template.

Steps

1. Create a blank new file and add in the following lines of code:

```php
<?php
if( !defined( '_VALID_MOS' ) && !defined( '_JEXEC' ) ) die(
'Direct Access to '.basename(__FILE__).' is not allowed.' );
?>
<table width="100%" align="center" border="0" cellspacing="0"
cellpadding="10">
  <tr valign="top">
<td width=53% align="left" class="Stil1">
      <?php echo ps_vendor::formatted_store_address(true) ?>
 </td>
 <td width="47%" align="right">
      <img src="cid:vendor_image" alt="vendor_image" border="0" />
 </td>
  </tr>
  <tr>
<td colspan="2" class="Stil1">
  <?php echo $order_header_msg ?>
</td>
  </tr>
  <tr bgcolor="white">
    <td colspan="2">
     <h3 class="Stil2"><?php echo $VM_LANG->_('PHPSHOP_ORDER_
PRINT_PO_LBL') ?>
      </h3>
```

```
        </td>
      </tr>
  </table>
```

2. Save the file with the name `order_header.tpl.php` and upload it to the directory `themes/packtpub/ templates/order_emails/includes/` in your VirtueMart frontend root. (You will need to create the `includes` directory yourself.)

3. Create a blank new file and add in the following lines of code:

```php
<?php
if( !defined( '_VALID_MOS' ) && !defined( '_JEXEC' ) ) die(
'Direct Access to '.basename(__FILE__).' is not allowed.' );
?>
  <tr bgcolor="#CCCCCC" class="sectiontableheader">
    <td colspan="2" class="Stil2">
  <b><?php echo $VM_LANG->_('PHPSHOP_ACC_ORDER_INFO') ?></b>
    </td>
  </tr>
  <tr class="Stil1">
<td>
  <?php echo $VM_LANG->_('PHPSHOP_ORDER_PRINT_PO_NUMBER')?>:
</td>
<td>
  <?php echo $order_id ?>
    </td>
  </tr>
  <tr class="Stil1">
<td>
  <?php echo $VM_LANG->_('PHPSHOP_ORDER_PRINT_PO_DATE') ?>:
</td>
<td>
  <?php echo $order_date ?>
</td>
  </tr>
  <tr class="Stil1">
<td>
  <?php echo $VM_LANG->_('PHPSHOP_ORDER_PRINT_PO_STATUS') ?>:
</td><td><?php echo $order_status ?>
</td>
  </tr>
```

4. Save the file with the name `order_customer_info.tpl.php` and upload it to the directory `themes/packtpub/ templates/order_emails/includes/` in your VirtueMart frontend root.

5. Create a blank new file and add in the following lines of code:

```php
<?php
if( !defined( '_VALID_MOS' ) && !defined( '_JEXEC' ) ) die(
'Direct Access to '.basename(__FILE__).' is not allowed.' );
?>
<table width=100% cellspacing=0 cellpadding=2 border=0>
  <?php
  foreach( $registrationfields as $field ) {
    if( $field->name == 'email') $field->name = 'user_email';
    if( $field->name == 'delimiter_sendregistration') continue;
    if( $field->type == 'captcha') continue;
    if( $field->type == 'delimiter') { ?>
<tr class="Still1">
  <td colspan="2">
    <b class="Still1"><?php echo $VM_LANG->_($field->title) ? $VM_
LANG->_($field->title) : $field->title ?></b>
  </td>
</tr>
  <?php
    } else { ?>
  <tr class="Still1">
<td>
  <?php echo $VM_LANG->_($field->title) ? $VM_LANG->_($field-
>title) : $field->title ?>:
</td>
<td>
<?php
    switch($field->name) {
      case 'country':
        require_once(CLASSPATH.'ps_country.php');
        $country = new ps_country();
        $dbc = $country->get_country_by_code($dbbt->f($field-
>name));
        if( $dbc !== false )
          echo $dbc->f('country_name');
      break;
      default:
        echo $dbbt->f($field->name);
      break;
    }
  ?>
    </td>
  </tr>
<?php
```

```php
    }
?>
<?php
    }
?>
</table>
```

6. Save the file with the name `order_billing_info.tpl.php` and upload it to
   the directory `themes/packtpub/ templates/order_emails/includes/` in
   your VirtueMart frontend root.

7. Create a blank new file and add in the following lines of code:

```php
<?php
if( !defined( '_VALID_MOS' ) && !defined( '_JEXEC' ) ) die(
'Direct Access to '.basename(__FILE__).' is not allowed.' );
?>
<table width=100% border=0 cellpadding=2 cellspacing=0
class="Still">
  <tr>
<td colspan="2">
     <b><?php echo $VM_LANG->_('PHPSHOP_ORDER_PRINT_SHIP_TO_LBL')
?></b>
    </td>
  </tr>
  <?php
  foreach( $shippingfields as $field ) {
    if( $field->name == 'email') $field->name = 'user_email';
    if( $field->type == 'delimiter') { ?>
  <tr class="Still">
<td colspan="2">
  <b class="Still"><?php echo $VM_LANG->_($field->title) ? $VM_
LANG->_($field->title) : $field->title ?></b>
</td>
  </tr>
  <?php
    } else { ?>
  <tr class="Still">
<td>
  <?php echo $VM_LANG->_($field->title) ? $VM_LANG->_($field-
>title) : $field->title ?>:
</td>
<td>
  <?php
    switch($field->name) {
      case 'country':
```

```
                  require_once(CLASSPATH.'ps_country.php');
                  $country = new ps_country();
                  $dbc = $country->get_country_by_code($dbst->f($field-
>name));
                  if( $dbc !== false ) echo $dbc->f('country_name');
                break;
                default:
                  echo $dbst->f($field->name);
                break;
              }
          ?>
            </td>
          </tr>
          <?php
            } ?>
          <?php
          }
          ?>
        </table>
```

8. Save the file with the name `order_shipping_info.tpl.php` and upload it to the directory `themes/packtpub/templates/order_emails/includes/` in your VirtueMart frontend root.

9. Create a blank new file and add in the following lines of code:

```
<?php
if( !defined( '_VALID_MOS' ) && !defined( '_JEXEC' ) ) die(
'Direct Access to '.basename(__FILE__).' is not allowed.' );
?>
 <table width=100% cellspacing=0 cellpadding=2 border=0>
  <tr align=left class="Still">
    <th><?php echo $VM_LANG->_('PHPSHOP_CART_QUANTITY') ?></th>
    <th><?php echo $VM_LANG->_('PHPSHOP_CART_NAME') ?></th>
    <th><?php echo $VM_LANG->_('PHPSHOP_CART_SKU') ?></th>
    <th><?php echo $VM_LANG->_('PHPSHOP_CART_PRICE') ?></th>
    <th><?php echo $VM_LANG->_('PHPSHOP_CART_SUBTOTAL') ?></th>
  </tr>
<?php
// CREATE THE LIST WITH ALL ORDER ITEMS
$order_items = "";
$sub_total = 0.00;
while($dboi->next_record()) {
  $my_qty = $dboi->f("product_quantity");
  if ($auth["show_price_including_tax"] == 1) {
    $price = $dboi->f("product_final_price");
```

```
        $my_price = $CURRENCY_DISPLAY->getFullValue($dboi->f("product_
final_price"), '', $db->f('order_currency'));
    } else {
        $price = $dboi->f("product_item_price");
        $my_price = $CURRENCY_DISPLAY->getFullValue($dboi->f("product_
item_price"), '', $db->f('order_currency'));
    }
    $my_subtotal = $my_qty * $price;
    $sub_total += $my_subtotal;
    ?>
    <tr class="Still1">
        <td><?php echo $my_qty ?></td>
        <td><?php $dboi->p("product_name")?> <?php echo ($dboi-
>f("product_attribute") ? ' ('.$dboi->f("product_attribute").')' :
''); ?></td>
        <td><?php echo $ps_product->get_field($dboi->f("product_id"),
"product_sku") ?></td>
        <td><?php echo $my_price ?></td>
        <td><?php echo $CURRENCY_DISPLAY->getFullValue($my_subtotal,
'', $db->f('order_currency')) ?></td>
    </tr>
    <?php
}
?>
    <tr class="Still1">
        <td colspan=4 align=right>  </td>
        <td> </td>
    </tr>
        <tr class="Still1">
            <td colspan=4 align=right><?php echo $VM_LANG->_('PHPSHOP_
ORDER_PRINT_SUBTOTAL') ?> :</td>
            <td><?php echo $order_subtotal ?></td>
    </tr>
            <?php
            // DISCOUNT HANDLING
        if ( PAYMENT_DISCOUNT_BEFORE == '1') {
            if ($order_discount > 0 || $order_discount < 0) {
                ?>
    <tr class="Still1">
        <td align="right" colspan="4">
            <?php echo $order_discount_lbl ?>:
        </td>
        <td>
```

```
        <?php echo $order_discount_plusminus .' '. $CURRENCY_
DISPLAY->getFullValue(abs($order_discount), '', $db->f('order_
currency')) ?>
      </td>
    </tr>
      <?php
        }
        if ($coupon_discount > 0 || $coupon_discount < 0) {
          ?>
    <tr class="Still">
      <td align="right" colspan="4"><?php echo $VM_LANG->_('PHPSHOP_
COUPON_DISCOUNT') ?>: </td>
      <td><?php echo $coupon_discount_plusminus. ' '.$CURRENCY_
DISPLAY->getFullValue(abs($coupon_discount), '', $db->f('order_
currency')) ?></td>
    </tr>
      <?php
        }
      }
      ?>
    <tr class="Still">
      <td colspan=4 align=right><?php echo $VM_LANG->_('PHPSHOP_
ORDER_PRINT_SHIPPING') ?> :</td>
      <td><?php echo $order_shipping ?></td>
    </tr>
    <tr class="Still">
      <td colspan=4 align=right><?php echo $VM_LANG->_('PHPSHOP_
ORDER_PRINT_TOTAL_TAX') ?> :</td>
        <td><?php echo $order_tax ?></td>
    </tr>
    <tr class="Still">
      <td colspan=4 align=right><?php echo $VM_LANG->_('PHPSHOP_
ORDER_PRINT_SHIPPING_TAX') ?> :</td>
        <td><?php echo $shipping_tax ?></td>
    </tr>
        <?php
    if ( PAYMENT_DISCOUNT_BEFORE != '1') {
      if ($order_discount > 0 || $order_discount < 0) {
        ?>
    <tr class="Still">
      <td align="right" colspan="4"><?php echo $order_discount_lbl
?>: </td>
      <td> <?php echo $order_discount_plusminus .' '. $CURRENCY_
DISPLAY->getFullValue(abs($order_discount), '', $db->f('order_
currency')) ?></td>
```

```
     </tr>
        <?php
        }
        if ($coupon_discount > 0 || $coupon_discount < 0) {
          ?>
  <tr class="Still">
     <td align="right" colspan="4"><?php echo $VM_LANG->_('PHPSHOP_
COUPON_DISCOUNT') ?>: </td>
     <td><?php echo $coupon_discount_plusminus. ' '.$CURRENCY_
DISPLAY->getFullValue(abs($coupon_discount), '', $db->f('order_
currency')) ?></td>
  </tr>
        <?php
        }
      }
      ?>
     <tr class="Still">
        <td colspan=4 align=right><b><?php echo $VM_LANG->_
('PHPSHOP_CART_TOTAL') .": " ?></b></td>
        <td><?php echo $order_total ?></td>
  </tr>
</table>
```

10. Save the file with the name `order_item_details.tpl.php` and upload it to the directory `themes/packtpub/ templates/order_emails/includes/` in your VirtueMart frontend root.

11. Create a blank new file and add in the following lines of code:

```php
<?php
if( !defined( '_VALID_MOS' ) && !defined( '_JEXEC' ) ) die(
'Direct Access to '.basename(__FILE__).' is not allowed.' );
?>
<?php
// EMAIL FOOTER MESSAGE
if( $is_email_to_shopper ) {
  $footer_html = "<br /><br />".$VM_LANG->_('PHPSHOP_CHECKOUT_
EMAIL_SHOPPER_HEADER2')."<br />";

  if( VM_REGISTRATION_TYPE != 'NO_REGISTRATION' ) {
    $footer_html .= "<br /><a title=\"".$VM_LANG->_('PHPSHOP_
CHECKOUT_EMAIL_SHOPPER_HEADER5')."\" href=\"$order_link\">"
    . $VM_LANG->_('PHPSHOP_CHECKOUT_EMAIL_SHOPPER_HEADER5')."</
a>";
  }
  $footer_html .= "<br /><br />".$VM_LANG->_('PHPSHOP_CHECKOUT_
EMAIL_SHOPPER_HEADER3')."<br />";
```

```
    $footer_html .= $VM_LANG->_('CMN_EMAIL').": <a href=\"mailto:" .
$from_email."\">".$from_email."</a>";
    // New in version 1.0.5
    if( @VM_ONCHECKOUT_SHOW_LEGALINFO == '1' && !empty( $legal_info_
title )) {
        $footer_html .= "<br /><br />
<br />";
        $footer_html .= '<h5>'.$legal_info_title.'</h5>';
        $footer_html .= $legal_info_html.'<br />';
    }
} else {
    $footer_html = '<br /><br /><a title="'.$VM_LANG->_('PHPSHOP_
CHECKOUT_EMAIL_SHOPPER_HEADER5').'" href="'.$order_link.'">'
    . $VM_LANG->_('PHPSHOP_CHECKOUT_EMAIL_SHOPPER_HEADER5').'</
a>';
}
echo $footer_html;
?>
```

12. Save the file with the name `order_footer.tpl.php` and upload it to the directory `themes/packtpub/templates/order_emails/includes/` in your VirtueMart frontend root.

13. Create a blank new file and add in the following lines of code:

```
<?php
if( !defined( '_VALID_MOS' ) && !defined( '_JEXEC' ) ) die(
'Direct Access to '.basename(__FILE__).' is not allowed.' );
?>
<html>
<head>
<title><?php echo $VM_LANG->_('PHPSHOP_ORDER_PRINT_PO_LBL') ?></
title>
<style type="text/css">
<!--
.Stil1 {
    font-family: Verdana, Arial, Helvetica, sans-serif;
    font-size: 12px;
}
.Stil2 {font-family: Verdana, Arial, Helvetica, sans-serif}
-->
</style>
</head>
<body>

<?php echo $this->fetch( '/order_emails/includes/order_header.tpl.
php'); ?>
```

```
<table border=0 cellspacing=0 cellpadding=2 width=100%>
   <!-- begin customer information -->

   <?php echo $this->fetch( '/order_emails/includes/order_info.tpl.
php'); ?>

   <!-- end customer information -->
   <!-- begin 2 column bill-ship to -->
   <tr class="sectiontableheader">
     <td colspan="2"> </td>
   </tr>
   <tr bgcolor="#CCCCCC" class="sectiontableheader">
     <td colspan="2"><b class="Stil2"><?php echo $VM_LANG->_
('PHPSHOP_ORDER_PRINT_CUST_INFO_LBL') ?></b></td>
   </tr>
   <tr valign=top>
     <td width=50%>
     <!-- begin billto -->

   <?php echo $this->fetch( '/order_emails/includes/order_billing_
info.tpl.php'); ?>

           <!-- end billto -->
     </td>
     <td width=50%>
     <!-- begin shipto -->

 <?php echo $this->fetch( '/order_emails/includes/order_shipping_
info.tpl.php'); ?>

        <!-- end shipto -->
        <!-- end customer information --> </td>
   </tr>
   <tr>
     <td colspan="2"> </td>
   </tr>
   <tr>
     <td colspan="2">
       <table width="100%" border="0" cellspacing="0"
cellpadding="1">

       </table>
     </td>
   </tr>
   <tr>
```

```
        <td colspan="2"> </td>
    </tr>
    <!-- begin order items information -->
    <tr bgcolor="#CCCCCC" class="Stil2">
        <td colspan="2"><b><?php echo $VM_LANG->_('PHPSHOP_ORDER_
ITEM') ?></b></td>
    </tr>
    <tr>
        <td colspan="2">

<?php echo $this->fetch( '/order_emails/includes/order_item_
details.tpl.php'); ?>

        </td>
    </tr>
    <!-- end order items information -->
    <!-- begin customer note -->
    <tr class="sectiontableheader">
        <td colspan="2"> </td>
    </tr>
    <tr bgcolor="#CCCCCC" class="sectiontableheader">
        <td colspan="2"><b class="Stil2"><?php echo $VM_LANG->_
('PHPSHOP_ORDER_PRINT_CUSTOMER_NOTE') ?>:</b></td>
    </tr>
    <tr>
        <td colspan="2">
            <?php echo $customer_note ?>
        </td>
    </tr>
    <tr class="sectiontableheader">
        <td colspan="2"> </td>
    </tr>
    <tr bgcolor="#CCCCCC" class="sectiontableheader">
        <td><b class="Stil2"><?php echo $payment_info_lbl ?></b></td>
        <td><b class="Stil2"><?php echo $shipping_info_lbl ?></b></td>
    </tr>
    <tr>
        <td><?php echo $payment_info_details ?></td>
        <td><?php echo $shipping_info_details ?></td>
    </tr>
</table>
<br />
<p class="Stil2"></p>
<p class="Stil2">
```

```
<?php echo $this->fetch( '/order_emails/includes/order_footer.tpl.
php'); ?>
</p>
</body>
</html>
```

14. Save the file with the name `confirmation_email.tpl.php` and upload it to the directory `themes/packtpub/templates/order_emails/` in your VirtueMart frontend root.

15. Go to the frontend to make an order through to final confirmation. You should receive the same message as in *Exercise 10.1* on the website. Check whether the order e-mail you receive is the same as before. In case there are any errors, you can compare the coding to make sure the template has been properly modified.

Notes

1. In this exercise, we created several new templates and placed them in the `includes` subdirectory of the `order_emails` template group directory. We then modified the `confirmation_email.tpl.php` template to make use of these new child templates. As a result, the size of `confirmation_email.tpl.php` became smaller and its content more clear.

2. In the process, we tried to keep the original content and layout so that the new template displays exactly as the old one. This helps to spot problems in case the new template breaks. Feel free to customize the template(s) as you please, if you are comfortable with it, or you can wait for the next Exercise.

3. We can identify a number of distinct sections in the order e-mail. They include header (vendor information, invoice number, and so on), footer (return policy, other fine print, order link, and so on), customer information, billing address, shipping address, order items, payment method, and shipping method. We created a child template for most of these sections. The payment method and shipping method are already built into the `ps_checkout` class. So, we don't bother to put them into separate templates here. If you think you will need to customize that, go ahead and put them into a child template as well.

4. Inserting the content of a child template is pretty straightforward. What we need is the `fetch()` function which accepts a `$file` parameter indicating the location of the child template relative to the theme directory (`packtpub` in our case). We don't need to put in the available fields as they are already added. That means that all the fields available in our current template can be used in the child template.

5. When we are certain that the new template works, we can introduce new content and a new layout.

Exercise 10.3: Modifying order e-mail layout

Now, we are ready to make modifications to the `confirmation_email.tpl.php` template. There can be infinite number of possibilities. Here we will demonstrate by making four changes:

- Some of the table cells do not have a CSS class, making them look different from the rest of the text. We will add/modify the CSS class as appropriate.

- We will move the payment and shipping information up, to before the order item details.

- We will add an "order status stamp" to the top of the administrator e-mail. This will help the shop administrator to easily distinguish orders with different statuses. Note that this additional information is restricted to the administrator e-mail only and is not included in the shopper e-mail.

- We will add the product thumb image to the e-mail.

Preparation

This exercise assumes you have worked on *Exercise 10.2*. If you have skipped that exercise, you may have difficulties in locating the lines to change.

Steps

1. Open your favorite text editor. Navigate to the VirtueMart frontend root.

2. Open the file `themes/packtpub/templates/order_emails/confirmation_email.tpl.php`.

3. Add the CSS class `Still` to the table cell in line 83 by replacing the line with:
   ```
   <td class="Still" colspan="2">
   ```

4. Add the CSS class `Still` to the table cell in lines 96 and 97 by replacing the lines with:
   ```
   <td class="Still"><?php echo $payment_info_details ?></td>
   <td class="Still"><?php echo $shipping_info_details ?></td>
   ```

5. Add the CSS class `Still` to the `<p>` tag in line 102 by replacing the line with:
   ```
   <p class="Still">
   ```

6. Move lines 88–98 (the payment and shipping info table rows) before line 50 (after the customer information):

```
<tr class="sectiontableheader">
  <td colspan="2"> </td>
</tr>
<tr bgcolor="#CCCCCC" class="sectiontableheader">
  <td><b class="Stil2"><?php echo $payment_info_lbl ?></b></td>
  <td><b class="Stil2"><?php echo $shipping_info_lbl ?></b></td>
</tr>
<tr>
  <td class="Stil1"><?php echo $payment_info_details ?></td>
  <td class="Stil1"><?php echo $shipping_info_details ?></td>
</tr>
```

7. Insert the following lines before line 18 (that is, at the beginning of the template.):

```
<?php
  if (!$is_email_to_shopper ) {
    echo '<div style="font-size:14pt;color:red">'.$VM_LANG->_
('PHPSHOP_ORDER_PRINT_PO_STATUS').
      ': '.$order_status.'</div>';
  }
?>
```

8. Save the file and upload it to your web server.

9. Open the file `themes/packtpub/templates/order_emails/includes/order_item_details.tpl.php`.

10. Replace line 31 (that is, the table cell for product `sku`) with the following lines:

```
    <td><?php echo $ps_product->get_field($dboi->f("product_id"),
"product_sku") ?>
    <?php
    $product_thumb_image=$ps_product->get_field($dboi->f("product_
id"), "product_thumb_image");
    $product_image=$ps_product->image_tag($product_thumb_image,
'', 0);
    echo '<br />'.$product_image;
    ?>
    </td>
```

11. Save the file and upload it to your web server.

12. Go to the frontend to make an order through to final confirmation. You should receive the same message as in *Exercise 10.1* on the website. The order e-mail you receive should have the new changes added. The shopper order e-mail will have a different layout, product image, and a more uniform text style.

13. For the administrator e-mail, you will see the order status stamp at the top of the e-mail:

Notes

1. As listed before, we made four changes to the template. Steps 3 to 5 were used to modify the CSS style so that the fonts are more uniform. This is just for illustrative purposes. You can choose a different style and font for this text.

2. In Step 6, we moved the payment and shipping info to a higher position after the customer information. Again, this is just an example. Actually, you can have a very different layout. If you are a supporter of using a tableless layout, you can remove the HTML table and use `<div>` to layout a different area.

3. In Step 7, we added the order status stamp. You can find similar coding within the Customer Info section of the original template. We just made a copy of it to the top and gave it a different style. As mentioned in the introduction, we want this order status stamp to be shown only in the administrator e-mail. That's why we added an `if` condition to check `$is_email_to_shopper` to see whether the e-mail is for the shopper or administrator. You can add other information together with the order status stamp as appropriate. You can even use a different color for each different order status by checking the order status before adding the CSS style.

4. In Step 10, we needed to modify the child template `order_item_details.tpl.php`. We used the `$ps_product` object to help us to retrieve the `product_thumb_image` and use the function `image_tag()` to get the actual thumb image URL. Note that this image is linked to your website and is not embedded in the e-mail. The image will show only if the shopper is online and the e-mail client allows the product images to be shown from the Internet. Although this is not the best way to add an image thumbnail to the e-mail, it is the simplest way to make this work. If you want to embed the image, you will need to override the `email_receipt()` function completely. You can check the original `ps_checkout.php` for the coding and add the embedded image code before sending the e-mail. While there is a sample of embedded image coding in the original code, to extend it to include product images is not straightforward. You will need to know the details of how e-mail clients can retrieve embedded images. Given the complexity, we will not be able to elaborate on this further here.

5. The product image is added to the product `sku` column. This is not mandatory. You can add this to the product name, column, or even add a new column for showing the thumbnail. If you do, make sure you insert a column header as well. Otherwise, the column header and the content will not match.

After you are done with testing the `confirmation_email` template, don't forget to reset the **Pause VM after order email** setting to no. Otherwise, the order will never be reset and the thank you page will not show.

Sharing child templates

Some templates will display common information. For these templates, we should try our best to build the template system to share the same child templates. There are two benefits in using this strategy:

- By using the same template, we reduce time writing and testing the template. While some templates can be straightforward to develop, they still take time to proofread and test.

- When there are changes needed, you only need to change one template and it will be modified in all parent templates that are using it.

For this reason, VirtueMart does group common templates into a template group called `common`. However, sharing templates does not require us to put them in the `common` template group. We can share templates wherever we place the child template.

Order detail template and order e-mail template

In the previous section, we mentioned that there are two big templates in VirtueMart. We discussed the order e-mail template in the previous section. It's time to take up the other one, the `account.order_details` template in the `pages` template group.

The order details template is used to show the order details online on the website. It shares a lot of common data with the order e-mail. Actually, in case the shopper lost his/her order e-mail, he/she can get a copy from logging into the website to print the online version. We cannot use the order e-mail template directly for the online version, however, because there are differences between them:

- The order e-mail template is for a complete HTML page. The order details template is just a part of the whole web page (recall that VirtueMart is only a component within the big context of the Joomla! site). The order e-mail template has `<html>`, `<head>`, and `<body>` tags that are not needed in the order details template. Including them may work in most browsers but is not XHTML compliant.

- The order details will need to cater for downloadable products and provide product download links as appropriate.

- The order details will need to cater for the case that the shopper has not paid. In case they need to pay, the order details page will provide a link for them to complete the order (whether a link is available will depend on the actual payment method).

- The product name in order details is clickable and will link to the product details page. The product name in the order e-mail does not have this function.

While we cannot share the whole template, it is possible to share some of the child templates which are the same. The following exercise will demonstrate how to do this.

Exercise 10.4: Sharing templates between order e-mail and order details

In this exercise, we are going to modify the `account.order_details.tpl.php` template to use some of the child templates we created for the order e-mail in the previous exercises.

Preparation

This exercise will build on the result of *Exercise 10.2*. If you have skipped that exercise, you will not be able to follow this one.

Steps

1. Open your favorite text editor. Navigate to the VirtueMart frontend root.

2. Open the file `themes/packtpub/templates/pages/account.order_details.tpl.php`.

3. Replace lines 130–158 (the shipping address section) with the following line:

   ```
   <?php include( $this->path.'/order_emails/includes/order_shipping_info.tpl.php'); ?>
   ```

4. Replace lines 93–122 (the billing address section) with the following line:

   ```
   <?php include( $this->path.'/order_emails/includes/order_billing_info.tpl.php'); ?>
   ```

5. Replace lines 70–85 (the customer info section) with the following lines of code:

   ```
   <?php
     $order_id=sprintf("%08d", $db->f("order_id"));
   ```

```
$order_date=vmFormatDate($db->f("cdate")+$time_offset);
$order_status=ps_order_status::getOrderStatusName( $db-
>f("order_status") );
include( $this->path.'/order_emails/includes/order_ info.tpl.
php');
?>
```

6. Replace lines 31–39 (the header section) with the following lines of code:

```
<?php
$result = $this->fetch('/order_emails/includes/order_header.tpl.
php');
$result = preg_replace('/<img [^>]+>/',$vendor_image,$result);
echo $result;
?>
```

7. Save the file and upload it to your server.

8. Log in to your frontend and browse to the **Account Management** page. Click the **View** button against any order you have made before. You should see the order details page now using some of the child templates of the order e-mail.

Notes

1. This exercise has demonstrated how we can share child templates between two template groups.

2. We do not need to share all the child templates. Just share those templates that are common to both parent templates. In this exercise, for example, we only share the top portion of the two templates, that is, the `order_header`, the `order_info`, the `billing_info`, and the `shipping_info`.

3. There are some subtle differences between the available fields of the two templates. So we will need to cater for these differences in order to share the templates.

4. In Step 5, we needed to create the three variables `$order_id`, `$order_status`, and `$order_date` before calling the `order_info` template because these three fields are not available in the original template.

5. In Step 6, we needed to replace the vendor image location. In the order e-mail, the vendor image is an embedded image. But in the order details, an embedded image makes no sense. We need to replace it with a link to the server location.

So far, we have introduced a number of techniques that we can use to extend or customize the theme functions. All these new features are inherent in VirtueMart itself and do not need external help. We can also make use of external utilities to help provide more features. In the next two sections, we are going to see how we can accomplish this.

More fun with advanced attributes

In *Chapter 4, Product Details Templates*, we worked on an exercise to use a radio button instead of the drop-down box for displaying the advanced attribute. The change was done by customizing the `addtocart_advanced_attribute.tpl.php` template. We can further customize the template to provide a lot more possibilities. In the following exercise, we will supplement the radio button with images.

Exercise 10.5: Showing advanced attributes as image radio button

In this exercise, we will modify the advanced attribute template to show the attribute as a list of radio buttons which include images in addition to text labels. We will also add an onclick event handler to change the product image to synchronize with the radio button selection. To illustrate the effect, we will use the product **Shovel** (`product_id=3`). This product has two advanced attributes: `Colour` and `Size`. We will show an image for each of the colors and the product image will change when the `Colour` selection changes. You can go to the backend to see the **Attribute List** on the **Product Status** tab of the **Shovel Update** page.

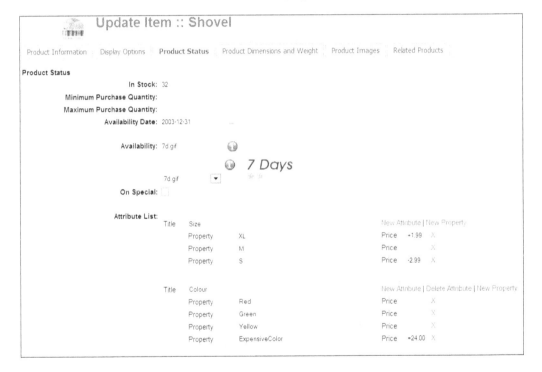

Note that **Colour** has four possible values: **Red, Green, Yellow**, and **ExpensiveColor**. We will need to prepare images to fit these four colors. (We try to use existing attribute without change. There is at least one inconsistency in the attribute: the attribute title `Colour` and property `ExpensiveColor` have different spellings. If you want to fix this, feel free to do so. If you change any of these values, however, the directory and image created in the *Preparation* will need to match.)

Preparation

This exercise assumes you have done *Exercise 4.7: Displaying advanced attribute as radio button*. If you skipped that exercise, you will not be able to follow this one.

You also need to prepare the images that we will use in the radio button as well as for the set of product images that will fit the color.

1. Open your favorite FTP client program and navigate to the `shop_image` directory of the VirtueMart frontend root. Create a subdirectory named `attribute`. Under the `attribute` directory, create a subdirectory named `colour`. (We use lower case for the directory and filename in order to conform with common standards.)

2. Create four image files `red.jpg`, `green.jpg`, `yellow.jpg`, and `expensivecolor.jpg` and upload them to the newly created `colour` subdirectory.

3. Make a copy of the **Shovel** image (the original filename is `520efefd6d7977f91b16fac1149c7438.jpg`) and rename it as `shovel.jpg`. Create four images to match the four attribute colors and name them as `shovel_red.jpg`, `shovel_green.jpg`, `shovel_yellow.jpg`, and `shovel_expensivecolor.jpg`. (It is not mandatory that the color of the images really match with the names for this exercise. But, in real-world usage, you definitely will want them to match.) Upload all five images to the `shop_image/product` directory of the VirtueMart frontend root.

4. The JavaScript code inserted will use the MooTools framework that should be enabled with the `default` theme (or also for the `packtpub` theme since it is just a clone of the `default`). If you are not using the default theme, you will need some modifications for the framework you are using.

Steps

1. Open your favorite text editor. Navigate to the VirtueMart frontend root.

2. Open the file `themes/packtpub/templates/product_details/includes/addtocart_attributes.tpl.php`.

3. Insert the following lines before line 18 (just after `endif`):

```
<?
  if ($has_image) {
    echo '<br />
      <img class="attribute_image" src="'.$attribute_image_
url.$option_value.'.jpg" />
        <br />
      ';
  }
```

```
?>
</label>
```

4. Replace line 13 (the `<input>` tag for the radio button) with the following lines:

```
    <input type="radio" id="<?php echo $attribute['titlevar'].
$i ?>_field"
        name="<?php echo $attribute['titlevar'].$attribute['produ
ct_id'] ?>"
        value="<?php echo $options_item['base_var'] ?>"
        <?php echo $onclick ?> />
    </><label for="<?php echo $attribute['titlevar'].$i ?>_
field">
```

5. Insert the following lines before line 13 (just after `foreach`):

```
<?php
  $onclick='';
  if ($has_image) {
    $option_value=strtolower($options_item['base_var']);
    $onclick='onclick="if (window.VM_ChangeImage) VM_
ChangeImage(\''.$option_value.'\')"';
  }
?>
```

6. Insert the following lines before line 12 (just before `foreach`):

```
$relative_path='attribute/'.strtolower($attribute['titlevar']);
  $attribute_image_path = IMAGEPATH.$relative_path;
  if (file_exists($attribute_image_path) && is_dir($attribute_
image_path)) {
    $has_image=true;
    $attribute_image_url = IMAGEURL.$relative_path;
  }
```

7. Save the file and upload it to your server.

8. Open the file `themes/packtpub/templates/product_details/garden_flypage.tpl.php`.

9. Replace line 29 (the `<td>` tag for product image) with the following line:

```
<td align="center" valign="top" rowspan="4"><img src="<?php echo
IMAGEURL.'product/'.strtolower($product_name).'.jpg' ?>" /></td>
```

10. Insert the following lines before line 3 (just after the `direct access` check):

```
<?php
  $custom_product_image=IMAGEURL.'product/'.strtolower($product_
name);
?>
```

```
<script type="text/JavaScript">
  var product_image="<?php echo $custom_product_image ?>";
  var VM_ChangeImage=function(option) {
    $("VM_Image").src=product_image+"_"+option+".jpg";
  }
</script>
```

11. Save the file and upload it to your server.

12. Go to the **Shovel** product details page (the URL is `index.php?option=com_virtuemart&page=shop.product_details&flypage=garden_flypage.tpl&product_id=3`), you will see the **Colour** attribute shown as a radio button with a color image below it. Click on the radio button and you will see that the product image changes color as well.

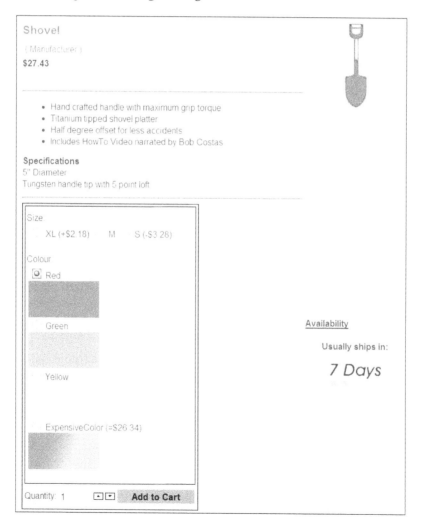

Notes

1. There are two major customizations in this exercise. The first one is to add the images for the radio buttons. The second one is to add the onclick behavior to the radio button and swap the product image accordingly. For the former one, we only need to modify the `addtocart_advanced_attribute` template. For the latter one, both the `addtocart_advanced_attribute` template and the flypage template will need to be changed. Each set of steps are listed in reverse in order to make sure the line number is correct.

2. In Step 6, we started to check whether we should use images for the radio buttons. There are a number of ways to do this. We can show images for a certain value of the attribute name (such as `Color`). We can assign the product to a certain product type and show images for that product type. Or we can use the file system like we did here. (You can probably think of other possibilities.) The trick we did was to create a subdirectory named `attribute` (or whatever name you can think of) under the `shop_image` directory of the frontend VirtueMart root. For the advanced attribute we planned to use images, and create a subdirectory under the attribute directory. For every possible value of the attribute, we needed to have an image file. In our case, the attribute we used was `Colour` and so we created a `colour` subdirectory. The attribute values we have are `Red`, `Green`, `Yellow`, and `ExpensiveColor` and so we named the four image files as `red.jpg`, `green.jpg`, `yellow.jpg`, and `expensivecolor.jpg`.

3. In the coding, we checked the existence of the attribute image directory to see whether we have images and set up the variable `$has_image` accordingly. We also initialized the variable `$attribute_image_url` for showing the image location in the browser.

4. Step 5 is related to the second goal of the customization (the `onclick` behavior). We created the `onclick` handler code only when we had images. Otherwise, the code would be an empty string. The `onclick` handler is to call the JavaScript function `VM_ChangeImage()` which will be created in the flypage template to swap the product image (see note 9 below).

5. In Step 4, we modified the `<input>` tag for the radio button to add the `onclick` handler to it so that when the radio button is clicked, we will swap the product image. We also inserted a `<label>` tag to link the label text and image to the radio button. This `<label>` tag made the label text and image respond to click just like the radio button is clicked.

6. In Step 3, we actually added the radio button image and closed the `<label>` tag. Note that the `</label>` end tag will have to come after the image, so that clicking the image will be the same as clicking on the radio button. We also inserted a couple of `<br/>` tags to break the lines because our images are big. You can use smaller images and the line breaks may not be necessary.

7. Steps 8 to 10 relate to the flypage template. The default flypage template for Shovel is `garden_flypage.tpl.php` and so we had to change this template. You certainly can use other flypage templates, if you want to. Just remember to change the category flypage template setting accordingly.

8. In Step 9, we replaced the product image tag. VirtueMart assigned a hashed number for all files you uploaded through the backend. This makes the product image file difficult to track. (As noted above, the original image file for Shovel is `520efefd6d7977f91b16fac1149c7438.jpg`. This is a legacy naming system used in VirtueMart 1.0. VirtueMart 1.1 made some improvements by adding the product sku to the name, but it is still difficult to track.). Just for the sake of this hack, we created a product image with a name the same as the product name (in our case, the product image is named `shovel.jpg`). Obviously, product name is easier for us human beings to match the product with the image. But this is not the only way we can name the image file. You can use `product_id`, `product_sku`, or any other naming system. Just make sure it is consistent and they agree with each other.

9. In Step 10, we added the JavaScript code to handle the `onclick` event of the radio button created in Step 4. We replace the `src` attribute of our image according to the value of the radio button. Again, we use product name (appended with the option value) to match the image file. All the image files have to put in the `product` subdirectory of the `IMAGEURL` (that is, `shop_image` of the VirtueMart frontend root) directory. You can place them in another directory. Just make sure its actual location is specified here correctly.

In the preceding exercise, we demonstrated a number of techniques in customizing VirtueMart:

- Name the product image file differently from standard VirtueMart. This can save us some trouble in matching the product image.

- Create various subdirectories to organize our files.

- Add image files that match the attribute values.

- Swap product images in accordance with the behavior of the user. We track the `click` event. You can extend this to other mouse movements such as `mouseover`, `mouseout`, `mouseleave`, `mouseenter`, `mousedrag`, `mousedrop`, and so on. If you are not sure about these events, just search the term on the Internet.

Product type templates

Product type is a very special feature in VirtueMart. It can be used for many different applications once you master it. However, it is also one of the VirtueMart features that many find hard to understand.

We all know that VirtueMart products have to be assigned to a product category. This is one way of classifying your products. You can assign a product to more than one category. So, other than the traditional categories (like clothes, shoes, and so on), you can create another dimension of classifying the products. For example, you can classify products in terms of brand name by creating each brand (such as Nike, Adidas) as a separate category. Consequently, a basketball shoes product can belong to a Shoes category and a brand category. By using categories of various dimensions, you can allow your shopper to find the product through different categories.

In addition to categories, you can also classify your products by product type. There are two major differences between product type and category:

- A product must belong to at least one category but may not belong to a product type.
- Classifying a product into a category does not add any new property to a product. On the other hand, a product type can have additional parameters defined. As a result, you will see a new tab in the Product Edit page. You can give a value for each parameter for the product. Let's say you created a product type called Books. (You can also have a Books category at the same time. But a Books product type and a Books category are not the same thing.). For this product type, you can add parameters like author, publisher, edition, ISBN, and so on. All these parameters will show up in the new Books tab of the product edit page.

It should be noted that the category and product type are two completely independent ways of classification. That means products of two different categories can belong to the same product type. For example, you can create a "Final Sale" product type where no return is accepted. This Final Sale product type can be applied to Clothes or Shoes or Books.

Another special thing about product type is that a flypage template can be assigned to a product type. You can use the product type template to make additional processing and/or add additional HTML code. We can use this special provision to make a lot of golden touch to the product details page, as we shall demonstrate in the following exercise.

File upload function in VirtueMart

VirtueMart has lots of features built-in. However, still there are many that are lacking. One feature people have long been asking for is a file uploading function. Some items will require shopper to upload a file to integrate into the final shipped product. It will be nice if this function can be added to VirtueMart. But up to the latest version, file upload is still a customization feature, not something built in.

There are several solutions provided for customizing VirtueMart to provide the file upload function. One is the Custom Attributes Extended hack which provides a lot of custom attribute type including the file type. So, you can configure the custom attribute to show a file input box in the product page to allow the user to upload a file. Custom Attributes Extended hack was originally developed by Ted Barnet for VirtueMart 1.0.x. The project was then ported by me to VirtueMart 1.1.x through a generous donation from Marco. Both the old and new hack are distributed in the VirtueMart forum. The new hack, available at `http://forum.virtuemart.net/index.php?topic=39666.0`, is the most active thread in the forum, with close to 900 posts and over 250,000 views at the time of writing. There are two major challenges in using that hack, though:

- This is an extensive hack. Every time a new version comes out, the hack needs a complete revision and the revision is not an easy task.

- The syntax for writing the correct attribute is pretty complex. There is a steep learning curve.

Another well-known hack that provides a file upload function is the VirtueUpload project. It comes with a separate Joomla! component and a Joomla! module. The component allows you to manage the upload in the backend and also provides an upload function in the frontend. The Joomla! module, on the other hand, is actually a code hack disguised as a module. You don't need to put it anywhere in your frontend. As you will see, we can put similar code into a VirtueMart template to achieve the same function.

The upload function is integrated into VirtueMart using the content plugin mechanism. The upload form coding is provided by the VirtueUpload module. You need to add a content plugin tag `{loadposition upload}` to your product description in order to have the upload form coding added. You can read the details from the website `http://www.bixie.org/extensions/virtueupload/7-virtueupload.html` where you can also download the free VirtueUpload version. In addition to installing the component and module, the download also comes with a set of five customized VirtueMart files:

- `/basket/basket_b2c.html.php`
- `/basket/ro_basket_b2c.html.php`

- `/pages/account.order_details.tpl.php`
- `/order_emails/confirmation_email.tpl.php`
- `classes/ps_checkout.php`

The first four are all VirtueMart templates and the last one is a class file. So they can be packaged as a VirtueMart theme without touching the core files. Actually, the latest VirtueUpload patch already packaged the hack as a theme.

While there may still be issues with the hack, VirtueUpload is a well-planned project and the mechanism is clever and clean. The code is almost 100 percent independent of VirtueMart. If you just need a quick and dirty trick to add upload file function, you only need to add the content plugin tag in your Product Description after installing the component and module. All the other hacks are needed only if you want additional information to be shown in the order details, order e-mail, and shop basket, respectively. If you don't need the file upload recorded in the order, you only need to make one change to the core file. The additional information can be incorporated in the order through a theme, if you want to. There are three major drawbacks of the hack:

- The content plugin tag has to be added to every product that needs the file upload function. This is not difficult but may prove to be an extra step if you have lots of products that need the function.
- You need to add a custom attribute named Upload to the product. While the attribute name can be customized, this has to be the same across all products. So you cannot name it as "Image File" for some products and "Word File" for another.
- You need to configure the Joomla! module to work with VirtueMart. The use of the module is not very intuitive and may cause confusion for some users.

Actually, VirtueUpload can be integrated with VirtueMart through the product type mechanism. This will remove the need for the Joomla! module completely. In doing this, we will be able to change the attribute name for different products as well. We will demonstrate how this can be done in the following exercise.

Exercise 10.6: Integrating VirtueUpload with VirtueMart using product type template

Product type can help to achieve many advanced functionalities. You can consider this as a tag to classify your products in different types in addition to categories. In this exercise, we will create a product type named VirtueUpload to associate with the products that need file upload function. Since each product type can have a custom flypage template (actually, it is just one child template of the flypage) that you can insert into the core flypage template, we can make use of this to add the file upload coding to the flypage.

Preparation

We want to associate our file upload template with a product type. So we need to create a product type and add product to this product type:

1. To create a product type in VirtueMart, log in to the VirtueMart backend. Click **Products** and then **Add Product Type** on the left menu. The **Add/Edit Product Type** screen will open up. Use `VirtueUpload` for the **Product Type Name** and `virtueupload/imagefile.tpl` for the **Product Type Flypage**. Click **Save** in the top toolbar to save the changes.

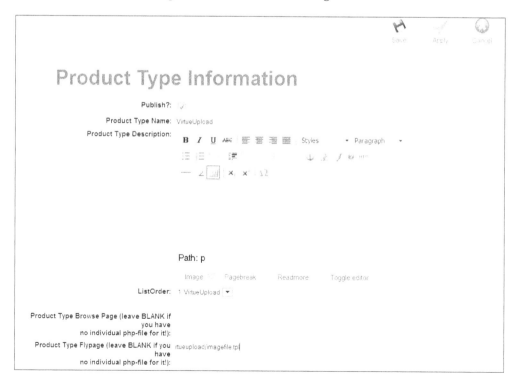

2. To add a product to the product type, click **List Product** on the left menu and then select **Chain Saw** in the product list. (We choose **Chain Saw** because this is the first one in the list. You can definitely select any other product you like.) Click **Add Product Type** in the top toolbar (not the **Add Product Type** menu link in the left menu). Select VirtueUpload from the drop-down and then click **Save** in the top toolbar.

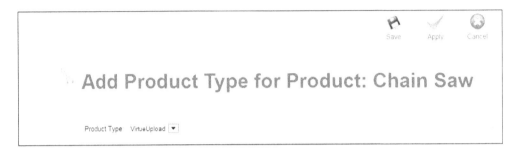

3. We need to add two fields to the **Custom Attribute List**. When you are back to the **Product List** page, click **Chain Saw** again to open up the **Update Item** screen. On the **Product Status** tab, add the field list Image Id;Image File Name to the **Custom Attribute List** textbox at the bottom of the page. We use the fields Image Id and Image File Name to store the upload file ID and the upload file name, respectively. (The upload ID is provided by VirtueUpload itself. We will add a feature to show the file name as well.)

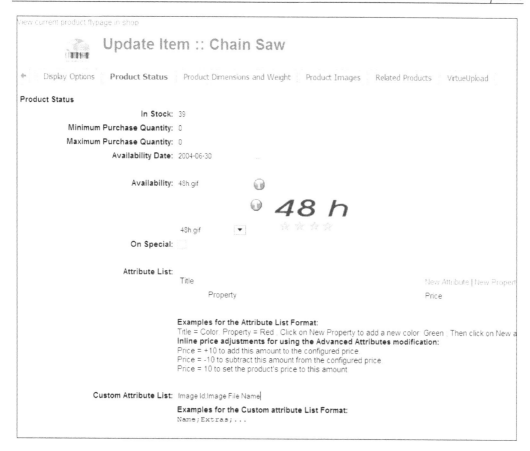

Steps

In this exercise, we adapt code from `mod_virtueupload` to be used in our template. For ease of discussion, we separate the section of code into a number of steps. Actually, you can combine all the steps into one, if you like.

1. Create a blank new file and add in the following lines of code:

```php
<?php
// most of the code are adapted from the the original VirtueUpload
code.
// you need to have VirtueUpload component installed to have the
code working

defined( '_JEXEC' ) or die( 'Restricted access' );

$upload_attr='Image_Id_field';
$upload_desc_attr='Image_File_Name_field';
```

```
ob_start();
?>
```

2. Append the following code to the end of the file. This section is basically code from the file `mod_virtueupload.php` that comes with the Joomla! module of VirtueUpload download.

```php
<?php
// code adapted from modules/mod_virtueupload/mod_virtueupload.php
if(!file_exists(JPATH_SITE.DS."components".DS."com_virtueupload".
DS."virtueupload.php")) {
  return '';
}
require_once (JPATH_ADMINISTRATOR.DS.'components'.DS.'com_
virtueupload'.DS.'classes'.DS.'output.class.php');
$config     = VUOutput::config();
$user       =& JFactory::getUser();
$document    =& JFactory::getDocument();
$jscript    = '';
$msg        = JRequest::getVar('msg', '');
$upload_id   = JRequest::getInt('upload_id', 0);
$uploadinfo  = false;
if ($upload_id) {
  $uploadinfo = VUOutput::UploadInfoId($upload_id, 'module'); //
original code to get html for display in frontend
}

$form->status    = VUOutput::getStatus($msg);
$form->ip       = $_SERVER['REMOTE_ADDR'];
$form->session_id   = session_id();
$form->uri_url   = VUOutput::_getUriString();
$form->prod_id   = JRequest::getInt('product_id', 0);
$form->cat_id   = JRequest::getInt('category_id', 0);
// code adapted from modules/mod_virtueupload/mod_virtueupload.php
ends
?>
```

3. Append the following lines of code at the end of the file. This section of code is adapted from the file `tmpl/default.php` in the `mod_virtueupload` module.

```php
<?php
// code adapted from modules/mod_virtueupload/tmpl/default.php
ends
global $Itemid;
JHTML::stylesheet('virtueupl_front.css','components/com_
virtueupload/assets/css/');
```

```
$document->addScript(JURI::base()."administrator/components/com_
virtueupload/assets/js/checkform.js");
?>
<div id="virtueupl_form">
<form id="adminForm" name="adminForm"  action="<?php echo
JRoute::_('index.php?option=com_virtueupload&view=form'); ?>"
method="post" enctype="multipart/form-data" onSubmit="return
checkForm();">
<table width="100%" border="0" cellpadding="0" cellspacing="0">
  <tr>
    <td colspan="2">
    <label for="file"><?php echo JText::_('VULANG_FORM_LBL_FILE');
?></label><br/>
    <input name="file" type="file" class="button" />
  </td>
    <td valign="bottom">
    <input id="upload_button" class="button" type="submit"
value="<?php echo JText::_('VULANG_FORM_SUBMIT'); ?>"
onclick="this.form.status.value = '<?php echo JText::_('VULANG_
STAT_INITUPL'); ?> '; $('spinner').style.display = 'block';  this.
form.status.style.color = '#339900';" />
  </td>
  </tr>
  <tr>
    <td height="50" align="left" valign="middle">
<label for="status"><?php echo JText::_('VULANG_FORM_STATUS');
?></label>
  </td>
  <td colspan="2">
    <input class="vu_status" size="50" type="text" id="status"
name="status" readonly="readonly" value="<?php echo JText::_
('VULANG_STAT_WAITTUPL'); ?>" />
    <img id="spinner" style="display:none; border:none; position:
relative; top: 3px;" src="components/com_virtueupload/assets/ajax-
loader.gif" alt="Loading..."/>
  </td>
 </tr>
<?php
 if ($uploadinfo) {
?>
  <tr>
    <td colspan="3">
    <?php echo $uploadinfo; ?>
  </td>
 </tr>
```

```
<?php
}
?>
 </table>
<?php echo $jscript; ?>

<?php echo JHTML::_( 'form.token' ); ?>
<input type="hidden" name="task" value="submit" />
<input type="hidden" name="prod_id" value="<?php echo $form->prod_
id; ?>" />
<input type="hidden" name="cat_id" value="<?php echo $form->cat_
id; ?>" />
<input type="hidden" name="uri_url" value="<?php echo $form->uri_
url; ?>" />
<input type="hidden" name="Itemid" value="<?php echo $Itemid; ?>"
/>
<input type="hidden" name="userid" value="<?php echo $user->id;
?>" />
<input type="hidden" name="session_id" value="<?php echo $form-
>session_id; ?>" />
<input type="hidden" name="controller" value="entry" />
</form>
```

4. Append the following lines of code at the end of the file. This section has highly customized code for the purpose of our current exercise. The code is based on the function prepareScript() of the VUOutput class file classes/output.class.php of the backend com_virtueupload directory.

```
<?php
//keep session alive while editing
JHTML::_('behavior.keepalive');
//JavaScript statusinput
echo $form->status;
$inputsize = 2;
$none = 'none';
if ($upload_id) {
  $uploadfile = VUOutput::UploadInfoId($upload_id);
}
$upload_desc = $uploadfile->file_name;
?>
<script type='text/JavaScript'>
  var upload_id=<?php echo $upload_id ?>;
  var upload_desc="<?php echo $upload_desc ?>";
  window.addEvent('domready',function(){
    var uploadattr = $("<?php echo $upload_attr ?>");
    var uploaddescattr =  $("<?php echo $upload_desc_attr ?>");
```

```
      if (uploadattr) {
        uploadattr.readOnly = true;
        uploadattr.className = 'readonly';
        uploadattr.size = <?php echo $inputsize ?>;
        if (uploadattr.value == '') {
          uploadattr.value = "<?php echo $none ?>";
        }
        if (upload_id) {
          uploadattr.value = upload_id;
        }
      }
      if (uploaddescattr) {
        uploaddescattr.readOnly = true;
        uploaddescattr.className = 'readonly';
        if (upload_id) {
          uploaddescattr.value = upload_desc;
        }
      }
    }
  });
</script>
</div>
<style type="text/css">
  #virtueupl_form {border:1px solid silver;margin:10px;padding:10p
x;margin-left:0}
</style>
<?php
// code adapted from modules/mod_virtueupload/tmpl/default.php
ends

$virtue_upload_html = ob_get_contents();
ob_end_clean();
return $virtue_upload_html;
?>
```

5. Save the file with the name `imagefile.tpl.php` and upload this to your web server in the `templates/virtueupload` directory of the `packtpub` theme root directory. The subdirectory `virtueupload` does not exist and you will have to create it yourself before you can upload the file.

6. Navigate your browser to the **Chain Saw** product page of your web server (URL is `index.php?page=shop.product_details&flypage=flypage.tpl&product_id=7&category_id=4&option=com_virtuemart`). You should see the `VirtueUpload` function working with the product type. Try uploading a file and you will see the Image ID and Image File Name textboxes filled up with proper values.

Notes

1. In this exercise, we integrated VirtueUpload with a product type template and provided some additional function that is not available in VirtueUpload itself. We basically cloned the code from the `mod_virtueupload` to the template. As a result, the `mod_virtueupload` is no longer needed to implement the file upload feature. However, you still need to have `com_virtueupload` installed to have the file upload function work.

2. In Step 1, we added the standard security checking code of Joomla!. Then we provided two configurable items `$upload_attr` and `$upload_desc_attr`. These two items were set to the two custom attribute they correspond to. Our code will fill up the custom attribute textboxes when the shopper uploads file to our server. By creating different product type templates with different values for these items, you can have the file upload feature working for products with different custom attribute names. This is an extension of the standard VirtueUpload function.

3. Note that the attribute name added here is different from the one you entered in the backend. HTML form fields do not allow names with space. So all the space is replaced with underscore `_`. Also, the string `_field` is appended to the attribute name. This is the protocol of VirtueMart to create `id` for form field elements.

4. It is also possible to create product type parameters to allow shop admin to change the attribute name per product. In that case, you can use a single template for all products and read the attribute name from the product type. Unfortunately, VirtueMart does not pass any product type properties (not even the product type ID) to the product type template. This is definitely a miss in the program design. This also means a lot more extra work for us, if we need to read the product type parameters in our template again.

5. Instead of using the `fetch()` function to parse the product type template content, VirtueMart used a non-standard way of adding the template as an include file. This will effectively treat the template file as a function and so we need to capture the HTML and return it as a functional value. That's why we need to use the `ob_start()` function to capture the template output ourselves.

6. The code in Step 2 is basically a replication of the code in `mod_virtueupload.php`. We removed code which is useful only in a module. We also changed the behavior in case the VirtueUpload component is not installed. The original coding will throw an error. However, I prefer to silently return an empty string to allow the user more flexibility.

7. Again, Step 3 is a replication of the file `tmpl/default.php` in `mod_virtueupload`. This is the area where most of the HTML is created. We did some customization on the code to make the form fit better with our template and removed the `prepareScript()` function call at the end. You can custom the HTML form further to make it fit with your own template. The various elements can also be moved around.

8. Step 4 is the code added to replace the `prepareScript()` function. Here we added code to make the `uploadattr` customizable with the value of `$upload_attr` set at the beginning of the file. We also added another attribute `uploaddescattr` for storing additional upload file description. We called the function `VUOutput::UploadInfoId()` to get all the information of the uploaded file. This function will return the `$upload_file` object of which we only used the `file_name` property in this exercise. You can make use of the other properties, if you need to. The properties are listed as follows:

   ○ `id` : The upload ID, an integer.

   ○ `file_name`: The filename of the upload with ID prepended.

   ○ `file_size`: The size of the file rounded to KB.

   ○ `upload_by`: The username of the logged in shopper.

   ○ `product_id`: The product ID and the image number (the number of the image that the shopper uploaded, not the same as `id`) associated with it, separated by the pipe (|) symbol.

   ○ `order_id`: The order ID that the upload is associated with. Can be zero if no order is associated with it or the order is not created yet.

   ○ `ip`: The IP of this shopper session.

   ○ `comment`: Comment with the file.

   ○ `date`: Date in format yyyy-mm-dd.

   ○ `cdate`: Date in Unix timestamp (an integer).

   ○ `file_ctype`: The mime type of the file.

   ○ `file_type`: The description of the file type.

   ○ `download_url`: The URL of downloaded file.

   ○ `link`: The file path of the uploaded file relative to the Joomla! root.

   ○ `path`: The file path including the Joomla! root.

   ○ `url`: The URL path of the uploaded file including the web root.

   ○ `thumb`: The file path for the thumb relative to the Joomla! root.

   ○ `thumb_path`: The file path for the thumb image.

   ○ `thumb_url`: The URL path of the thumb image.

- ○ thumb_img: The `<a>` tag to download the file with the file type thumb image enclosed.

- ○ thumb_img_small: The `<a>` tag to download the file with the small file type thumb image enclosed.

9. We used two custom attributes to correspond to the upload ID and the upload file description. The upload ID is mandatory as it is needed to associate the image file with the order. The upload file description is added in this exercise to make it easier for the shopper to know which file has been uploaded. Both attributes are readonly and cannot be modified by the shopper directly. The purpose of the prepareScript() function is to create the JavaScript to fill in these data to the custom attribute on the web page. We need to replace this function to provide our additional features. In addition to these, custom attributes ensure that the data will be recorded in the shop basket and the order, in case one is created.

10. You can add more custom attributes to provide more information (such as file size). You only need to extend our JavaScript code to include the additional fields.

11. In Step 5, we created a subdirectory virtueupload for storing the VirtueUpload template files. Of course, the directory name can be changed. The subdirectory is not mandatory. You can save the file anywhere within the templates directory. The subdirectory is just for better organization. The only thing you need to take note of is that the directory path of the template must be correctly entered in the **Product Type Form** (Preparation 1).

Hacking into core VirtueMart functionalities

We've been working on a lot of template customizations. We've also touched on a couple of class file customizations. So far, we didn't talk too much about hacking the core VirtueMart functionalities and logic. This is because template and theme are usually meant for presentation and not core processing logic. With the introduction of theme class files, however, hacking into core VirtueMart functionalities is possible. But you must have some thorough understanding of the working of VirtueMart before you can make good use of this. As we are coming to the end of the book, I would like to show you two more customization possibilities. These two examples may or may not seem too useful at first unless you happen to have a project that needs a similar feature. But they will serve to illustrate the basic principle. You should be able to further extend or apply the principles in your projects to do something interesting.

Exercise 10.7: Creating new VirtueMart module pages

The customization and creation of VirtueMart module pages are not the subject of this book. As you are aware, we have been trying to avoid changing any core VirtueMart files in order to independently maintain our changed version, as much as possible. However, it is still interesting to see how we can create a new VirtueMart module page. We will need a custom shop page to test our customization in the next exercise, which provides a reason why we will introduce the creation of the VirtueMart module page here.

As you will recall, VirtueMart module pages are named in the format `module.page.php`. We will be creating a new page for the `shop` modules named `shop.featured` that shows a list of featured products.

Steps

1. Create a blank new file and add in the following lines of code:

```php
<?php
  $_REQUEST['featured']='Y';
  ob_start();
  require_once(PAGEPATH.'shop.browse.php');
  $html=ob_get_contents();
  ob_end_clean();
  $html=str_replace('shop.browse','shop.featured',$html);
  echo $html;
?>
```

2. Save the file with the name `shop.featured.php` and upload it to the directory `html` in the VirtueMart administrator root of your website.

3. Navigate your browser to the URL `index.php?option=com_virtuemart&page=shop.featured`. You will see the product list showing all the featured products in your shop.

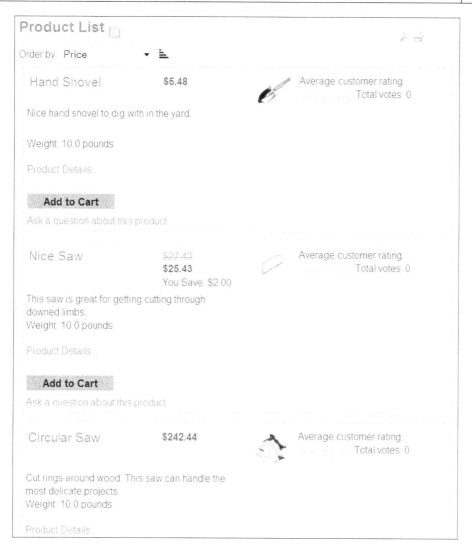

Notes

1. In this exercise, we used the little known secret of the VirtueMart search function. There are two special parameters that will show different types of product list. The first one is `discounted` and the second one is `featured`. When you add `discounted=Y` to the `shop.browse` page URL, you will restrict the list to discounted products only. Similarly, when you add `featured=Y` to the `shop.browse` page URL, you will get a list of featured products instead.

2. In Step 1, we created the coding for the `shop.featured` page. We programmatically added the `featured` parameter to the `$_REQUEST` variable. This is equivalent to putting the parameter in the URL. We then included the `shop.browse.php` page to process the product list as usual.

3. Everything should be fine except that the URL built on the page will still use the `page=shop.browse` parameter. So all the navigation links (including the sort and page links) on the page will point back to `shop.browse` without the `featured` parameter. In order to make sure the page works for the navigation links as well, we captured the HTML output by `shop.browse.php` and replaced all links with `shop.browse` by `shop.featured`. This will fix the problems.

4. You can extend this method to create a VirtueMart module page called `shop.discounted`. The same trick can be extended to include `category_id`, `manufacturer_id`, `keyword`, and other parameters.

Exercise 10.8: Custom price calculation

You may encounter some situations where you want to modify the price calculation logic provided by VirtueMart for certain products. There are two functions in the `ps_product` class that are related to this. The function `get_price()` is used to calculate the price that will be displayed in the product catalog (both the product list page and product details page). The function `get_adjusted_attribute_price()` is used to calculate the price in the shop basket and checkout. You can modify one or both of these functions according to your own needs. In this exercise, we will modify the logic to give a 50 percent discount to all featured products.

Steps

1. Create a blank new file and add in the following lines of code:

```php
<?php
if( !defined( '_VALID_MOS' ) && !defined( '_JEXEC' ) ) die(
'Direct Access to '.basename(__FILE__).' is not allowed.' );
class ps_product extends vm_ps_product {

  function get_price($product_id, $check_multiple_prices=false,
$overrideShopperGroup='' ) {
    $price =parent::get_price ($product_id, $check_multiple_
prices, $overrideShopperGroup);
    if ($this->get_field($product_id,'product_special')=='Y') {
      $price["product_price"] *= 0.5;
      $price["product_base_price"] *= 0.5;
    }
    return $price;
```

```
    }
  }
```

2. Save the file with the name `ps_product.php` and upload it to the directory `user_class` of the `packtpub` theme root directory.

3. Navigate your browser to the URL `index.php?option=com_virtuemart&page=shop.featured`. You will see the product list of the featured products showing a 50 percent discount for each product.

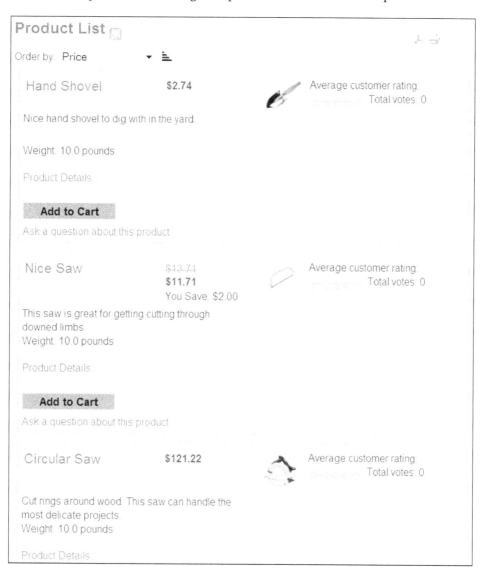

Notes

1. In this exercise, we created a custom theme class `ps_product` to modify the `get_price()` function.

2. We first get the value of `$price` by calling the original `get_price()` function. After that we check the `product_special` field of the product. If the value equals `'Y'`, it will be a featured product. If this is true, we multiply the `product_price` and `product_base_price` by 0.5 to get 50 percent of the original price. Otherwise, we just return the original price.

3. Note that the hack only modified the product price and had no effect on the discount. So, the discount for **Nice Saw** is still minus $2.00 as the discount set in the backend is an absolute value of 2. Also, the calculated price does not affect the attribute price as `get_price` only returns the price without attributes. You will need an additional hack to the `ps_product_attribute` class to affect this.

4. As you anticipated, the price calculation logic in VirtueMart is not that simple. Our hack only works perfectly for simple cases. For more complex cases, you will need additional changes. (For example, if you have different price for a different shopper group and would like to have a different discount for each, you will need to check the shopper group ID and return the appropriate discounted price.)

Summary

In this chapter, we rounded up our discussion on VirtueMart themes and templates by providing some additional customization possibilities. We considered the template hierarchy and ways to break big complex templates into smaller manageable ones. We then took a look at how to share child templates with two templates. We also looked at adding images to display advanced attributes and how to change the product image in response to changes in the attribute. We explained what a product type template is and used it to add a file upload function to the product details page by integrating the product type with VirtueUpload. Finally, we investigated how to hack into the core VirtueMart functionalities by creating new VirtueMart module pages and extending the VirtueMart class file.

Index

C

quantity element 161

R

radio button
  adding, to ask seller page 151, 152
  advanced attribute, displaying as 119, 120
recent.tpl.php template 125
Recommend To Friend page
  template file, creating for 292-297
refactoring 300
reflect() function 275
reflection effect
  adding, to product images 269, 270
reflectionHeight config 275
reflection.js file 268
reflection.js JavaScript
  inserting, into theme.php file 272
registration information 180, 181
relatedProducts.tpl.php template 125, 224
reviewform.tpl.php template 109
reviews.tpl.php template 108
root VirtueMart directory 16

S

scope
  determining, of project 31
Search Engine Friendly. *See* SEF system
Security Settings subsection 45
Security tab 45
SEF system 17 139
SEF URLs 139
set_cfg() function 230
set() function 230, 231
shipping address list
  modifying 187-191
shipping information 180, 181
shipping methods 192
Shipping tab 46
shop.ask.php file 40
shop basket 160, 161
  functions 166, 167
  product thumbnails, adding to 167-169
  templates 162-166
  versus Shop Cart page 170
shop basket data 160
shop basket display 160

shop.basket_short.php page 207, 208
shop basket templates 162-166
shop.browse.php file 39
shop cart 39
shopcart
  image, modifying for 134, 135
  pop-up duration, modifying for 137, 138
shopcart image
  modifying 134, 135
Shop Cart page
  about 170
  Ajax, used for updating 170-172
  versus shop basket 170
shop.cart.php file 39
shop.cart.tpl.php template 170
shop.index.php file 38
shopIndex.tpl.php template 153, 154
shop.infopage.php file 41
shop.manufacturer.php file 41
shop module 27
shopping digression 40
shopping life cycle, VirtueMart
  about 38
  account maintenance 40
  checkout presentation logic 40
  landing page 38
  product detail 39
  product listing 38
  shop cart 39
  shopping digression 40, 41
shop.product_details.php file 39
shop.recommendation.php file 41
shop.waiting_list.php file 41
showRecommendationForm() function 297
site configuration, VirtueMart
  about 46
  display subsection 47, 48
  layout subsection 48, 49
Site tab 46
snapshotReflection config 279
snapshot template
  configuring 218-222
sql directory 17
stars images 239, 240
statement separator 69
str_replace() function 186

W

web page design, VirtueMart
  structure 127, 128
web technology 160

X

XML 251
XML documents
  rules 251

Thank you for buying
Joomla! Virtuemart 1.1 Theme and Template Design

About Packt Publishing

Packt, pronounced 'packed', published its first book "*Mastering phpMyAdmin for Effective MySQL Management*" in April 2004 and subsequently continued to specialize in publishing highly focused books on specific technologies and solutions.

Our books and publications share the experiences of your fellow IT professionals in adapting and customizing today's systems, applications, and frameworks. Our solution based books give you the knowledge and power to customize the software and technologies you're using to get the job done. Packt books are more specific and less general than the IT books you have seen in the past. Our unique business model allows us to bring you more focused information, giving you more of what you need to know, and less of what you don't.

Packt is a modern, yet unique publishing company, which focuses on producing quality, cutting-edge books for communities of developers, administrators, and newbies alike. For more information, please visit our website: www.packtpub.com.

About Packt Open Source

In 2010, Packt launched two new brands, Packt Open Source and Packt Enterprise, in order to continue its focus on specialization. This book is part of the Packt Open Source brand, home to books published on software built around Open Source licences, and offering information to anybody from advanced developers to budding web designers. The Open Source brand also runs Packt's Open Source Royalty Scheme, by which Packt gives a royalty to each Open Source project about whose software a book is sold.

Writing for Packt

We welcome all inquiries from people who are interested in authoring. Book proposals should be sent to author@packtpub.com. If your book idea is still at an early stage and you would like to discuss it first before writing a formal book proposal, contact us; one of our commissioning editors will get in touch with you.

We're not just looking for published authors; if you have strong technical skills but no writing experience, our experienced editors can help you develop a writing career, or simply get some additional reward for your expertise

Joomla! 1.5: Beginner's Guide

ISBN: 978-1-847199-90-4   Paperback: 380 pages

Build and maintain impressive user-friendly web sites the fast and easy way with Joomla! 1.5

1. Create a web site that meets real-life requirements by following the creation of an example site with the help of easy-to-follow steps and ample screenshots

2. Practice all the Joomla! skills from organizing your content to completely changing the site's looks and feel

3. Go beyond a typical Joomla! site to make the site meet your specific needs

Mastering Joomla! 1.5 Extension and Framework Development Second Edition

ISBN: 978-1-849510-52-3   Paperback: 560 pages

Extend the power of Joomla! by adding components, modules, plugins, and other extensions

1. In-depth guide to programming Joomla! 1.5 Framework

2. Design and build secure and robust components, modules, and plugins

3. Customize the document properties, add multilingual capabilities, and provide an interactive user experience

Please check **www.PacktPub.com** for information on our titles

www.ingramcontent.com/pod-product-compliance
Lightning Source LLC
Chambersburg PA
CBHW080148060326
40689CB00018B/3894